Transforming Trauma

A Gift to Bowdoin's
Women's Resource Center
from
Safe Space, June 1995

For Corey

❖ ❖ ❖

Anna C. Salter

Transforming Trauma

A Guide to Understanding and Treating Adult Survivors of Child Sexual Abuse

SAGE Publications
International Educational and Professional Publisher
Thousand Oaks   London   New Delhi

For information address:

SAGE Publications, Inc.
2455 Teller Road
Thousand Oaks, California 91320

SAGE Publications Ltd.
6 Bonhill Street
London EC2A 4PU
United Kingdom

SAGE Publications India Pvt. Ltd.
M-32 Market
Greater Kailash I
New Delhi 110 048 India

Printed in the United States of America

Library of Congress Cataloging-in-Publication Data

Salter, Anna C.
    Transforming trauma : A guide to understanding and treating adult survivors of child sexual abuse / Anna C. Salter ; with chapter by Hilary Eldridge and Jenny Still.
        p.   cm.
    ISBN 0-8039-5508-1 (cloth : acid-free paper). — ISBN 0-8039-5509-X (pbk. : acid-free paper)
    1. Adult child sexual abuse victims—Rehabilitation. 2. Child sexual abuse. 3. Child molesters. I. Title.
    RC 569.5.A28S25   1995
    616.85'836906—dc20   95-7710

This book is printed on acid-free paper.

95 96 97 98 99 10 9 8 7 6 5 4 3 2 1

Sage Production Editor: Tricia K. Bennett
Typesetter: Janelle LeMaster

Contents

Foreword

John N. Briere

Anna C. Salter's last book, *Treating Child Sex Offenders and Victims: A Practical Guide*, established her as an important thinker in the area of sex offender treatment. The popularity of that book (in its 12th printing at the time of this writing) reflected Dr. Salter's awareness of the need for practical, yet research-based information on the treatment of sexual abusers.

Those of us who know Anna often wondered, "What would happen if someone this bright and this open to complexity were to write on adult survivors?" It was a reasonable question, on one level, because Anna has worked with survivors for years. On another level, however, the question was unacceptable because we needed her where she was—writing and synthesizing knowledge on the treatment of one of society's most pressing social problems. I personally asked Anna on multiple occasions to write more on sex offenders, to continue to share her extensive knowledge base with the vast majority of clinicians who have contact with, but tend to undertreat, sex offenders.

Luckily for all of us, Anna ignored my (and, no doubt, others') request. She has written another book, but not a book on sexual abusers per se. Instead, she has applied her understanding of victims and perpetrators to produce a fascinating text on the treatment of adult sexual abuse survivors.

This latest effort comes to us at an interesting time. Of late, our culture has become especially preoccupied with false accusations, false memories, and other issues that clearly deserve attention but that do not resolve the larger problem of child abuse and its effects. There appears to be a creeping, subtle question: What if most abuse reports are merely hysteria, or the products of badly done therapy? Because those adults who allege childhood sexual victimization often have psychological problems and attend therapy, how credible can they be? If it is true that children confuse fantasy and reality, how do we know anything really bad is even going on? If the media are right, and there are false memories of abuse everywhere, how many memories of abuse are true in the first place?

These questions reflect, in part, the fact that the primary source of information the public has about abuse is victims and survivors. Yet such "self-report" is subject to easy attack by those who seek to either protect themselves from a charge of sexual abuse or discount the likelihood of sexual abuse per se. In many cases, because there are no witnesses to child maltreatment other than the victim and the perpetrator, the final judgment may come down to who is more credible—an adult without obvious psychological dysfunction who mounts a convincing defense, or an accuser who is either very young or already suffering psychological effects?

There is, however, another source of information on whether abuse is common and likely to be deleterious to its victims. Beyond the reports of abuse victims or survivors, we have the voluminous and detailed admissions and confessions of convicted sex offenders. In my experience, no one who has listened to the stories of self-admitted pedophiles comes away from the experience unaffected. When faced with the actual incarnate source of the victim's pain, it is much harder to pretend (or assert) that sexual abuse is less than a tremendous evil. This second body of information directly informs the book before you.

Although we continue to struggle with a system that often works to deny the extent or importance of child abuse as a social problem, we continue to make progress on the clinical front.

Books on the treatment of adults abused as children have become increasingly sophisticated and useful. There has been a growing recognition that therapy for child abuse trauma is not an entry-level activity but rather something that requires specialized training, supervised experience, and both intellectual and empathic resources. In this sense, the "backlash" has done us an inadvertent service: By challenging clinicians on so many fronts, it has forced us to examine our assumptions, question our techniques, monitor our peers, and challenge any complacency we might have developed. By exposing us to harsh evaluation, society's response to abuse-focused therapy and therapists has forced us to become better at what we do. Like the abuse survivors we serve, we are faced with the choice of folding up our tents and leaving (at the various levels in which that can occur), or capitalizing on the opportunity to become smarter and stronger. Although the jury is still out, my bet is on the latter.

It is from this complex system of therapeutic challenge, alienation, and growth that Anna Salter's new book emerges. Building on the insights of her last volume and her considerable clinical experience, Dr. Salter refines what we know and provides new tools and perspectives. This new book constantly acknowledges the micro and macro social environments in which the abuse occurred and the survivor lives, and incorporates this awareness into therapeutic theory and practice.

Most important, Dr. Salter moves us into important new areas by crossing the bridge between the experience of the victim and the psychology of the perpetrator. By tracking the ways in which the abuser's grooming of the victim, gratification of distorted needs, and abuse-justifying cognitive processes become imprinted on the victim, Dr. Salter helps us to understand aspects of the survivor's experience and injury that heretofore may have eluded us. By exposing us to the actual thinking processes of the repetitive sex offender, she reminds us that the work we do has its basis in almost unspeakable acts, rather than faddishness or the malevolent influence of self-help manuals.

Anna Salter reminds us of another world—the world of the sexual predator. This information is bound to be disconcerting, if not disheartening, to those who have not encountered this domain because it highlights the essential narcissism and willingness to harm of those who sexually abuse children. But this information is critical to the provision of abuse-focused therapy because it tells us why and how the survivor is traumatized. It is as if we have been treating oppressed expatriates of a foreign country without any understanding of what that country is, how its government works, or what impacts it has on its subjects. Dr. Salter offers us the travel guide, as much as we might not always want to read it.

In a field of several recent good books on understanding and treating sexual abuse survivors, Anna Salter offers something truly new. At times dispassionate and scientific, at other times impassioned and lyrical, Dr. Salter keeps the reader moving, if not on edge. As if challenging extant social forces that seemingly require conservatism in the face of adversity, she emphasizes the art as much as the science of therapy, and surprises us, in the end, with something akin to poetry. This is an important book, and our field is exceedingly lucky to have it.

Foreword

Roland C. Summit

With *Transforming Trauma*, Anna Salter establishes a milestone in the expanding consciousness of sexual victimization. By choosing to relate therapeutically with the offender as well as the victim, she provides the essential crossover viewpoint between victim/survivor experience and the impositions of the intruder. This book makes it clear that it is not enough to study one polar aspect of the victim-perpetrator syncytium. In fact, we can learn from Dr. Salter that the destinies of overpowering adult and annihilated infant are so intertwined that it is only an artificial intellectualization that teases them apart. Until now, we have dared look only at pieces of the victimization picture puzzle, like gathering corners, frames, and central clusters without risking the difficult moves that would integrate the several fragments into a coherent picture. *Transforming Trauma* puts these pieces together.

Human society, no less than the professionals in charge, and hardly different from the victims and offenders themselves, has depended on excuses and clever devices to scatter the pieces of the victimization agony into trivialized, tolerable shards. As the puzzlemaker dices a meaningful image into intriguingly shaped, potentially interlocking bits, so have all of us succeeded in atomizing the abuse experience. We have done this like a dissociating child, not in a conscious preference for ignorance but in the relentless avoidance of insufferable pain. An integrated consciousness of victimization allows for a picture of conjoint human savagery and vulnerability that shatters civilized notions of a just and fair society. Such consciousness offends the conscience of all of us wise fools who are charged to address human nature and who have consistently missed the point. Child sexual abuse, in its partially recognized dimensions, is already an intolerable mote in the eye of an idealistic society. Framing those dimensions more coherently, as Anna Salter has so carefully and compassionately accomplished, will move some to understand, many to wonder, and some to retaliate.

Through most of this century, child sexual abuse was either simply ignored or elaborately reconstructed. Either it didn't really happen and all children tended to imagine it, or occasional miscreant kids followed their wishful thinking into seductive conquest. In that psychological wonderland the real experience of survivors and offenders alike was obscured by professional mythology. Both aspects of the myth were created and maintained not from a reflection of a child's vulnerability but through reframing by self-protective and empowered adults. By accepting the thinking errors of child predators, the wise elders cast the children as predators and liars, attractive nuisances capable of destroying the noble destiny of men with their siren song of irresistible innocence. With the "discovery" of parental child abuse and through the feminist revolution of the 1960s and 1970s, the picture was abruptly reframed: Children can't help it and adults are entirely answerable for any form of maltreatment. Unlike the gender parity assumed for other forms of child abuse, children became defined as daughters, and abusers were presumed to be fathers. The victim-perpetrator dichotomy defined by the protective service and rape crisis models left boy victims and nonfamily offenders in relative obscurity. Boy victims and their chicken hawk predators were the concern of vice cops. A corollary group of sexual exploitation and sex ring specialists was ignored and sometimes erased in the rush to concentrate on incest. Cracks appeared in the solidarity of the CPS-feminist efforts as one side pushed family reunification and treatment while the other demanded incarceration for father-rapists.

Even as sociologists and journalists succeeded in exposing the awful prevalence of child sexual abuse, there was no coherent interest in the demographics and ecology of an adult society populated by a substantial bloc of invisible survivors. Those survivors who chose to reveal themselves were defined by the mind-set of whatever service system they happened to select. In rape crisis centers, they were victims of crime who should empower themselves through collective protest and court reform. Strong women were welcome, but there was no audience for the inner voice of a helpless, hungry child. Traditional psychotherapeutic systems defined that hidden child as borderline character pathology. Twelve-step addiction programs and human potential groups defined "inner children" while pioneers in the treatment of dissociative disorders discovered "child alters." The more exotic and complicated the concepts of dissociation and multiplicity became, the more such ideas were shunned by conservative psychiatrists and incest specialists alike. Senior psychiatrists labeled multiple personality as an iatrogenic fraud. Women's advocates resented the emergence of a "treatment industry" that turned victimized women into mental patients hugging teddy bears. But in all service sectors there was a common recognition of something unexpected: Many survivors had managed at some time not to know of their history of childhood trauma.

The foregoing summary is at risk of irresponsible stereotyping. It is presented in hopes of illustrating the conceptual chaos generated by the unexpected and fragmentary discovery of child sexual abuse. The explosive awareness was unanticipated but hardly unprecedented. It was the century-old censure of previous discoveries that had reinforced a preference for deliberate ignorance, or *nescience*. Real science, valid consciousness, and reasonable conscience, all of which are named after the root *to know*, are all distorted and misguided where they are infused with nescience, that which is proclaimed as unspeakable, officially not to be known.

Is it any wonder, then, that the painful experience of the victimized child has not yet achieved parity with the discomfort of adults who are forced to share it? Is it not important that the child's voice is stifled both by an offender who hides from his own offending and a society that offends by hiding its own capacity for perversity? We are willing dupes for the blandishment of offenders: We have always welcomed their reasonable explanations and applauded the discretion of silent children.

As many of us are unprepared for the depth of our societal ignorance, so are we nonplussed by the entrenched power in society to punish impertinent knowledge. It should not be surprising that well-meaning professors and lab-bound researchers have joined with insulted parents to champion the preexisting backlash. They all denounce the therapeutic upstarts who treat recovered memories of abuse as real. We who once attacked the perpetrators of sexual abuse as the enemies of the people are now fair game as the greater enemy, accused of perpetrating an international hysteria in our relentless hunt for victims and for victim-related pathology.

In this topsy-turvy, Chicken Little gaggle of claims and counterclaims, accusations and counteraccusations, one fact should stand unquestioned: There is and always has been more power and credibility afforded to those who deny sexual abuse than to those who claim it is real and dangerous. And because sexual abuse is mostly a private, one-on-one contest of grotesquely unbalanced power, there is no "trustworthy" or "objective" testimony to prove beyond a reasonable doubt that it exists. We have advanced too many ideas among too many fields in too short a time to present a coherent diagnosis. And although the competing idealogues among survivor advocates abandon one another in search of their own peculiar truth, a wider diversity of more confident adults achieves an unlikely resonance in voicing a simple, kill-the-messenger solution: Banish the therapeutic upstarts who have coached the complaints.

Unlike an initiate, who may look at the cover to guide in the assembly of all the pieces in the picture puzzle box, society has never had access to the picture, only the pieces. Unlike the puzzlemaker, who prints both the fractured puzzle and the congruent solution, there is no trusted proprietor of the real design for sexual victimization. We have arrived at our different pictures by ignoring the spaces within our partial solutions. Adult society as a whole stands in judgment against our errors without offering to help in bridging the obvious gaps.

Among all these divisive players and disillusioned observers, there is only one proprietor of the picture, only one group that has direct, experiential access to the solution. If anyone has seen the picture before cutting it apart, it is the cunning designers of the puzzle. Throughout history, a few adults have wreaked havoc among the whole of society to create a multitude of disenfranchised victims. This elite corps is not the mental health upstarts and not the feminist revolutionaries; it is the child molesters. They are the ones who *know* the picture and they are the ones who can obscure it, even from themselves. We could learn from offenders if we would only risk challenging our own prejudicial avoidance and deciphering their deliberate misconceptions.

In recent years, there has been a growing body of knowledge among offender therapists who have managed to work uphill against the wrath of victim advocates. Despite divided sympathies and mutual estrangement, some offender therapists and victim advocates have found rapprochement in daring to talk with one another and with their opposite clienteles. These crossover therapists propose a revisionist, more ambitious aggregation of our divergent views of the picture: Neither the offender nor the victim has an objective, fly-on-the-wall view of the victimization process. The offender brings an idealized, self-fulfilling prophecy to the encounter with a preselected, noncomplaining victim. The child becomes something of a partner by incorporating the intruder's deceptive scenario. Just as there is no fingerprint definition of the typical pedophile, there is no single portrait to identify the victim. To understand the misconceptions and the assaulted identity of the victim/survivor, we must recognize the footprints on the soul that are the stamp of the misguided trespasser.

Anna Salter is one of those intrepid crossover therapists. Although she has no protective sympathy for the acts of the child molester, she achieves a painful awareness of the chimerical complexity of their self-fulfilling drives. She has confronted and defined the chimera of abuse through her gut-wrenching therapeutic immersion in the life experience of every sort of victim and offender. She has also tasted and spit back the wrath of the backlash in a courtroom assault on her professional integrity.

At this point in our recent and troubled history, no one can or should claim to be the universal and undisputed custodian of the truth. We have no right to presume that the FMS Foundation consists mainly of false deniers any more than that organization can brand all recovered memories as false. Such presumptions are not scientific, merely mutually antagonistic, and the smoke of that battle can only help the real child predators to maintain their cover in both camps.

The only way to escape the smoke is to rise above it in the persistent search for objective truth. The many colors of our partial enlightenment must be integrated into a coherent outlook. The spectrum of credibility and the dividing line between deceiver and deceived have never been more indistinct nor more deliberately blurred.

Dr. Salter has sought to look at every visible shade of the spectrum and to illumine the imposing shadows. If there are many colors of light in the spectrum of science, there is a greater complexity of darkness hiding in the blind spot of our continuing nescience.

Transforming Trauma is aptly named. By taking us into the dark side of offenders, beyond our bright, collective idealism, and by acknowledging the footprints such offenses leave on the untrammeled innocence of children and on our own wishful naïveté, Dr. Salter helps transform murky and unutterable horror into a source for enlightenment. By defining the smelter of entrapment, she forges new keys to release.

A backlash book of the moment condemns the treatment of trauma as the making of monsters. *Transforming Trauma* brings together exquisite clinical and scientific illustration to unmake the monsters each of us may have imagined. The proven child molesters are not so hideous and cunning that we dare not confront them. They are a ragtag band of opportunists who either can continue to hide in the deliberate ignorance they help to sustain or allow us to find the missing pieces that could blow their cover.

Dr. Salter has opened the window to such enlightenment and widened the door to more effective, more empathic treatment of survivors and offenders alike. I hope the much-maligned "treatment industry" as well as the larger world of skeptical onlookers will be equally inspired by her efforts.

Acknowledgments

I would like to thank the following colleagues who graciously took the time to read and critique the manuscript: Ellen Bass, John Briere, Jon Conte, Laura Davis, Rob Freeman-Longo, Steven Kairys, Cynthia Monahon, Tony Morrison, Lloyd Sinclair, and Regina Yando. They are all busy and talented folk whose generosity with their time and expertise were gifts that strengthened this book.

I would like to especially thank Roland Summit, who, in the middle of a frantic schedule, read this manuscript carefully on planes and in motel rooms all the way to Hong Kong and sent back detailed, thoughtful notes on nearly every page. This book is immeasurably enriched by his clinical acumen.

I would like to express my appreciation to Andrew Garrod, who edited this book as well as my first. Andrew brought to the task not only a precise command of good English but an unusually good grasp of the subject matter. He also brought a high level of professionalism and dedication. This book is clearer and more gracefully written for his help.

I would like to thank the Bay Foundation, whose support at a crucial time was pivotal. In particular, I would like to thank Fred Bay, whose assistance with a variety of projects over the years has been singularly helpful.

I would like to thank my secretary, Judy MacNeil, a woman of many talents, who has been simultaneously secretary, research assistant, travel agent, bookkeeper, and loving baby-sitter. In the midst of chaos, she is always calm, supportive, and warm.

I would like to thank Tumpale Kilindu, my research assistant, for her competence and her carefulness.

Finally, I would like to thank George Vaillant for his wisdom.

Introduction

In the past decade, the field of child sexual abuse treatment has polarized into sex offender treatment and victim treatment specialties for good cause. Although some clinicians maintain that offenders and victims have the same dynamics, and others believe that they can be treated with the same techniques and even in the same groups (Giarretto, 1982), it is more common for offender and victim treatment specialists to take radically different perspectives on the theoretical underpinnings, methods of treatment, and even the nature of the therapeutic contract between therapist and client.

With sex offenders, aversive conditioning techniques are frequently used (Maletzky, 1991; Marshall, Laws, & Barbaree, 1990; Quinsey & Marshall, 1983), as are confrontational techniques, both applied individually and in groups (Abel et al., 1984; Salter, 1988), and even techniques that use shame (Knopp, 1984). Court involvement is often required. Pressure is exerted on sex offenders to take plethysmograph and polygraph examinations, sign liberal releases of confidentiality, and cooperate fully with treatment at the risk of incarceration should they not.

Although some sex offender treatment specialists emphasize the necessity of trust within the therapeutic relationship (Maletzky, 1991), it is more common for clinicians to warn against the dangers of trust (Knopp, 1984) and to suggest external monitoring instead (Pithers, 1990). Sexual offending is frequently noted to

1

have some similarities with addictive behavior (Carnes, 1983), a comparison that makes the folly of relying on trust and self-report all too obvious.

With adult survivors, however, even the most aggressive treatment does not include aversive conditioning techniques. Confirmation is emphasized over confrontation, and the reduction of shame, not its cultivation, is a primary goal. Techniques that might take away control from the survivor are considered emergency measures to be used only in life-threatening circumstances (Briere, 1992a; Herman, 1992). The reduction of the underlying pain associated with sexual abuse is often the primary focus of treatment rather than the control of specific symptoms.

By contrast, sex offender treatment programs universally see the reduction of the specific symptom—sexual offending—as the primary, if not only, focus of treatment. Outcome of sex offender treatment is not measured in terms of increased self-esteem or decreased personal distress, but rather reduced recidivism.

Thus far, outcome research on both groups suggests that focused therapy is promising (Foa, Rothbaum, & Steketee, 1993; Maletzky, 1991; Marshall et al., 1990; Pithers, 1990; Resick, 1993), although there are those in the sex offender field who feel the research at present is insufficient to say one way or the other (Quinsey, Harris, Rice, & Lalumière, 1993) and those who feel there is no evidence that anything works with sex offenders (Furby, Weinrott, & Blackshaw, 1989).

So what is wrong with this picture? Treatment has become more focused and specific, supported by outcome research that generally suggests improved efficacy.

What is wrong is that in the profusion of separate books, separate treatment providers, and separate conferences, there is little emphasis on the links between sex offenders and victims. It is a premise of this book that some of the harsh, self-punitive thinking patterns of adult survivors can be traced to an internalization of the thinking errors of sex offenders. In addition, different types of sex offenders think in different ways and leave different "footprints" (Hindman, 1989) within adult survivors.

Adult survivor specialists who are not aware of the thinking patterns of offenders are at risk of dealing superficially with the echo of those patterns in survivors. It is not enough to tell an adult survivor, however kindly, that she is wrong in her self-blame for the abuse. As Briere (1992a) points out, the metamessage implicit in such a communication may simply reinforce her belief that she is once again in error. "I know it's wrong," many survivors say with embarrassment and guilt, "but I still feel it's my fault." Victim treatment specialists who do not recognize an internalized offender when they hear one are often frustrated by the tenacity of the survivor's self-blame. At its worst, an argument ensues.

Likewise, the seeming normality of offenders, their frequent high status in the community, their denial patterns, and their extraordinary compulsivity around sexual abuse affect victims in very specific ways. This vital knowledge is unavailable to the survivor treatment specialist who does not study offenders.

On the other side, without a knowledge of victim dynamics, sex offender therapists cannot effectively monitor offender apologies to prevent them from reoffending. In addition, offender therapists cannot help their clients appreciate the harm they have done without understanding the thinking patterns of adult survivors.

Unquestionably, the development of specialized treatment services for offenders and victims has yielded far better results than the generic, insight-oriented psychotherapy common 10 years ago. But at present, there is unmapped territory between these two approaches that has crucial significance for healing in survivors and change in offenders.

Although it is my hope that this book will be useful to both those who treat sex offenders and those who treat adult survivors, my focus will be on the treatment of survivors. What does the clinician who treats adult survivors need to know about sex offenders? How do sadistic and nonsadistic offenders think differently, and what are the different footprints they leave in the heads of survivors? How does trauma affect the worldview of victims? Exactly how can clinicians help their clients shake free of an internalized perpetrator? What are the steps of therapy for adult survivors? Finally, how can trauma not be just endured, but transformed? Answering those questions will constitute the bulk of the book.

A bridge between the world of offenders and victims, however, is only one of the links this book will explore. It will also move between the research literature and clinical impression. It will review the research on the compulsivity of offenders and on the sequelae in victims. Ultimately, however, the healing properties of therapy cannot be explained with tables. In the end, it is necessary to simply assert what therapy with adult survivors is and suggest how to do it.

In moving from the research to the clinical, the book also moves from the measured tones of academic writing to more metaphoric rhythms. For some, no doubt the change of tone will surprise. But I change it unapologetically. I believe the scientist and the clinician, the academic and the poet must both be brought together if we are to enter the arena of healing. Without a research scaffolding, our clinical impressions are mere daydreams. But, like a superhighway that simply stops, the research will take us only so far. "In ghostlier demarcations," Wallace Stevens wrote, "keener sounds" (Stevens, 1969, p. 130). The human heart is not explained by an analysis of muscle; health is more than the absence of symptoms; joy is not only a lack of depression. We must bring not just our left-brain logic to bear—and the prose that accompanies it—but whatever we can muster for poetic imagination.

I end the book with an epilogue in the form of a personal essay on the nature of safety for adult survivors. As I reflect on writing this book, I think safety was on my mind for a reason. In many ways, this entire book is about safety. Few will read the chapters on offenders without subsequently feeling less safe for themselves and their children. The chapter on cognitive changes in adult survivors documents how unsafe survivors feel, and the chapter on affective sequelae describes attacks from within as well as without. Inevitably, studying sex offenders, and the havoc they wreak, diminishes one's own sense of safety in the world.

But if working in this field decreases one's sense of safety, it increases the sense of awe. The starfish is not the only creature that can grow new limbs. The human capacity for recovery is astounding. "How can you do this work?" the layperson asks (endlessly, it seems). I think for most clinicians, the answer is that we are fascinated by transformation and by change. We hear of death, but we see birth.

I

What Do We Know About Sex Offenders and What Does It Mean?

Compulsivity and Repetitiveness

If the widespread sexual assault of children and adult women has historically been, in Rush's words, "the best kept secret" (Herman, 1981; Rush, 1980; Summit, 1988)—so well-kept that some have termed it a "shared negative hallucination" (Goodwin, 1985a, p. 14; Summit, 1988)—then surely the second largest societal blind spot has been the compulsiveness and repetitiveness of the sexual offender. Certainly sex offenders themselves have little reason to emphasize the intransigence of their behavior. Legal sanctions and societal disapproval have virtually guaranteed that sexual offenders accused of child molestation or rape either deny the offense altogether or admit to the minimum possible even while they justify to the maximum possible.

Wormith (1983) found, for example, that only 65% of a sample of 205 sex offenders (53% rapists, 7% attempted rapists, 36% child molesters, and 4% miscellaneous sexual offenders) who had not only been charged and prosecuted but also convicted and incarcerated for a sexual offense, admitted to it. Likewise, Becker, Cunningham-Rathner, and Kaplan (1986) found in their sample of 67 adolescent sex offenders seen in an outpatient setting that 31% denied the act entirely, 42% admitted part of what they were accused of, and only 27% admitted entirely to what they had been accused of.

Those who do admit something characteristically admit to the single offense for which they are caught and deny a history of other similar or dissimilar sexual offenses. They deny, too, a history of deviant thoughts and fantasies. Becker and Quinsey (1993) agree that "frequently, the alleged child molesters distort information, falsely deny that the alleged offence occurred, and report difficulty in recalling events surrounding the offence" (p. 170). The denial of a sex offender sometimes strains the credulity of the most gullible.

> A 14-year-old male was charged with sexual assault after grabbing a female classmate while walking her home from school and dragging her halfway into the woods. He wrestled her to the ground, tore her blouse half off, and produced a knife, which he drove toward her face but diverted at the last moment so that it stuck into the ground by her ear. The girl managed to free herself and ran home. The entire event was witnessed by another schoolmate, a male friend of the offender who was also walking home with them, and he testified against his classmate. Prior to the evaluation, the examiner obtained police interviews with a number of other classmates and younger children who, while being interviewed in regard to this offense, described to the police other assaults by this same individual as well as a pattern of chronic sexual harassment and sexual intimidation that had increasingly terrorized a rather large circle of children. All in all, the examiner had 34 documents on her desk that testified to her client's previous deviant sexual behavior and his predilection for knives. He admitted to owning 28.
>
> Upon interview, the offender denied he had assaulted his classmate on the walk home, denied that he had ever assaulted or intimidated anyone, denied other sexually deviant behaviors, denied any deviant fantasies, denied that he had ever had a single nondeviant sexual thought or fantasy, and denied that he had masturbated. He further volunteered that he had never held his penis while urinating.

Indeed, the entire category of regressed offender (Groth, Hobson, & Gary, 1982) must be viewed with some suspicion because it is based on self-report and is difficult to verify independently. Sex offenders sometimes use such categorization to deny responsibility and to claim they are not "real pedophiles." Indeed, the denial of sex offenders is so well-established and well-entrenched that norming of the Multiphasic Sex Inventory has established that deviant scores typically go up rather than down after treatment (Nichols & Molinder, 1984). Nichols and Molinder believe that this reflects the increased honesty of the offenders after treatment rather than any increased deviancy.

However, self-report differs in its reliability depending on the circumstances. An offender facing legal sanctions or familial confrontation has more reason to deny or minimize his offenses than does an incarcerated offender who is guaranteed anonymity. An outpatient offender not facing legal sanctions or one who is guaranteed immunity from prosecution for newly disclosed offenses may have less reason yet to deny. Increasingly, research that guarantees anonymity and/or confidentiality to sexual offenders has revealed a high degree of repetitiveness and compulsiveness to their behavior. Table 1.1 summarizes a number of studies that have obtained information under conditions designed to optimize offender reliability.

Bernard (1975) reported on a sample of 50 predominantly male-oriented pedophiles (96% preferred male children) who were members of the Dutch "Working Group of Pedophilia," presumably a pedophilic organization. Thirty percent claimed to have molested 10 children or less; 28% had molested from 10 to 50 children, and 14% admitted to molesting from 50 to 300 children. (The remainder answered "some" or "many.") Fifty-four percent stated they had at least one child whom they were molesting at the time they filled out the questionnaire. Many of the sample had traveled to foreign countries to obtain boys for anal intercourse, and although more than half had been sentenced for child molestation and 38% had received psychiatric treatment, 90% had no desire to reduce or eliminate their sexual interest in children.

TABLE 1.1 Charged and Anonymously Admitted Sex Offenses

Name	N	Sample	Arrested	Admitted		Victims
				Acts		
Bernard (1975)	50	Male-oriented pedophiles				30% had fewer than 10; 28% had 10-50; 14% had 50-300
Weinrott and Saylor (1991)	37 / 67	Rapists / Child molesters	66 rapes / 136 child victims	433 rapes / > 8,000 contacts		959 child victims
Freeman-Longo (1985)	23	Rapists	43 sex offenses	5,090 sex crimes including 178 rapes and 319 child molestations		Rapists plus child molesters = 17,392 victims
	30	Child molesters	45 sex offenses	> 20,000 sex crimes including 213 rapes and 5,891 child molestations		
Groth, Longo, and McFadin (1982)	83 / 54	Rapists / Child molesters	232 sex offenses / 92 sex offenses	1,162 rapes		594 child victims
Marshall, Barbaree, and Eccles (1991)	129	Outpatient child molesters		< 5 victims each		
Abel et al. (1987)	561	Sex offenders		291,737 paraphilic acts including 63,965 child molestations		195,407 victims including 27,777 child victims

8

Weinrott and Saylor (1991) studied an incarcerated sample of 37 rapists and 67 child molesters. The rapists had been arrested a total of 52 times and charged with 66 rapes. The mean number of victims was 1.8. These same 37 men self-reported 433 rapes, with a mean of 11.7 victims and a median of 6 victims each. The 67 child molesters were known to have molested 136 victims, with a median of 1 victim per man. However, they admitted to more than 8,000 sexual contacts with 959 children. The number of victims ranged from 1 to 200 with a median of 7.

Freeman-Longo (1985) distributed anonymous questionnaires to 23 rapists and 30 child molesters in an institutional forensic mental health program. All inmates had been in treatment at least a month and were guaranteed confidentiality. He found that the rapists had 43 arrests total, or 1.86 arrests per subject. However, they admitted to 5,090 sex crimes (221 per person), including 319 child molestations and 178 rapes. The child molesters had averaged only 1.5 arrests per man, whereas they admitted more than 20,000 sex offenses, including nearly 6,000 child molestations and 213 rapes. This sample of 53 men had more than 17,000 victims.

Groth, Longo, and McFadin (1982) found that an incarcerated sample of 83 rapists and 54 child molesters admitted anonymously to 2 to 5 times more offenses than had come to the attention of the criminal justice system. The child molesters alone reported an average of 11 sexual offenses for which they were not charged.

Other studies have not found the high numbers cited above, although they all found undetected recidivism. Marshall, Barbaree, and Eccles (1991), in their study of 129 child molesters in an outpatient treatment setting, found that the offenders reported, on average, fewer than 5 victims each. Older studies by Frisbie, Vanasek, and Dingman (1967) and Gebhard, Gagnon, Pomeroy, and Christenson (1965) found even lower rates among incarcerated sex offenders—fewer than two different paraphilic acts per offender.

The most comprehensive study in this area, however, found the highest rates of all (Abel et al., 1987; Becker & Quinsey, 1993).

The astounding rates of sexual offending documented in this study has galvanized clinical and research interest equally. A sample of 561 sex offenders reported that they had completed a total of 291,737 paraphilic acts with a total of 195,407 victims. (Although Abel et al. included ego dystonic homosexuality in their figures, if we were to remove the 3,701 homosexual acts and the 2 "victims," there would be little effect on the totals.) The subgroup of 377[1] extrafamilial child molesters in the sample were responsible for 48,297 acts against a total of 27,416 victims. Those who molested female children averaged 19.8 victims; those who molested male children averaged 150.2 victims. The 203 incest offenders in the group committed 15,668 acts against 361 victims.

Abel et al. (1987) calculated the chances of getting caught for child molestation at approximately 3%. But perhaps this is not surprising given Russell's (1984) findings that fewer than 5% of the 647 child molestations reported in her study of adult females were ever reported to the police.

Why are there such dramatic differences in the literature? It is tempting to consider the Abel et al. study the anomalous one because its figures are higher than all the others. However, there are reasons why the Abel et al. study may prove to be the most accurate, despite its staggering figures and its current lack of replication.

Specifically, none of the other studies to date has taken as much care to ensure offenders that their information was both anonymous and confidential. First, Abel et al. only accepted voluntary subjects not under court order for evaluation or treatment. Second, each subject read and signed a detailed consent form explaining the need to avoid specifics about any given offense that would allow the victim to be identified. Third, subjects were given confidential identification numbers and charts were coded only by number. The master code matching names and numbers was kept outside the United States to prevent any attempts at subpoena. Fourth, a Certificate of Confidentiality was obtained from the Secretary of Health, Education and Welfare that ensured that no city, county, state, or federal agency could seek the identities of the subjects. In addition, subjects entered the building from a common entrance frequented by many other individuals. Finally, subjects were told that a primary goal of the study was to help them understand their own behavior and gain control over it. They were given reports if requested, but such reports were released only to them or to those they specified.

All of these protections were included in a 1-hour videotape that each participant watched prior to signing the consent form. He was then given the chance to ask questions and express concerns before signing. Prior to the structured interview beginning, he was reminded that he could withdraw without penalty at any point.

By contrast, the study by Marshall et al. (1991) relied on the rapport between offender and therapist to ensure accurate reporting. No offender was asked questions before at least five interviews had occurred and until the therapist felt that he or she had the patient's confidence. Therefore, the offenders were by no means anonymous and were reporting to a therapist with whom they had a therapeutic relationship.

It could be argued that individuals in therapy typically want to be liked by their therapists. Asking such a client to come up with information about his deviant past could be seen as putting the client in a bind. If he wants to please the therapist, he will come up with something, but will he come up with everything if he thinks that the extent of his deviancy is so great that it might alienate the therapist? Clinical experience suggests that offenders typically "test the waters," that is, give some information and see how it is received over time before they reveal more extensive deviancy.

In addition, some offenders were referred by child protection agencies and probation and parole officers in the Marshall study, which suggests that they may have been under scrutiny by outside agencies and possibly even under court order. Those within the criminal justice system tend to be hypervigilant about providing information that could be used against them, particularly in determining or maintaining probation or parole. Kaplan (1985) found, for example, that offenders who were guaranteed confidentiality by probation and parole officers revealed only 5% of the reports to those officers that they revealed to mental health workers in a nonjudicial setting.

Most of the studies cited here were on incarcerated offenders. However, both the Bernard (1975) study and the Abel et. al (1987) study were on offenders without current ties to the judicial system, and both found unusually high rates of offending. Their figures, therefore, are likely to be more accurate than those given by prisoners.

Support for the supposition that sexual offending is a particularly tenacious and compulsive behavior can be found in the clinical as well as academic realm:

> A California optician who molested boys while giving them eye exams molested his last victim 2 hours before he was due in court for sentencing.

> In Dallas, a stepfather molested his leukemia-stricken 9-year-old daughter for the second time while awaiting sentencing for the first offense. In both cases, he molested her following a chemotherapy session that left her ill and weakened.

> In Virginia, an evangelical preacher admitted to molesting more than 100 boys during his 20 years of preaching.

> On Long Island, two people in their late teens, already charged with "numerous" accounts of sexual abuse of children, were charged with an additional 302 counts.

> In Kentucky, a minister, incarcerated for molesting his two grandchildren, was asked, "What excuse or rationalization did you have that made it possible for you to suspend your conscience and do what you did right at the time?" He replied, "I didn't suspend my conscience. I carried it right into the action with me. . . . I suppose that, being a devout religious person, if I had of believed with all of my mind and heart that the earth was going to open up and swallow me up in hell, I would have went ahead and done it anyway."

Conclusions

Increasingly, research and clinical experience both suggest that sexual offending is a highly compulsive and repetitive behavior. Typically, the offense for which an offender[2] is caught is by no means his first assault, even if the offender is an adolescent. Awad and Saunders (1991), for example, found that 61% of their sample of 49 adolescent sexual assaulters and 40% of their sample of 45 adolescent child molesters had a history of prior sexual offending. As will be seen, the tenacity of sexual offending behavior will have repercussions for victims in a number of areas, including family reunification, perpetrator remorse and apologies, and safety of the victim's children around the perpetrator.

Sex Offenders: Specialists or Generalists?

Several years ago, a police officer approached me with the question, "Is it true if a man is a rapist, he can't be a child molester?" "Why do you ask?" I replied. "Well, we have this guy for abducting a 12-year-old in a van and molesting her, but he has previous convictions for rape, and he's saying everybody knows he's a rapist so he can't be a child molester. Also, his therapist is agreeing with him."

Putting aside for the moment definitional issues of whether someone who abducts a 12-year-old in a van and has forced intercourse with her is a child molester or a rapist, clinical experience until recently would have agreed with the offender's main point —that rapists rarely molest children. Few accused or even convicted sex offenders admitted to more than the offense for which they had been caught, if they admitted to that. Although therapists usually inquire about other offenses of the same type, they have rarely looked for different types of offenses.

That this failure to ask only about the current offense could result in gross clinical error was pointed out by Abel, Mittelman, and Becker (1985), who described an 18-year-old sex offender caught for touching women's buttocks in the subway. Although

TABLE 1.2 Child Molesters' and Rapists' Paraphilias (in percentages)

Paraphilia	Child Molesters	Rapists
Pedophilia	100.0	50.6
Rape	16.8	100.0
Exhibitionism	29.7	29.2
Voyeurism	13.8	20.2
Sadism	5.6	11.2
Frottage	8.6	12.4
Obscene phone calls	0.0	4.5

SOURCE: Adapted from Abel, Mittelman, and Becker (1985).

he admitted a 2-year interest in frottage, he denied other deviant arousal. However, when presented with audiotaped descriptions of a (fictional) offender describing sexual interactions with an 8- to 10-year-old girl, he developed 60% of a full erection.

After confrontation with the plethysmograph results, he admitted that when he was 15 years old, he had sexually attacked an 8-year-old girl and murdered her while he was on cocaine. He was subsequently incarcerated for 3 years. Since his release, he had found himself sexually attracted to very young girls but had told no one for fear of reincarceration.

In fact, there is considerable research evidence at present that multiple paraphilias should be considered in every case of sexual offense. The crossover can perhaps be seen most easily by looking at the percentage of offenders in each category who had other paraphilias in addition to the index offense. In a report on a sample of 411 sex offenders, Abel et al. (1985) summarized the percentages of child molesters and rapists who had additional paraphilias (see Table 1.2).

As can be seen, 51% of rapists had also committed child molestation, whereas 17% of child molesters had also raped. Almost 30% of both child molesters and rapists were exhibitionists. Fully one fifth of rapists were also voyeurs.

In a later publication that reported results on an enlarged sample of 561 men, Abel and Rouleau (1990) noted the percentage

TABLE 1.3 Percentage of Multiple Paraphilias Among Sex Offenders by Type (in percentages)

Diagnosis	Number of Paraphilias			
	N	1	2-4	5+
Pedophilia				
Extrafamilial female	224	15	58	27
Extrafamilial male	153	19	59	22
Incest female	159	28	49	23
Incest male	44	5	55	41
Rape	126	27	49	24
Exhibitionism	142	7	58	34
Voyeurism	62	2	52	47
Frottage	62	21	45	34
Sadism	28	0	61	39
Obscene phone calls	19	5	48	48

SOURCE: From Abel et al. (1988). Reprinted after revision with permission of the American Academy of Psychiatry and the Law.

who had one or more paraphilias. Table 1.3 summarizes those data.

As can be seen in Table 1.3, only a minority of offenders in each category had a single paraphilia. More than 80% of extrafamilial child molesters and more than 70% of incest offenders had more than one paraphilia. Within the category of 5+ paraphilias, the sadists and the incest offenders who molested male children particularly stood out. Abel et al. (1988) reported that fully 7% of the former and 9% of the latter had 10 paraphilias.

Freund (1990) corroborated Abel et al.'s findings. Multiple paraphilias were common in his sample of 440 exhibitionists, voyeurs, frotteurs/touchers, and rapists seen at a psychiatric teaching hospital. Table 1.4 summarizes his findings.

Table 1.4 indicates that a majority of voyeurs, exhibitionists, and frotteurs had other forms of paraphilia. Only among rapists did a minority admit to other paraphilias, and rape was the least-admitted-to offense among the other paraphiliacs.

However, as Freund pointed out, his population consisted of sex offenders who were not promised confidentiality. In fact, the

TABLE 1.4 Percentage of Types of Multiple Paraphilias Among Sex Offenders

Type	N	Voyeur	Exhibitionist	Toucher/ Frotteur	Rapist	Other
Voyeur	94	—	82	38	19	90
Exhibitionist	241	32	—	30	15	56
Toucher/frotteur	119	30	61	—	22	77
Rapist	195	9	19	13	—	28

SOURCE: From Freund (1990). Reprinted after revision by permission of the author.

outcome of the clinical interview and test results was to be reported ultimately to the courts or to the offenders' lawyers. He noted, "Many patients who freely admit to exhibitionism are nonetheless reluctant to admit to having raped" (Freund, 1990, p. 200). Given that, it is remarkable that the figures on multiple paraphilias are as high as they are—with as many as 90% of voyeurs, 56% of exhibitionists, and 77% of frotteurs admitting to some other type of paraphilia.

Weinrott and Saylor (1991) likewise found a high incidence of multiple paraphilias in their incarcerated sample of sex offenders. Based on criminal records, 85% of the sample of 99 men could be classified as having one class of victims—either adult female, extrafamilial child, or intrafamilial child. However, only 48% could be classified as having one type of victim based on confidential self-report. Thirty-two percent of the rapists also admitted to child molestation, but only half of those (16%) had been arrested for it. Twelve percent of the child molesters admitted to at least one attempted or completed rape, none of which was in their official records. Thirty-four percent of the extrafamilial offenders had also committed incest. Half of the known incest offenders admitted to child abuse outside the home, none of which had been detected.

Lower rates have been reported by some researchers. Marshall et al. (1991) found that only 14% of the extrafamilial female-oriented child molesters and 12% of the male-oriented child molesters had more than one paraphilia, whereas 8% of the incest offenders had more than one. None of this sample of offenders admitted to more than three additional paraphilias.

Conclusions and Cautions

The occurrence of multiple paraphilias, particularly the co-occurrence of voyeurism and exhibitionism, has been reported frequently in the past (Gebhard et al., 1965; Rooth, 1973; Smukler & Schiebel, 1975; Yalom, 1960). The contribution of research in the past 5 years has been to establish that far higher numbers of sex offenders may have multiple paraphilias than previously thought, including as many as 25% or more who may have five or more (Abel et al., 1988). Although contrary evidence exists (e.g., Marshall et al., 1991), the preponderance of evidence at present appears to be on the side of those who report that sexual offending is a generic problem. Sex offenders averaged 2.02 paraphilias, according to Abel et al. (1987), leading him to conclude that "individuals with one and only one paraphilia are rather uncommon" (Abel & Rouleau, 1990, p. 16).

Given the probabilities, it seems clear that men who commit one sexual offense should be carefully assessed for others. Although a thorough assessment will include both plethysmograph and polygraph examination, simply asking the sex offender about other categories of victims and other types of sexual offenses will sometimes yield results. I was asked to consult on an exhibitionist who had written a threatening letter to his therapist and who was hospitalized in a psychiatric inpatient unit. The conversation included the following:

Dr. Salter: *What other sexual deviant behaviors have you engaged in?*

Patient: *None.*

Dr. Salter: *What about child molestation?*

Patient: *Well, there was the 9-year-old I got undressed and had her in bed with me but her mother walked in.*

Dr. Salter: *What other deviant behaviors?*

Patient: *None.*

Dr. Salter: *What about obscene phone calls?*

Patient: *Well, yes, I like them a lot.*

Dr. Salter: *How often do you make them?*

Patient: *I'll go on a tear and do 50 a day for a week or so. Then I won't do any for a few weeks.*

Dr. Salter: *What other sexual behaviors?*

Patient: *None.*

Dr. Salter: *What about rape?*

Patient: *I've just had a few fantasies.*

Dr. Salter: *Tell me about the fantasies.*

(Patient leans forwards in animated manner, stares straight at the examiner, and starts to graphically describe the physical attack itself.)

Dr. Salter: *Hold it. Do not pass go. Do not collect $200. Tell me about the fantasies leading up to the rape. How do you find your victim? How do you get control of them?*

Patient: (Patient sits back, apparently disappointed.) *I go to town and follow a female backpacker to the woods.* (The Appalachian trail runs through this patient's town.)

Dr. Salter: *Have you done that?*

Patient: *Yeah.*

Dr. Salter: *In the fantasy, how do you overcome the backpacker?*

Patient: *With a knife.*

Dr. Salter: *Have you bought the knife?*

Patient: *Yeah.*

Dr. Salter: *Do you carry it when you follow the backpackers?*

Patient: *Yes.*

Although this patient would not admit to having raped anyone, he did admit enough for it to be clear that he is not simply an exhibitionist, but at minimum has multiple paraphilias and is currently involved in the "rape walk," a planning and rehearsal technique used by rapists prior to committing rape. Of course, it is possible, perhaps even probable, that he is simply a rapist smart enough to deny actually breaking the law.

Unfortunately, all too often, sex offenders are not asked about types of sexually deviant behaviors other than the index offense.

Abel et al. (1985, pp. 193-194) reported the following conversation with a rapist.

Dr. Abel: *What other sexual behaviors have you been involved in?*
Subject: (No reply)
Dr. Abel: *Have you been attracted to kids?* (Long pause)
Subject: *Oh yeah, I've been involved with kids about 4 years.*
Dr. Abel: *How many times have you been involved with them?*
Subject: *More than 30 or 40 times.*
Dr. Abel: *What did your previous doctor say about that?*
Subject: *Well, he didn't say anything.*
Dr. Abel: *Did you tell him?*
Subject: *Well, no!*
Dr. Abel: *Why didn't you tell him about your interest in kids?*
Subject: *Because, he didn't ask.*

Worse, it appears that some interviewers do not even ask important questions about the offense for which the offender is seeking treatment. Maletzky (1991), with a sample of more than 5,000 sex offenders treated by his clinic, found that "a number of sexual offenders, once involved in treatment, have confided that their therapist did not ask them about aberrant arousal patterns and masturbatory practices during the course of the evaluation" (p. 40).

Nonsexual Offenses

Rapists

One of the most startling findings to come out of the recent literature on sex offenders is the extent to which even incest offenders have committed high numbers of nonsexual crimes. That rapists frequently engage in criminal behavior has long been known. Abel et al. (1985) found that 29% of their sample of 89 rapists met *DSM-II* criteria for antisocial personality disorder, whereas Marques,

Day, Nelson, and Miner (1989) found that as many as three fourths of their sample of 135 rapists met the criteria. Prentky and Knight (1991) determined that 40% of their sample of 106 incarcerated rapists not only met the criteria for antisocial personality according to *DSM-III*, but also met the criteria for psychopathy on Hare's Checklist for Psychopathy (Hare, 1980).

Even in adolescent samples, high numbers of those who commit sexual assaults have been found to have engaged in antisocial behavior as well. Lewis, Shanock, and Pincus (1979) found in a sample of juvenile sex offenders that all but one of their sample of 17 had records of nonsexual juvenile offenses prior to committing the sexual assaults. The one who had no previous court record had burned down his house, set fire to another, and stabbed a child in his kindergarten class, but was sent to hospital rather than court because of his age. Awad and Saunders (1991) found that 63% of their sample of 49 adolescent sexual assaulters had a history of antisocial behavior, and most of those had a delinquency record. Likewise, Pithers, Beal, Armstrong, and Petty (1989) found that 44% of 64 rapists had a prior arrest for a nonsexual offense.

Even in nonclinical samples, undetected rapists have been found to commit other antisocial acts. Rapaport (1984) found that sexually aggressive male undergraduates were more likely to have engaged in antisocial conduct of all types than were nonsexually aggressive college males. Malamuth (1989) found that the proclivity to engage in forced sex and to rape correlated with the self-reported proclivity to steal and to murder.

Still, even for rapists, the numbers found by Weinrott and Saylor (1991) were strikingly high. Thirty-seven incarcerated rapists admitted to more than 11,000 nonsexual offenses in the year preceding incarceration, which averaged roughly one crime per day per man. Every rapist reported at least one nonsexual crime, with the average number of different types of crimes being 10.5 out of a possible 22. More than half the sample had burglarized (victim-absent theft) and almost half had committed robberies (victim-present theft). The 37 rapists committed those two types of crimes 380 times during the preceding year. Sixty-two

TABLE 1.5 Nonsexual Crimes Reported by Known Rapists in the Year Prior to Commitment (N = 37)

	% of Men	Total Offenses	Mean
Used hard drugs	57	376	10.2
Hit partner	46	197	5.3
Hit another woman	89	297	8
Shoplifted	46	777	21
Stole property	62	976	26.4
Extortion	24	47	1.3
Supplied drugs to minors	46	1,009	27.3
Theft > $100	59	159	4.3
Sold hard drugs	27	554	15
Public drunkenness	84	2,231	60.3
Aggravated assault	62	120	3.2
Breaking and entering	57	315	8.5
Concealed weapon	43	2,089	56.5
Kidnapping	78	172	4.6
Robbery	46	65	1.8
Stole < $100	73	1,535	41.5
Aggregate	100	11,277	304.8

SOURCE: From Weinrott and Saylor (1991). Reprinted after revision by permission of Sage Publications, Inc.

percent of the sample admitted committing aggravated assault without a sexual component. One rapist alone (who had also molested children) admitted to 2,038 nonsexual crimes in the year preceding his arrest. Table 1.5 shows those crimes that more than 20% of the rapists admitted committing.

Child Molesters

Although it is no surprise that rapists frequently engage in nonsexual crimes, child molesters have less frequently been thought to engage in other antisocial behaviors. For example, one study (Abel et al., 1985) found that only 12% of 232 child molesters were diagnosed as antisocial personalities. Nevertheless, the Weinrott and Saylor (1991) study found that the 67 child mo-

TABLE 1.6 Nonsexual Crimes Reported by Known Child Molesters in the Year Prior to Commitment (*N* = 67)

	% of Men	*Total Offenses*	*Mean*
Hit partner	28	170	2.7
Shoplifted	27	183	2.9
Stole property	33	358	5.6
Supplied drugs to minors	23	923	14.4
Hit child in household	36	539	8.4
Hit another child	22	106	1.7
Theft > $100	23	133	2.1
Public drunkenness	44	1,360	21.2
Aggravated assault	23	63	1.0
Breaking and entering	22	223	3.5
Concealed weapon	22	1,412	22.1
Kidnapping	20	270	4.2
Stole < $100	39	759	11.8

SOURCE: From Weinrott and Saylor (1991). Reprinted after revision by permission of Sage Publications, Inc.

lesters committed more than 8,000 nonsexual crimes in the year preceding incarceration. As Table 1.6 indicates, a solid 20% or more engaged in a number of purely criminal acts, including breaking and entering, kidnapping, aggravated assault, stealing property, carrying a concealed weapon, and supplying drugs to minors. These figures are consistent with Awad and Saunders's (1991) data on adolescent child molesters. Fifty percent had a history of antisocial behavior prior to the sexual offenses.

Even when the incest offenders were isolated in the Weinrott and Saylor (1991) study, the number of nonsexual criminal acts fails to drop to zero. In fact, although reporting fewer offenses than either rapists or extrafamilial offenders, every incest offender admitted to at least one nonsexual crime. Table 1.7 reports the crimes that more than 20% of the sample of incest offenders admitted committing. It would seem that sexual offenders, even incest offenders, engage in a wide variety of nonsexual crimes.

TABLE 1.7 Nonsexual Crimes Reported by Known Incest Offenders in the Year Prior to Commitment ($N = 21$)

	% of Men	Total Offenses	Mean
Used hard drugs	24	180	8.6
Hit partner	43	38	1.8
Shoplifted	29	105	5
Stole property	29	92	4.4
Supplied drugs to minors	24	131	6.2
Hit child in household	62	456	21.7
Public drunkenness	43	162	7.7
Aggravated assault	24	23	1.1
Stole < $100	33	265	12.6

SOURCE: From Weinrott and Saylor (1991). Reprinted after revision by permission of Sage Publications, Inc.

Incest Offenders:
Are They Really Sex Offenders?

The data on multiple paraphilias and on nonsexual crimes committed by incest offenders challenges the widespread assumption that incest offenders are somehow different from other sex offenders. Traditionally, incest has been thought to be the result of family dysfunction (Alexander, 1985; de Young, 1982; Gutheil & Avery, 1977; James & Nasjleti, 1983; Lutz & Medway, 1984; Mrazek & Bentovim, 1981; Taylor, 1984).

Giarretto (1982), for example, writes in one of his chapters, "Treatment Premises Regarding the Incestuous Family," that "incestuous behavior is one of the many symptoms of a dysfunctional family" (p. 19). He further states that an offender did not make a choice to abuse. "Self-abusive and abusive behavior was the *only* [italics added] response he could make to discharge the chronic state of low self-worth caused by unmet needs" (p. 18). Trepper and Barrett (1989) go so far as to recommend the following reframing with "incestuous families": "The incestuous abuse may indicate that your family loved each other too much, and so

we'll have to find another way for you all to show your love"
(p. 46).

The thesis that families, rather than offenders, are responsible for incest has been extensively documented as well as chal-
lenged by Becker and Coleman (1988), Herman (1981), and Salter
(1988). Nevertheless, incest offenders continue to enjoy shorter
prison sentences and to be put on probation more often than child
molesters.

Because the law does not recognize the notion that families
rather than perpetrators are responsible for crimes, the presumed
justification is that incest offenders are less dangerous than other
child molesters and therefore can be safely contained within the
community or returned to it early. But how well supported is the
theory that incest offenders are not a risk outside the home?

Not very. As noted above, Weinrott and Saylor (1991) found that
half of their sample of incest offenders had molested outside the
home. Likewise, Faller (1990) found that one third of her sample
of 65 biological fathers in intact families molested outside the home,
whereas four fifths of the sample molested more than one child.

In a series of reports on an expanding sample of outpatient sex
offenders, Abel and his colleagues (Abel et al., 1988; Abel et al.,
1987; Abel & Rouleau, 1990) noted varying, but always high,
numbers of incest offenders who perpetrated outside the home.
Becker and Coleman (1988) noted that 44% of the men in their
sample who had molested female children in the home had also
molested female children outside the home. In addition, 11% had
molested male children outside the home, 18% had raped, 18%
were exhibitionists, 9% were voyeurs, 4% were sadists, and 21% had
other paraphilias. Abel et al. (1988) reported that 49% of the incest
offenders who molested girls within the family molested girls
outside the family as well, and 19% were rapists. Of those who
molested male children within the family, 61% molested females
outside the family and 68% molested males outside the family.
Finally, Abel and Rouleau (1990) wrote that 68 men (12%) in their
sample of sex offenders engaged in incestuous behavior alone,
whereas 131 (23%) had molested both in and out of the home.

Age of Onset

Emerging data regarding the age of onset of the offender's deviant arousal pattern also argue against the theory that situational variables such as current stress, alcohol addiction, or marital difficulties are responsible for child molestation. Forty-two percent of Abel et al.'s (1985) 411 subjects developed a deviant arousal pattern prior to age 15, and the majority (57%) had done so by age 19. The earliest onset subgroup was the male-oriented pedophiles. More than half (53%) had developed an interest in male children by age 15, and almost three fourths (74%) by age 19. In a later report of this study with a sample of 561 men, Abel and Rouleau (1990) found that 54% of the total sample had developed at least one deviant sexual interest before age 18. Fifty percent of extrafamilial, male-oriented pedophiles had developed a deviant interest by age 16, whereas 40% of extrafamilial, female-oriented sex offenders, 40% of male-oriented incest offenders, 25% of female-oriented incest pedophiles, and 30% of rapists had developed their interests prior to age 18.

Marshall et al. (1991) found that 38 offenders (30%) in their sample of 129 child molesters admitted to having sexual fantasies of children before the age of 20. However, only 68 men in the total sample admitted to *ever* having fantasies of children. Therefore, more than half of those who acknowledged fantasies admitted that the fantasies began in adolescence. As in Abel's research, the extrafamilial, male-oriented pedophiles had the earliest onset. More than 40% fantasized about sexual interactions with boys before age 20, whereas more than one third of the extrafamilial, female-oriented pedophiles had an onset of their deviant arousal pattern in adolescence. However, only 11% of the incest offenders admitted to such an early onset.

Longo and his colleagues (Longo & Groth, 1983; Longo & McFadin, 1981) found that approximately 35% of rapists and child molesters had progressed beyond simply developing a deviant arousal pattern and had committed their first deviant acts in early adolescence. In an unpublished study (Freeman-Longo,

1985), Longo noted that the average age of first offense for 30 incarcerated child molesters was 15, although their first conviction was not until age 28. The ages for first offense and first conviction for rapists were 18 and 24, respectively.

Other studies have produced congruent findings. More than one third (35.7%) of Marshall et al.'s (1991) sample admitted committing their first offense in adolescence. Groth (Groth, Hobson, & Gary, 1982) found that more than half of the men he and his group had treated ($N > 500$) had attempted or committed their first offense by age 16, whereas in his sample of 149 incarcerated child molesters (Groth, 1979), 7% had committed their first offense *before* adolescence. Likewise, Freund and Kuban (1993) found a difference in sexual interests prior to age 11 among pedophiles versus adult hetero- and homosexuals. Freund and Kuban conclude that "in a substantial proportion of pedophiles (and possibly in all of them) the occurrence of this paraphilia is predetermined at least from early childhood" (p. 323).

A sizable proportion of sex offenders, including incest offenders, develop their interest in deviant sexuality in adolescence, and even begin their offending careers while still in their teens.

Who Are They?

The television program *60 Minutes* once began a segment on the McMartin preschool case by filming a group of defendants chatting informally. The voice-over asked whether they looked like child molesters. This perception—that child molesters somehow look different, speak differently, or act differently—appears to be ubiquitous. Likewise, an evaluation of a man eventually convicted as a serial rapist stated that as he walked with the therapist to his office, he "stayed back to close one of the doors, a very solicitous gesture that, as it turned out, is consistent with his general pattern of behavior." The alleged offender was found by the examiner to be "kind, thoughtful and considerate, a person who seemed to take pleasure in being helpful and caring." The examiner used this as evidence that he was innocent. Evidently, rapists were expected to have bad manners, even in an evaluation destined for court.

In a survey of families who contacted them for information (Remembering "Repressed" Abuse, 1992), the False Memory Syndrome Foundation of Philadelphia found that four fifths of the parents were still married and four fifths of those happily so. Most of the parents were well-educated. Two thirds of the fathers and half of the mothers had obtained a college or graduate school degree. Median family income was between $60,000 and $69,000. The parents reported that they routinely ate together, vacationed together, and were actively involved with their children growing up. The results were used to support the parents' contentions that their adult children's accusations of child sexual abuse were false. " 'These appear to be families that have realized the American dream,' " Hollida Wakefield is reported to have said (Remembering "Repressed" Abuse, 1992, p. 7).

Setting aside for a moment the issue of whether the parents were exaggerating the degree of early harmony, what evidence is there that child molesters can be recognized by their level of education, their vacation plans, or their dining arrangements? On the contrary, sex offenders appear to come from every occupational and socioeconomic group. Table 1.8 lists, for example, the defendants' occupations in a U.S. Customs sting operation on child pornography.

These occupations appear to represent a cross-section of American vocations, and therefore educational and income levels. Socioeconomic level cannot be used to predict sexual deviancy; neither can mental health as defined by currently available tests and measures. Becker and Quinsey (1993) stated flatly,

> The question of determining whether or not a person has committed a sexual offence is not one that clinical assessment can address. There are no psychological tests or techniques that indicate whether someone has engaged in sexual behaviors with children; such questions are best left to detectives and the courts. (p. 169)

TABLE 1.8 Occupations of Child Pornography Suspects

Actuary	Manager, paper company
Attorney (2)	Marketing analyst
Baker/maintenance worker	Musician (2)
Bank courier	National Weather Service employee
Bar operator	Owner, foreign car repair shop
Bartender	Owner, funeral home
Butcher	Owner, hair salon
Caretaker	Parole and probation officer
Carpet installer	Payroll auditor
Chemical company employee	Police/juvenile probation officer
College music teacher	Police officer (2)
College professor	Police officer, retired
Computer installer	Railroad inspector
Defense contractor	Retired (2)
Dentist (2)	Retired truant officer/former Scout
Detention center employee/	leader
Boy Scout leader	Sales (3)
Electrical technician	School bus driver
Electrician	School librarian
Engineer	Schoolteacher
Factory worker (2)	Service station attendant
Farmer	Shipping clerk
Film distributor	Shrimp fisherman
Food service trainee	State auditor
Graphic artist (2)	Structural engineer
Hospital attendant	U.S. Navy civilian employee
Housepainter	U.S. Navy enlisted man
Janitor	Utility worker
Job service representative	Video engineer
Loan officer	Video producer
Machinist	Waterfront worker
Maintenance worker	

SOURCE: From Sullivan (1986).

Nichols and Molinder (1984) summed up the literature on psychological tests in this area by noting that "no test, no device, has the power to pick out a sexually deviant person from any other person in a crowd" (p. 3). Myers et al. (1989) concluded in their review that

Sex offenders are a heterogeneous group with few shared characteristics apart from a predilection for deviant sexual behavior. Furthermore, there is no psychological test or device that reliably detects persons who have or will sexually abuse children. . . . There is no profile of a "typical" child molester. (p. 142)

Barnard, Fuller, Robbins, and Shaw (1989) attributed the "declining use of traditional assessment procedures with sex offenders" to the "apparent failure of traditional psychological tests to distinguish sex offenders from other types of offenders or to differentiate among types of sex offenders" (p. 50). However, given the number and variety of nonsexual crimes that sex offenders commit, the failure of psychological tests to distinguish nonsexual and sexual offenders may be due to the amount of crossover in the two groups rather than the lack of specificity of the tests.

Maletzky (1991) concluded in his sample of more than 5,000 sex offenders that

There has been no documentation of a typical "offender personality." . . . Rather, these men were characterized by their diversity: An offender could as well have been a professor as a pauper, a minister as an atheist, a teetotaler as an alcoholic, a teenager as a septuagenarian. Moreover, an offender . . . might as well have had an extensive history of arrests or none at all, and might as well have had associated diagnoses as none. . . . In retrospect, these patients did not seem to share any definable demographic or personality traits to render them distinctive. (pp. 16-17)

Herman (1990) agreed. "The most striking characteristic of sex offenders, from a diagnostic standpoint, is their apparent normality" (p. 180). Berlin explained the confusion somewhat by noting that

People often confuse issues of traits of character with issues of sexual orientation or the type of sexual interest an individual has. Persons who may be compulsive pedophiles, for instance, may obey the law in other ways, may be responsible in their work, may have concern for other persons. So you can describe character traits independent of sexual orientation. (Berlin, quoted in Knopp, 1984, p. 9)

Perhaps, however, no one can describe the distinction between traits of character and sexual deviancy better than the man who wrote the following:

> I want to describe a child molester I know very well. This man was raised by devout Christian parents. As a child he rarely missed church. Even after he became an adult he was faithful as a church member. He was a straight-A student in high school and college. He has been married and has a child of his own. He coached little league baseball. He was a Choir Director at his church. He never used any illegal drugs. He never had a drink of alcohol. He was considered a clean-cut all-American boy. Everyone seemed to like him. He was a volunteer in numerous community civic functions. He had a well-paying career job. He was considered "well-to-do" in society. But from the age of thirteen-years-old he sexually molested little boys. He never victimized a stranger. All of his victims were friends. He is now serving a five-year term in prison for sexual abuse. I know this child molester very well because he is me!!!
>
> (child molester of up to 100 male children)

Research confirms the fact that many sex offenders have no pathology discernible by generic psychological tests or clinical interview. Abel et al. (1985) found that, according to the *DSM-II* criteria available at the time, 60% of the 232 child molesters and 45% of the 89 rapists in their outpatient sample had no psychopathology other than the sexual deviancy.

However, personality disorders were found in a significant minority of the population. Twelve percent of the child molesters and 29% of the rapists met the criteria for antisocial personality disorder. Indeed, personality disorders have been found frequently in criminally identified sex offenders as well (Henn, 1978; Knight, Rosenberg, & Schneider, 1985). For example, Pithers, Kashima, Cumming, and Beal (1988) found in a sample of 136 pedophiles and 64 rapists (all of whom had been adjudicated and some incarcerated) that 61% of the rapists and 35% of the pedophiles had personality disorders. Marques et al. (1989) diagnosed fewer than half of their child molesters as having a personality disorder, but three fourths of their rapists. The most frequent disorder was antisocial personality. However, the presence of a personality disorder is by no means diagnostic of sexual deviancy, nor is its absence proof against it.

Nowhere is the issue of a sex offender profile more important than in court. I have seen a number of forensic evaluations in which claims were made that an alleged offender was unlikely to have committed the crime because he lacked certain characteristics, mental traits, or behaviors thought to be part of a sex offender profile.

In one case, the absence of a criminal history was used as evidence that the defendant was not a sex offender, despite the fact that most nonsexual crimes by sex offenders are never detected. In another, the offender's admission that he and his wife had sexual problems and that he had a drinking problem was used to discredit his son's otherwise credible account of sexual abuse. The examiner felt the father was "very forthright" during the interview and that this forthrightness supported his overall "truthfulness." The son was so convincing that the interviewer concluded he had been abused, but given her opinion of the father, decided he could not have been the offender.

These attempts to use a sex offender profile are more often made by the defense simply because the prosecution in such cases is formally prohibited from introducing profile evidence. Nevertheless, there have been some attempts to make "end-runs" around this restriction by the prosecution (Myers et al., 1989, pp. 142-144), although they are not generally successful. On either side, the use of sex offender profiles is not warranted. They cannot be justified by the relevant research literature. Legally, Myers et al. (1989) have termed such evidence "prejudicial and confusing" (p. 144). Evidently, offender profiles not only represent bad psychology, they make bad law.

As I write these words, the phone rings and a therapist calls to tell me that her client, a bright, capable, charming physician, could not have molested his 3-year-old daughter, as the daughter has reported. "Why not?" I ask. I do not know whether he has or not because I am just beginning the forensic evaluation of his daughter. However, it seems interesting that she, who has not heard the child's story, is sure that it is false.

Because, she tells me, he has a crazy, paranoid wife. This is, in fact, true, but I point out to her that many child molesters marry impaired women. It gives them better access to children and a better cover if they are caught. Having an impaired wife does not prove you are or are not a child molester. And it is, I tell her, less easy to coach 3-year-olds than many think.

No, she tells me, she has worked with him for 3 years and she has very good antennae for psychopathic traits. He does not have any. I remind her of the literature that suggests that only a percentage of offenders have anything wrong with them other than the sexual deviancy, and tell her of the numerous offenders who have fooled therapists for years. "Were they in good therapy?" she asks. She does not believe the therapists could have been competent.

I do not convince her. She states that she has never seen any boundary violations between him and the child. I grow impatient and wince at the annoyance in my voice. Why, I ask, would she expect to? Does she think a child molester would necessarily be stupid enough to encroach on the child's boundaries in the office or would report such activities at home? We are each alarmed—she that I would consider the possibility that her client might be a child molester, and I at the fact that she would not.

It is the therapeutic fallacy—the notion that one can tell whether or not someone is a sex offender—and it is unfortunately not restricted to therapists. I am reminded of the several times I have seen members of a community write letters or sign petitions insisting that an outstanding member of the community could not have been a sex offender—only to have the offender eventually confess.

I am reminded, too, of the child molester who had tried to disclose to his minister by first saying that someone else had said he was a child molester. The minister had laughed, the offender reported years later when he was finally caught, and said he could never believe anything like that about him.

I recall a conference at which a presenter showed a video of an alleged offender playing with his 5-year-old child. She argued that because the child was not afraid of his father, his father could not have molested him. "Why not?" I asked, and pointed out that offenders are often proud of their ability to groom victims sufficiently that the children remain attached to them. There are numerous cases, I told her, in which children have lied to protect offenders, have even warned them of inquiries. "If that man were a child molester," she told me later, "I would know it."

In her presentation, she showed the pictures that the child was still drawing 2 years later while visiting with his mother. At the presenter's recommendation, the alleged offender had custody. The pictures were graphic descriptions of anal intercourse that the now 7-year-old child insisted was still occurring. The pictures, she said, must have been drawn by the mother. The child couldn't have drawn them. After all, the father was not a child molester.

Conclusions

Current data on sexual offending draw a sobering picture. This appears to be a highly compulsive and repetitive behavior, the tenacity of which is truly impressive. In addition to committing a wider variety and a higher number of sex offenses at an earlier age than previously thought, sex offenders also commit an extensive number of nonsexual crimes as well, thus adding to the overall picture of antisocial and irresponsible behavior.

Despite this, the most chilling aspect of this behavior is its invisibility. Abel et al. (1987) set the likelihood of detection at 3%. Russell (1984) found that only 5% of crimes were ever even reported to the police, and fewer than 1% resulted in arrest, conviction, and imprisonment of the offender. A number of research studies have reported that large numbers of victims never told anyone before adulthood, and sometimes not before being queried by the researcher (Donaldson, 1983; Finkelhor, 1984; Russell, 1984; Salter, 1988).

Adding to the difficulty of detection is the failure of psychological tests to identify sex offenders reliably. This is less likely because of deficiencies in the tests—in general, they measure what they were designed to measure—rather than the fact that sexual deviancy often stands alone. Frequently, there is simply nothing wrong with sex offenders other than aberrant sexuality, which offenders usually deny. There is little reason to expect, for example, that tests designed to measure depression, schizophrenic thinking, or alcoholism will distinguish sex offenders from others if, in fact, sex offenders are not uniquely depressed, schizophrenic, or alcoholic. Tests specifically designed to measure sexual deviancy must rely on self-report, which has been shown to be less than ideal in sex offenders, particularly those involved in the legal arena.

Given the devastation wreaked by sexual assault (see Chapters 4, 5, and 6), it is sadly ironic that something so malignant could be so silent. In part, this is due to the fact that offenders can be, and often are, well-educated, highly respected members of their communities. Unfortunately, legal cases often pit such pillars of the community against victims suffering from a variety of difficult sequelae of sexual assault. For example, I have repeatedly seen lying and emotional disturbance in an adolescent used to discredit her testimony, when in fact, such reactions can be sequelae to the repeated assaults she endured.

A major national magazine once pictured on its cover a couple portrayed as victims of false accusations by their adult daughters. The accompanying article failed to cite any evidence that the couple had not committed the offenses that the daughters had charged except the facts that they were Caucasian, middle class, and most importantly, grandparents. It was apparently unthinkable to the authors that such individuals would sexually abuse children.

Sexual assault is a strange psychic hurricane in which the victims must, despite the evidence of uprooted trees and roofless houses, argue to the disbelieving that something happened. Frustrated with the claim that his adolescent client made up her tale of paternal rape in order to please her mother—when in fact the young woman had been hospitalized in a psychiatric ward for the entire preceding year—one lawyer stormed, "You don't get that kind of trauma from imagination." That may be so, but the invisibility and isolation of the child sexual assault victim are major contributors to the distress and confusion of the adult survivor. This book will examine the impact of the characteristics explored in this chapter on child sexual abuse victims and the adult survivors they become.

Notes

1. Figures for the number of extra- and intrafamilial child molesters in the larger sample were not made available in the 1987 article. However, Becker provided them in a more recent description of the 1987 study (Becker, 1993, p. 379).

2. Male pronouns will be used throughout this book to describe offenders because all existing studies find that the majority of offenders are male. Male and female pronouns will be alternated when describing victims and therapists.

2

The Deviant Cycle

Sexual abuse is frequently thought to be an accident or happenstance. It is more accurate to think of it as a deviant cycle, an interlocking series of thoughts, feelings, and behaviors that culminate in sexual assault. This chapter will review the concept of the deviant cycle, the separate components that compose it, as well as the thinking errors that are found throughout. I will also discuss the recent trend toward considering sexual offending an addictive behavior as well as some of the negative consequences of applying that model. Finally, some of the implications of the deviant cycle for survivors and survivor therapists will be considered.

Throughout this chapter I will rely heavily on the use of the offender's own words to describe his thoughts, feelings, and behavior. No one speaks as clearly about sex offenders as offenders themselves.

Sexual Assault: Accident or Plan?

A Tonawanda, New York, man spent 8 weekends in jail for raping a 13-year-old girl, a sentence that his lawyer felt was justified given that " 'it was an alcohol-based offense' " ("Father Knows Best," 1992). At the time of sentencing, the judge was unaware that the offender had admitted to police that he knew the girl was 13 years old, had given her alcohol, and had videotaped the rape and played it for his 8- and 11-year-old sons, telling them he had " 'dirty pictures' " of the neighborhood girl.

The contrast here between the naïveté—or the sophistry—of the offender's lawyer and the extensive deviancy that the actual facts of the case suggest is one that occurs repeatedly in sexual assault cases. Sex offenders routinely blame the sexual offenses on stress, impulse, happenstance, marital problems, alcohol, or even the victim herself (Salter, 1988).

> I remember one 5-year period where I went through that I had no involvements at all during that time, and then another period of stress would develop that would throw me back into it, stressful situation, and then I would retreat back onto that.
>
> (extrafamilial child molester)

Sometimes they claim that offenses "just happen" and blame them on nothing at all.

> My first involvement was not something that I thought, well, gee, I want to plan this. I want to get involved with another kid. That was not it. It just sort of happened the first time. It was a situation where it just happened.
>
> (extrafamilial child molester)

Unfortunately, such rationalizations are frequently believed. A Wisconsin judge sentenced a 24-year-old man to 3 years' probation after he was found guilty of first-degree sexual assault on a 5-year-old girl, commenting that, "I am satisfied that we have an unusual sexually promiscuous young lady and that this man just did not know enough to knock off her advances" (Hannah, 1982). More typically, judges offer lighter sentences to "situational" offenders, even though these incest offenders may have molested the same victim over a period of many years. Donaldson and Gardner (1985), for example, found in their sample of 26 women that the average duration of incest was more than 8 years. Abel et al. (1987) found that the men in their sample who molested their sons averaged 62 different sexually abusive acts, whereas men who molested their daughters averaged 81 such acts.

As Pithers (1990) has pointed out, the notion that sexual offending is a momentary aberration in an otherwise rational person is somehow comforting for society. It is easier to accept the notion of error rather than evil, and coldly plotting the sexual molestation of children strikes most people as something very close to evil. However one labels it, discussions with admitting sex offenders reveal that sexual offending is anything but impulsive.

> When a person like myself wants to obtain access to a child, you don't just go up and get the child and sexually molest the child. There's a process of obtaining the child's friendship, and, in my case, also obtaining the families' friendship and their trust. When you get their trust, that's when the child becomes vulnerable and you can molest the child. . . . As far as the children goes, they're kind of easy. You befriend them, you take them places, you buy them gifts. . . . Now in the process of grooming this child, you win his trust, and I mean the child has a look in his eye that it's hard to explain. You just have to know the look and you know when you've got that kid and you know when that kid trusts you.
>
> (intra- and extrafamilial child
> molester of "40 to 100" victims)

> I will tell you about my latest situation. I'm sure you have heard and read about how addictive crack cocaine is and how sex is being traded for crack by hookers and other women who don't always have the money to buy it. Well, as you probably guessed, that is the kind of situation I have. I have mentioned to you many times that, for me, the ultimate sex thrill is to get a mother and daughter who are vulnerable and desperate and just take outrageous sexual advantage of them. . . . I have been having a great time with mama and her sexy young little nookie daughter.
>
> (This sex offender, unknowingly corresponding
> with a federal marshal in a sting operation,
> went on to describe graphically coercing
> mothers into sexual acts with their daughters.)

As illustrated by the above, sexual offending is frequently carefully thought out and well-planned. Sex offenders sometimes plan their assaults around a category of child, such as single-parent mothers looking for "father figures" for their children, parents having marital problems, or even drug-addicted parents who will trade their children for drugs. Of course, access is easiest to the offender's own child, but that approach, too, may be carefully thought out.

> He, at that time, was only seven. And it was sort of in that close relationship I had lost control of my family and I had control of him. And I had, you know, he would do just about anything I would ask him to do. I wouldn't have to tell him to do anything. I'd tell him to go take a bath or get out of the bathtub or go to his room or whatever and he'd do it. And I had a lot of times I would wait for my wife to go to work, tell him to go take a bath, and he had been outside playing, which was normal. Something normal to do, and then I would remove the towels from the bathroom so he would have to come out of the bathroom without any clothes on. Setting him up. . . . Otherwise, I would say his clothes were all dirty. And all he'd have on would be a towel. And I would fondle him.
>
> (intra- and extrafamilial child
> molester describing the beginning
> of his molestation of his stepson)

Even when the circumstances make it obvious that planning took place, offenders are often quick to agree with the myth that sexual offending "just happens." One offender entered an apartment and forced the 13-year-old girl he found there alone to strip at knifepoint. He stabbed her and left the apartment when she began screaming. Even with two previous charges related to assaults on 12- to 13-year-old girls, he denied knowing there was a 13-year-old girl in the apartment beforehand and denied deliberate planning or intention to commit the offense. In his version, he found the apartment door open, went in to ask for directions, and concocted the offense on the spur of the moment. He just happened to be carrying a knife. He did not consider the offense to be sexually motivated and maintained the stabbing was accidental. The girl had made a break for the door, he said, and ran into the knife. Because she was stabbed in the back, she was presumably running backwards, in her underwear, toward the offender when it occurred. This offender was outraged that he was incarcerated for simply "an irrational two minutes of my life" and insisted that he did not need treatment.

This chapter will explore the reality of sexual offending as a compulsive, repetitive behavior rather than the myth of sexual offending as an isolated, impulsive act. It will describe current theories of sexual abuse as an addiction or, at the least, a highly compulsive behavior, explore the deviant cycle, and discuss the implications for adult survivors.

Sexual Offending as an Addiction

If the impulsive model of sexual offending simply does not fit the evidence—the compulsive, repetitive aspects of the behavior as evidenced by the research cited in Chapter 1, the careful planning described by admitting offenders or implied by their behavior—then what is the nature of sexual offending and how can we conceptualize it?

Recent efforts in the field (Carnes, 1983; Laws, 1989; Marques & Nelson, 1989b; Pithers, Buell, Kashima, Cumming, & Beal, 1987; Pithers et al., 1988; Pithers, Marques, Gibat, & Marlatt, 1983) have centered on the addiction model as one that successfully captures many aspects of sexually deviant behavior. Sexual offending shares with other addictive behaviors a focus on short-term, immediate gratification at the expense of delayed, long-term, negative consequences—a problem referred to in the literature as the Problem of Immediate Gratification (PIG) (Marlatt, 1989a, 1989b).

In addition, both addictive behaviors and sexual aggression tend to be highly repetitive, to be reliable ways to alter and enhance mood, to be shrouded in secrecy and denial, to involve thinking errors that justify the behavior, to be manageable but not curable, to be compulsive and driven even when the negative consequences are potentially catastrophic, and to be subject to frequent relapse (Laws, 1989; Miller, 1980; Pithers, 1990; Pithers et al., 1988).

It appears that relapses in both sexual aggression and in addictive behaviors may be triggered by similar types of precipitants (Marlatt & Gordon, 1980; Pithers et al., 1987). Some authors also count as similarities the fact that neither sexual abuse nor addictive behaviors have known etiologies or a single method of treatment that has proved superior (Laws, 1989; Pithers et al., 1988), although these latter criteria would lump together any disorders about which little is known and therefore would seem less specific.

Other authors (Carnes, 1983) follow the addiction logic to the point of construing sexual aggression as a disease. This view is certainly controversial, most probably for heuristic rather than theoretical reasons. As Laws (1989) points out,

> Such an externalization of blame and treatment responsibility can backfire with offenders who are already reluctant to take any responsibility for their misdeeds and choose to view this so-called addiction as a convenient excuse before and after a reoffense. (p. 12)

Indeed, Laws has termed the entire addiction model a "mixed blessing" (p. 12), pointing out that in addition to the similarities with addictive behaviors, there are salient differences. Specifically, every single occurrence of a sexual offense involves the victimization of another person. Although addictive behaviors inevitably victimize others at some point, the behaviors themselves may occur many times before the cumulative effect on the family or friends of the addict occurs.

Because of this, ethical and legal considerations are more prominent and more problematic with sexual aggression than with other addictions. If an offender discloses other sexual offenses for which he was not caught, does the therapist disclose those to the authorities? Does she insist the client give the kind of detail that would allow the police to identify the victim and thereby potentially charge him with a new offense? If she does, will any other offenders in the group ever admit the extent of their deviancy, or will they stay in denial? Will the first admission by a member of the group be the last? On the other hand, is it ethical for her not to press for detail or not report the offenses to the authorities? These issues simply do not exist when an addict describes a more extensive drug or alcohol history than he previously revealed.

Finally, fantasy is far more prominently featured in sexual aggression than in addictive disorders. Although addicts in general may fantasize about the compulsive behavior, the fantasy in other disorders is unlikely to be as satisfying as the real event, that is, the fantasy of smoking a cigarette or having a drink does not produce the physiological satisfaction that the real event does. However, because offenders can masturbate to orgasm while fantasizing about sexually deviant behavior, the difference between the fantasy and the reality for the offender in sexual assault is less dramatic. Indeed, some offenders seem to prefer the fantasy and use the reality more to fuel the fantasies than the other way around. Consider, for example, the following comments from an incarcerated rapist talking in a group session:

Rapist: *You know, there was this little scene, fantasy that I played out in my mind, and when I committed rape, the fantasy did not live up. I mean, the rape did not live up to the fantasy . . . but the rape was part of the next fantasy. The fantasy wasn't all the same thing, like the same picture of a woman and the same sexual acts. It was different acts. It was different situations. But the rape became part of the next fantasy, you know, and in my mind—and these pictures are so vivid and so clear that I had, and these fantasies are so strong and now I still have trouble with them. They come to me when I'm at sleep, going to sleep at night before I go to sleep I have them but I don't dwell on them. See, there's the key. You know, they'll come into my mind and I have never been able to stop them, but when they do come I don't dwell on them. Anyway, I would think about the rape and how I didn't do this or that, and part of the new fantasy is, you know, well, I'm going to do this or that. You know, take the old rape, put in some new parts, and I've got a new, fresh fantasy that is like the pot of gold at the end of the rainbow, kind of. You know, this is what I'm going to do this time.*

Second Rapist: (softly) *Perfect.*

Rapist: *Right. The perfect rape. This is what's going to make it work. This is what's going to be exciting or this is what I need to have that total fulfill-ment or that total excitement.*

(incarcerated rapist)

Through the use of fantasy, the offender can maintain the de-viant arousal even while incarcerated. This is one of the reasons that prison alone does not stop sexual offenders from resuming their activities when they emerge. As long as the offender is con-tinuing to masturbate to deviant fantasies, there is no "detox" from sexual aggression, no natural extinction curve. And in prison, or even in the early stages of treatment programs, offend-ers do not automatically stop masturbating to such fantasies as the following two offenders admit:

Interviewer: *So how often do you find yourself masturbating to sexual fanta-sies with boys now?*

Offender: *Now? I would say now that maybe a third of the time I masturbate.*

(incarcerated child molester in a treatment program)

Interviewer: *Before you got into actual involvement, sexual involvement with these boys, was there any masturbation that was going on with fan-tasy about having sex with them?*

Offender: *All the time. That's a constant thing with me. It's something I'm still working on right now. I have to get, I have to calm that down. I believe if I can get a hold of that, I'll do a lot better.*

Interviewer: *How much of the time do you fantasize about boys?*

Offender: *I'd say about half of the day; it's when I'm not doing anything.*

(incarcerated child molester in a treatment program)

In the end, the most valuable reason for acknowledging that sexual offending seems like an addictive behavior—at least in some ways—is the usefulness of the addiction model in guiding treatment. The addiction model, by its very nature, confronts the most frequent denial of the admitting offender, that is, that the sexually deviant behavior was a single, isolated event or series of events that "just happened" and will never happen again. The very use of the term *addiction* implies that the offender has an ongoing attraction to the disordered behavior that will be very difficult to change and is unlikely to remit spontaneously. In addition, use of the addiction model opens the door to treatments that have proved efficacious with other addictions, most notably, relapse prevention.

Relapse prevention focuses on the identification of precursors to the sexually deviant behavior that can be used as early markers, or warning signs, that the offender is likely to commit another sexual offense. Thus relapse prevention focuses not only on the sexually deviant behaviors themselves but on the thoughts, feelings, behaviors, attitudes, and beliefs that precede and follow the offending behavior.

Whatever model one uses to describe sexual assault, the bad news is that sex offenders premeditate the assaults; the good news is that the behavior is potentially controllable (never curable) because of the premeditation. If sexual aggression were truly impulsive, then treatment would be almost impossible. There would be no warning signs that an assault was about to occur, and therefore no way for anyone (even the offender) to anticipate the offense and to intervene. However, by identifying a deviant cycle that leads up to the sexual assaults, the offender can potentially learn to interrupt the cycle early, before he has the opportunity to offend, and therefore, before he is maximally tempted to do so.

Summary

Although sex offenders frequently claim that sex offenses "just happen," or are temporary aberrations resulting from stress, in fact, interviews with treated offenders reveal that extensive planning and/or grooming of the victim is more the norm. It may be that sexual offending has more in common with addictive disorders than with truly unplanned, impulsive acts. However, it may be most accurate to describe sexual offending as a driven and compulsive behavior, but not actually an addiction. In any case,

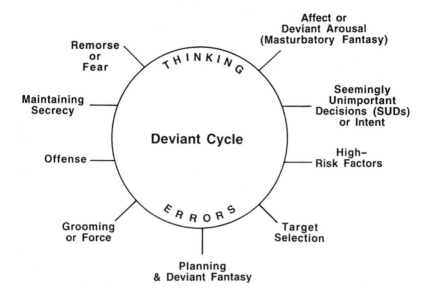

Figure 2.1. The Deviant Cycle

techniques such as relapse prevention, which were developed for use with addictions, are gaining in popularity.

Components of the Deviant Cycle

Affect or Deviant Arousal With Masturbatory Fantasy

As can be seen in Figure 2.1, there are typically a number of both precursors and sequelae to the actual assault. This is true of both sexually deviant behavior and addictions. Cummings, Gordon, and Marlatt (1980), for example, found in a study of 311 addicts (alcohol abusers, smokers, heroin addicts, compulsive gamblers, and overeaters) that 71% of all relapses were precipitated by one of three precursors: (a) negative emotional states not occasioned by a particular social interaction (35%); (b) interpersonal conflict, such as a recent argument (16%); or (c) social pressure, that is, situations in which other individuals pressured the addict, either directly or indirectly, to violate the rules (20%).

Some research suggests that sex offenders also often experience strong negative emotional states prior to committing an offense. In one study (Queen's Bench Foundation, 1976), 77% of the rapists experienced emotions such as anger, rejection, frustration, or depression prior to their assaults. Day, Miner, Nafpaktitis, and Murphy (1987) found that 45% of their sample were angry at the time of the attack or molestation. This included three fourths of the rapists, although less than a third of the child molesters. Pithers et al. (1987) found that 89% of their sample of 136 pedophiles and 64 rapists experienced strong negative emotional states prior to the offense. Ninety-four percent of the rapists stated they were angry, whereas 46% of the pedophiles were anxious and 38% felt depressed.

All of these data, however, are based on retrospective self-report from sex offenders, many of whom were incarcerated—a group whose historical accuracy is somewhat fragile. Although Pithers et al. (1988) have stated that "the similarity of results across the subject sample mitigates this concern" (p. 135), it does not appear to do so entirely. The similarity of results could be due to the tendency of sex offenders to use similar thinking errors to justify their behavior. It may be that to many sex offenders, committing a crime in a highly emotional state seems less reprehensible than simply being sexually attracted to children, or simply enjoying violence against women. Indeed, Yochelson and Samenow (1976) found in their sample of incarcerated criminals, many of whom had committed sex offenses, that

> If a criminal did not tell us he was a victim of environmental circumstances, he said he was a victim of his own character structure, but put it in terms of "feelings." A man might try to explain away his violations by saying that he had been depressed, tense, or upset. (p. 33)

> He determines how to assume the victim stance so that it will be most acceptable—shall it be presented in terms of feeling or thinking? In a psychiatric setting, it sounds authentic if he talks

in terms of feelings, because thinking is often considered "intellectualizing." Therefore, he says that he was bored, angry, scared, or depressed; this is the acceptable currency in most transactions at many mental health centers. (p. 368)

In addition, although Pithers and colleagues emphasized the role of anxiety and depression as precursors to sexual acting out, their study also found that more than one fourth of pedophiles and almost half of rapists were bored prior to committing the assault (Pithers et al., 1988, p. 136). Certainly, many sex offenders and criminals frequently speak of the excitement of committing illicit acts.

Did you ever get this feeling like, you know, you're going to break into a house, and it's dark and everything like that, and you find your little window or door or whatever where you can make that lock move and open and smell the air, how the air was different inside the house than it was outside the house, and just get a feeling of exhilaration . . . here's more excitement, you know, you're getting excitement. It's like shooting a drug and here's some more.

(voyeur/rapist)

Moreover, emotion does not appear to be the only way in which the deviant cycle begins. Research consistently indicates that a percentage of sex offenders can be demonstrated to have a deviant arousal pattern (Abel, Barlow, Blanchard, & Guild, 1977; Barbaree, Marshall, & Lanthier, 1979; Freund, 1967; Marques & Nelson, 1989a; Quinsey, 1977). These offenders develop erections in a laboratory situation when slides of children are shown, or when audiotapes describing sexual molestations of children, violent sexual attacks on adults, or violent, nonsexual assaults on children or adults are played.

Marques and Nelson (1989a), for example, found that 66% of their sample of 67 sex offenders evidenced deviant sexual arousal in the lab (21% did not respond and only 13% showed a nondeviant arousal pattern). Pithers et al.'s (1988) research found that 57% of the 136 pedophiles in their sample had a disordered sexual arousal pattern (p. 136). More pedophiles had a deviant arousal pattern than reported being anxious or depressed. Sixty-nine percent of the 64 rapists (Pithers et al., 1988) had a disordered arousal pattern, and whereas 94% of the rapists were angry prior to committing the offense, in only 6% of the cases was that anger due to an event or an interpersonal conflict. In the other 88%, the anger was generalized and global.

In short, a chronically disordered arousal pattern with ongoing deviant sexual fantasies may play as great a role in sexual offenses as a preceding, more transitory emotional state. Certainly, admitting sex offenders often describe a long history of deviant fantasies coupled with masturbation, sometimes to the exclusion of all other fantasies. The following responses are typical of many child molesters.

Q: *How old were you when you first began to have sexual fantasies about children?*

A: *About 13 or 14.*

Q: *When you masturbated in the three months prior to the commission of your offenses, how often would you say during masturbation you had sexual fantasies involving children?*

A: *All the time.*

(32-year-old intra- and
extrafamilial child molester)

And then over the next couple of years, I'd say probably 70 or 80 percent of the time I masturbated would be to child fantasies.

(intrafamilial child molester)

Some offenders appear to use masturbation almost constantly in order to manage negative moods and to self-soothe.

I've been making myself feel good through some form of masturbation since I was six years old. . . . And by the time I was 15 years old, I was into masturbation pretty heavy. Could range anywhere from 3 to 10 times a day. There was days when it went more than that, but those days, you know, it wasn't very many of them. . . . I would just need, when I masturbated, I really didn't do it for the sex part of it. I done it because I needed to feel good and because maybe my stepfather cussed me or something like that when I didn't really think I'd done nothing to deserve that kind of treatment. Maybe I'd done something that I should have been called down for, but to stand there for ten minutes and take a pretty hard cussing and things like that, I didn't think I deserved that. And in a situation like that, I'd usually get to hurting and want to go somewheres alone, and that was my way of stopping the hurting, I guess.

(extrafamilial child molester)

Compulsive masturbation combined with deviant fantasy could develop, as it did with this offender, into a stable, disordered arousal pattern that resulted in high numbers of victims. Although the above offender began by self-soothing with masturbation, he soon found that sexual acting out was highly gratifying in itself and that it provided more material for his deviant fantasies, as shown by his description of his fantasy life:

I always fantasized to the most recent victim. I'd never sit around and fantasize about children that I hadn't been involved with. There are a few times, you know, that I seen a few that I kind of thought, you know, might be good to have sex with him or something like that. And I might think about it and fantasize once or twice, but I didn't get off into a lot of unknown fantasies. Usually, when I masturbated, it was some sexual experience that I'd had.

(extrafamilial child molester)

Thus the deviant cycle can begin with either an affective state or a deviant arousal pattern. Some offenders are anxious, depressed, or angry prior to beginning the chain of thoughts and behaviors that lead to an offense, although other emotions may be implicated as well. On the other hand, there is no question that a percentage of sex offenders have a disordered arousal pattern, that is, they are simply sexually attracted to children or to violence, and they do not need any particular affect to act on that attraction any more than normal, adult-oriented, hetero- or homosexuals need to be anxious or depressed to act on their interests. In fact, deviant sexual interest, when accompanied by emotion, may be paired with a very different type of emotion. Day et al. (1987, p. 400) found that approximately half of their sample of child molesters reported some sort of positive emotional state immediately prior to the sexual offense.

Finally, there is a third possibility for beginning the deviant cycle. Some offenders do not necessarily have a deviant arousal pattern but are willing to use anyone or anything without regard to age or sex in pursuit of sexual gratification.

> At one point, when I was younger, I remember an instance where I guess I was maybe nine, ten years old, where I was masturbating in a barn. I was up in the hayloft playing with myself and there was a kitten in there, and I took the kitten and the fur felt real good against my penis, and I tried to have vaginal sex with the animal. The cat wasn't in heat, but I didn't know nothing about being in heat at that time, so there wasn't anything happening, but I tried to have—I don't know. It was just a stimulation, something that I was looking for and it was more or less the same thing with my daughter. It was just a little added stimulation.
>
> (intrafamilial child offender who
> molested his 2-year-old daughter)

Likewise, other criminals may see little difference in the videocassette recorders they steal and the people they assault. Both are objects to be used. The following conversation occurred in an incarcerated sex offender treatment group:

Offender 1: *In my case, I think it was more or less the availability. . . . I was doing a lot of home invading prior, I was doing a lot of burglary, stealing, stereo equipment and all this stuff. Somewhere back here, I was thinking what if someone's home one of these times, what am I going to do, and this time somebody was home. It happened to be a female. Okay. So the thought was grab her. So I grabbed her. We wrestled around and I'm thinking, okay, I'll just tie this woman up and I'll go about my business and go on. I came here to rob. I'll just go on and do that. So as I drug her back toward* *the bedroom and remove her from the room because I had, my face was covered. I wanted to get this off my head so I can go on and do what I was going to do and get on out of the place. Somewhere during the overpowering, I guess the feeling of here I am in total control of this person, overpowering, I don't know. I got sexually turned on, and that's when I raped the woman. . . . It was almost the thrill of getting away with it. . . . Maybe I can rape this woman and get away with it. It came out. It was like regurgitating. It just exploded out of me. . . . It happened to be a woman. If it had been a male, I probably would have tried to beat the snot out of the guy. It just happened to be a woman home at the time.*

Offender 2: *If the girl had been—hey, if the girl—was she attractive or was she ugly or what? If she had been repulsive to you, you wouldn't have raped her?*

Offender 1: *I don't even—truthfully I can't remember what this woman looks like. I haven't the slightest idea whether she's ugly, fat, or skinny.*

Offender 2: *Why were you burglarizing homes?*

Offender 1: *Money at the time. It's a source of easy income.*

Offender 2: *You didn't have a job?*

Offender 1: *Yeah, I had a job. I was greedy. I could get away with burglary. You know, I'd done it and we got away with it and I kept doing it. It was my addiction.*

As was demonstrated in Chapter 1, not every sex offender is exclusively or even primarily a sex offender. For some, sexual offending is part of a pattern of irresponsible and exploitative living that makes no distinction between the animate and inanimate. Both are to be used. Sexual offenses occur simply when there is opportunity, often in the middle of a burglary. The general criminal/sex offender takes no more responsibility for the sexual attack than he does for any other aspect of his exploitative lifestyle. One incarcerated general criminal/sex offender said angrily in regard to his burglary/rape victim, "If she hadn't been at home in her own bed at the time, this never would have happened!"

Summary

The deviant cycle is generally triggered by (a) an affective state, such as rage, anxiety, depression, or boredom; (b) a chroni-

TABLE 2.1 Components of the Deviant Cycle

Affect or deviant arousal with masturbatory fantasy	Drive
Seemingly unimportant decisions or intent	Access to potential victims
High-risk situations	
Target selection	Sexual access to a specific potential victim
Planning and deviant fantasy	
Grooming or force	
Sexual offense	Offense
Maintaining secrecy	Hangover
Remorse or fear	

cally disordered sexual arousal pattern in which the offender is sexually attracted to children or to violence; or (c) an antisocial attitude in which the offender is willing to use anyone or anything for sexual gratification and for fulfillment of his need to have power and control over others. In either case, the next step in the cycle is for the offender to place himself in a situation in which he can gain access to potential victims.

Seemingly Unimportant Decisions (SUDs) or Intent

A seemingly unimportant decision is an internal lie—an attempt by an offender to convince himself that the action he is taking to place himself in a position where he has access to and power over potential victims has nothing to do with sexual aggression. Table 2.1 illustrates the relationship of the deviant cycle to the issue of access to victims.

The sex offender who announces his wish to become a scoutmaster again because the Boy Scouts really need scoutmasters and he was really a very good one is making a seemingly unimportant decision. The anesthetist who raped women while they were unconscious but is convinced there is no reason he cannot return to his old job is making a seemingly unimportant decision. So is the child pornographer who got to know children by photographing them and who immediately resumes his "hobby" upon release from prison. When confronted, he replies angrily that there is nothing illegal about taking pictures of children and nobody is going to tell him what to do. The therapist who fondled a woman during a therapy session and who reopens his counseling practice because "counseling is what I'm good at" is not attending to the real issues. Most certainly, the child molester who wants to get involved with youth services in the church again because it would be good to "test" himself is one step short of relapse.

In order to molest children, sex offenders must obtain access to them. That process can occur by conscious intent or by unconscious SUDs. The use of SUDs occurs when an individual is consciously attempting to control the behavior, because there is no need for internal subterfuge otherwise. The drug addict who wants heroin and who decides to get it simply goes to his dealer's house with that intent in mind. Later, in treatment or after a vow of abstinence, he may feel a sudden urge to stop by his dealer's house to pick up the sports jacket he left there. It was, after all, a very good sports jacket and there's no reason to lose a good sports jacket simply to avoid seeing his dealer. He is sure he can handle it.

This process is familiar to anyone who has struggled with a problem behavior such as overeating. It may suddenly become very important that cookies or chips be bought for the children. After all, why should they suffer just because the adult is dieting?

Vocational or Avocational Access

At this stage of the cycle, the offender must access potential victims for the pattern to continue. Access is obtained most commonly through the use of a vocation or avocation, an adult relationship, physical proximity, or emotional proximity (Jenkins-

Hall & Marlatt, 1989). Child molesters commonly choose vocations or avocations that place them in contact with children.

> What you do want to watch for is a person who centers his, all of his relationships on children, doesn't seem to have many relationships with people his own age group. . . . My whole life was dedicated to children. You'll notice my jobs, all my jobs seem to put me in contact with children. And my whole life has just centered around them.
>
> > (child molester who had been a youth choir leader, an emergency room technician in a children's hospital, a music teacher, and a social worker in a boy's club)

None of the child molester's professions would be termed SUDs because he was entirely aware that these choices were made in order to obtain access to children. However, the following exchange occurred when he was in prison in a treatment program and applying for parole.

Therapist: *When you met the parole board here, had you at one time thought about obtaining employment that would again have given you access to victims?*

Offender: *I don't think so. I believe when I first met the parole board I was going to work in a Christian book store.* (Long pause.) *Okay. Yes, perhaps being a music teacher. I guess I was. Yes. I just, that's the first time I've even thought about that in three years. I guess perhaps I was.*

Of course, it is possible that the above is not an example of a SUD, but of masked intent. The offender certainly could have deliberately chosen an occupation that would give him access to children, and he could certainly be lying about it. However, in that case, he would have been unlikely to tell the parole board about it.

Adult Relationships

Some offenders use their relationships with adults rather than, or in addition to, their professions or hobbies in order to obtain access to children. It is not uncommon for a parole officer to discover that a sex offender has moved in with a woman with children of the same age and sex as the previous victim(s).

> It was through her child that I met her, and I was so attracted to her child that I began grooming her as well as her child. And she kind of fell in love with me, and the next thing I knew, we were living together. And I guess I used her child as a stepping stone because I primarily molested my children, her children's friends. However, I did molest her child also, but her child was only molested a couple of times. The rest of it was through his friends. So I guess you could say I did use her to gain access to other children.
>
> I feel like my marriage was a cover-up for what I really was. My sexual relationship with my wife, I would almost have to fantasize being with a child in order to fulfill the sexual role of a husband.
>
> (intra- and extrafamilial child molester)

It is important to remember that the same behaviors—those that will gain the offender access to victims—can occur either by intent or by SUDs. And in either case, the offender will often vehemently deny that the function of the behavior was to gain access to potential victims. Offenders simply make excuses such as, " 'it's hard to find a woman my age without children these days' " (Jenkins-Hall & Marlatt, 1989, p. 51).

Likewise sex offenders will use friendship with adults as a method of access.

> Their parents were always my friends. And their fathers, you know, we went hunting together and fishing together and things like that. And there was a lot of times, you know, that me and the father and the sons would all go fishing or hunting, and then there would be times that just me and the boys would go hunting and fishing or whatever. And the parents, you know, pretty much, you know, allowed me to have a lot of time with their children and everything. They made it pretty easy as far as having access to their children.
>
> (extrafamilial child molester of male children)

Thus the offender preys not only on the trust of the child, but on the trust of the parent and friend as well.

Interviewer: *How about the parents of the child, was there any suspicion there that you know of?*

Offender: *No. No. That's the most painful part of this, because they were friends of mine and they trusted me. Yes. All of them.*

(child molester/minister)

Physical Proximity

Physical proximity refers to the tendency of sex offenders to frequent places where children are likely to be found. Child molesters, for example, are drawn to arcades, shopping malls, circuses, carnivals, parks, toy stores, department stores, and public restrooms. They visit them at times when children are likely to be there. The offender with a compulsive urge to visit an arcade somehow manages to restrain it during school hours. One child molester termed the hours between 3 p.m. and 6 p.m. as his "prime time."

Those who gain access to children in this way are, of course, unlikely to have ongoing access to a particular victim, as the following child molester notes:

I had abused a number of other children, picking them up in parks, playgrounds, public swimming pools, with enticements of money or rides or just anything that was going on during the time, took them to the park, and I would entice them with these things. . . . And there were two in particular that lasted any length of time. Most of them were just one night, one time things. Never saw them again.

(intra- and extrafamilial child molester)

Rapists also must find access to victims. A rapist who had robbed a bar at shotgun point, kidnapped a woman, and raped her repeatedly, announced to his outpatient treatment group one night that he had had a terrible fight with his wife that evening and had done the right thing by leaving and driving to group. When asked what he would have done had it been a night when group was not held, he said he would have simply gotten in his car and driven around. The therapist confronted him with the obvious fact that it was a poor plan for an angry rapist to be cruising the streets in his car alone, one that suggested he had in all probability obtained previous victims by that method. The client became enraged and refused to answer.

Rapists appear to use intent more often than SUDs to obtain access to victims. As Jenkins-Hall and Marlatt (1989) note,

> When a rapist makes the decision to rape, it is often a conscious one, not precipitated by a chain of AIDs [Apparently Irrelevant Decisions], because he has little or no concern about the impact of his behavior on others, and there are no immediate threats to his self-esteem. (p. 53)

Nevertheless, rapists do appear to use SUDs on occasion. The following offender raped 28 women. His excuse for being in the places where he obtained access to the victims was that he was looking for his wife, who, as he knew, was home at the time.

> I felt that she was evading me or hiding from me in some abstract way. I went looking for her. I looked for her in the places that in our past life when we were first married. I was in the service, would spend a lot of time together at laundromats. Because I always took her and helped her with the baby's clothes and whatever, and helped her, and I enjoyed doing that and those were happy times. So I looked for her in places like that. Like small apartment complexes, because during the time in the service, we rented many different places. Through all the moving. So and I looked for her at bus stops, because . . . whenever I could, depending on what shift I was on, I would sit at a bus stop with her to protect her.
>
> (rapist)

Does it matter whether the offender is lying, and he simply frequented places where he could find potential rape victims with the conscious intent to rape them, or whether he successfully convinced himself—even after the 27th rape—that he was simply looking for his wife? Not from a treatment point of view. The relapse prevention treatment approach would assume that this offender could never in his lifetime safely frequent such places again, no matter what the excuse. For this man to visit a laundromat alone, for any reason and under any circumstances, would be to court disaster.

Emotional Proximity

Finally, some offenders obtain access to victims by befriending them or offering assistance in some way. Such an approach lends itself naturally to the use of SUDs because the offender will often, in retrospect, point out he only molested "a few" of the many children in his care. This he will see as proof that his intentions were honorable and that the sexual offenses "just happened."

Offender: *I'm a rescue person. I'm going to save the cotton-pickin' world, yes, that's me. I'm always looking for the kid that's struggling, doesn't have anybody to grab him and pull him up out of the mud, that's got problems that are overwhelming him, and I'm going to save the world.*

They were kids that for some reason or another, and I think that the rescue parts of me were reaching out to kids that had similar problems that I had when I was younger, similar feelings of being isolated from family, being lonely, needing someone to care about them. These are kids that I would single out as kids needing special attention, and in many instances, I was able to do that and not get sexually involved with the kids, but in some kids, I did take it the other end and get involved with them sexually.

It just seemed to be that it would, I would gravitate toward certain kids. There would be kids that would gravitate toward me. We just really would hit it off towards each other and I fulfilled a need for some of these kids in that I became a substitute parent for them or a substitute friend.

Interviewer: *They sought you out or you sought them out?*

Offender: *I think if there was any seeking, I was seeking more than they were because I so identified with their hurt, and of course as a justification for my action, I loved these kids. Anybody that says how could you bring yourself to do it, but I convinced myself what I was doing was out of an expression of love. Not exploitation. I never thought about it that way.*

Emotional involvement is where I got into trouble, not with the physical attraction.

(child molester/minister)

In the "newspeak" of the sex offender, molestation is love, exploitation is rescue. The problem is his altruistic heart, not his perverted sexual interests.

Summary

Offenders take steps, either consciously or unconsciously, to place themselves in high-risk situations where they have access to potential victims. Initially, this behavior tends to be intentional, but may continue in covert form once the offender tries to exercise control over it. For a rapist, the use of intent, and occasionally the use of SUDs, may be as simple as getting in a car and driving around while angry. For a child molester, SUDs and intentional decisions are more complicated and require the offender to find an arena in which he can legitimately have contact with children and acquire power over them. Vocations or avocations, adult relationships, physical proximity, and emotional proximity are all ways by which child molesters gain access.

High-Risk Factors

High-risk situations, as described in the preceding section, have both generic elements (situations that are risk factors for all sex offenders) and idiosyncratic elements (situations that are risk factors for only a few sex offenders). For child molesters, generic high-risk situations are those that allow offenders access to children. Public places such as malls, parks, and arcades are generic high-risk situations, as is involvement in community organizations such as Boy Scouts, Big Brothers, church youth groups, and sports teams.

Idiosyncratic elements might include photography (if this was part of the offender's grooming pattern), alcohol and drugs (if it increased his deviant arousal), or pornography (if used to increase his arousal or as part of his grooming pattern). Many offenders are not involved with these elements, but all child molesters are involved in getting access to children.

To a certain extent, treatment programs can set limits on an offender's access to such places and activities, at least for the period of time in which he is in the program. Unfortunately, however, the easiest way to gain access to a child is to live with one. In a study at Atascadero State Hospital, more than half of 27 child molesters reported that they had lived in the same household as their victims (Day et al., 1987). As seen in Chapter 1, many offenders move back and forth between intra- and extrafamilial victims:

Offender: *I'd like to bring out that I was arrested as a juvenile for sex abuse and I have been, had been abusing other children before I was married, but after I was married it was just my own family unit that I abused.*

Interviewer: *And so it sounds like then that access . . .*

Offender: *Access had a big part to do with it.*

(intra- and extrafamilial child molester)

Because of the numbers of incest offenders who are, in Sanford's terms, "lazy pedophiles" (L. Sanford, personal communication, October 25, 1994), and because living with a child is the quintessential high-risk situation, many treatment programs require incest offenders to move out of their homes. Moving out will assist them in gaining some control over their behavior and allow time for the spouse and child to become better able to protect themselves. Likewise, the treatment team needs time to understand the dynamics involved and thus be better able to note movement along the deviant cycle.

External control and supervision of offenders helps them avoid high-risk situations. Initially, external supervision is very important because access is all that is required for some sex offenders to commit another offense:

Interviewer: *Can you tell me what would make the difference for you . . . whether or not that you would attempt to molest them again?*

Offender: *It was primarily had to do with the access that I had to the victim. Some victims I might get to see every single day. And might, you know, if I had access to that victim every day, I might actually molest that child every day. Some victims I might only see on weekends. Some I might be lucky enough to take that victim somewhere once a month, and it primarily had to do with a family allowing me to have access to the victim.*

(intra- and extrafamilial child molester)

Nor does getting caught and incarcerated alone change the offender's proclivity to offend at the first opportunity:

Interviewer: *Do you think that you are capable of committing another sexual offense?*

Offender: *Right now?*

Interviewer: *Yes.*

Offender: *Depending on circumstances, yes.*

Interviewer: *Now what circumstances would it take to allow for that to happen?*

Offender: *I would have to start to be back around children again. . . . Just having the opportunity, if the opportunity was there to be alone with a child.*

(incarcerated extrafamilial child molester)

Summary

High-risk factors include some universal aspects. In general, situations that permit access to victims, particularly those that allow child molesters to groom children or rapists to isolate women, are by definition high risk. However, in addition, some offenders find their proclivities to offend increased by drugs, alcohol, pornography, or specialized hobbies, whereas other offenders do not use these as part of their deviant cycle. For rapists, possession of a weapon or even access to a car may be high-risk elements.

Target Selection

Once the offender is in a high-risk situation where he has access to potential victims, he begins the process of targeting one. This appears to involve two elements: choosing a victim that appeals to the offender and picking someone the offender believes he can safely victimize. This section will summarize what is known about the risk factors for becoming a victim, and it will specifically address child molesters' preferences for a specific age, sex, or certain personal characteristics. This section will also discuss which sex is abused more often; whether lonely children are more often chosen; whether the mother's absence, illness, or incapacity are factors; whether the nature of the child's relationship with the mother is an issue; and whether conflict between the parents is correlated. It will highlight as well the role played by opportunity and victim characteristics in the target selections of rapists.

Child molesters differ dramatically in terms of their specificity. Some child molesters will target any child within their age and sex preference to whom they have access. Others have particular characteristics they seek in the children. Still others are influenced almost entirely by their appraisal of the chances of success.

Interviewer: *How did you pick them out?*

Offender: *Very friendly.*

Interviewer: *The ones that were friendly toward you?*

Offender: *Extremely. Yes. Overfriendly.*

Interviewer: *Did they have anything in common in addition to sounds like being fairly open kids?*

Offender: *The ages were approximately ranging from eight to ten. . . . And one victim I molested for, what was it, a year and a half. Up until he was, the time he was twelve and a half or so. And then he started going into puberty and I just cut it off. I just wasn't interested anymore. But as far as other background, to my knowledge there was none. Because they were random picked. I didn't know anything about them except that they were very open and very, I had probably met them someplace and I had said hi, and they had opened up to me and said hi, I'm so-and-so and, well, and* *then I'd set myself up to see them again. And say hi and then entice them with something.*

> (intra- and extrafamilial offender of
> 8- to 10-year-old boys he met in parks)

Other offenders are drawn toward children with certain physical characteristics or personality attributes.

Interviewer: *Was there a particular physical type that you had?*

Offender: *Usually athletic, very athletic kids, kids that were popular, almost all of them fell in that category. . . . I never was attracted toward a weak, feminine little boy. That never had anything to do with it.*

> (extrafamilial child molester of
> 12- to 15-year-old boys he coached)

For still others, target selection is based simply on the child's looks and whether or not the offender can identify some vulnerability that he can exploit:

For me, it might be nobody fat, have to be a nice-looking child, wasn't fat, I had preferences to maybe blond hair, but that didn't, really didn't have a lot to do with it. You maybe look at a kid that doesn't have a father image at home. You start deducting, well, this kid might not have a father, a father that cares about him. Some kids have fathers but they're not there with them. I guess it's hard to, it's really hard to say how you decide what child is appealing to you because, say, if you've got a group of 25 kids, you might find nine that are appealing, well, you're not going to get all nine of them, but just by looking you've decided just from the looks what nine you want. Then you start looking at the family backgrounds. You find out all you can about them, and then you find out which ones are the most accessible, and eventually you get it down to the one that you think is the easiest target, and that's who you do.

> (intrafamilial and extrafamilial offender of
> boys ages 8 to 16 whom he met through the
> church and related community activities)

Sex of Victims

Although these words are from men who primarily molested male children, more offenders actually target girls than boys. Marques et al. (1989) reported that 64% of their sample of 301 child molesters molested female children, whereas 26% molested male victims and 11% molested both. Abel and Rouleau (1990) found that 67% of their sample of 561 sex offenders (rapists, child molesters, and other paraphiliacs) preferred females and 12% preferred males. Twenty percent targeted both sexes. The latter study, however, included rapists and other paraphiliacs. Rapists almost exclusively select females; thus the inclusion of rapists in the Abel and Rouleau study would result in an overall higher number of female victims than would have been the case had the subjects all been child molesters.

However, the number of offenders who target each sex can be misleading. As seen in Chapter 1, although there may be fewer men who prefer male victims, the male-oriented pedophiles have higher numbers of victims per person. For example, the 224 men in the Abel and Rouleau study who molested female children out of the home had a total of almost 4,500 victims, whereas the 153 men who molested males outside the home had approximately 23,000 victims.

Thus more offenders select female victims than male, but those who do target males have higher numbers of victims. It turns out that this mix still produces more female victims than male. Across eight epidemiological studies, the ratio of females to males molested was 2.5 to 1; thus 29% of victims were male (Finkelhor & Baron, 1986).

The reason for this ratio may lie in the prevalence of incest. Far more men commit incest against female children than against male children. In the Abel and Rouleau (1990) study, 159 of their sample molested females in the home, whereas only 44 men molested males in the home. However, perhaps due to the limited number of victims available in the home, the average number of victims was approximately equal for men who molested girls and those who molested boys. Men who molested females averaged

1.8 victims, and those who molested boys, 1.7 victims (Abel & Rouleau, 1990).

In summary, more offenders target female children than male children. However, those that do target male children have higher numbers of victims per person. Nonetheless, the studies of victims suggest that overall, more girls are molested than boys.

Vulnerable Children

A number of child molesters report that their assessment of the child's degree of loneliness and distress is a factor. One minister would counsel couples who were having marital problems, then offer to work with their children, pointing out that the marital difficulties were likely to have an impact on them. A teacher handed out self-esteem questionnaires at the beginning of the school year and chose his victims based on those who had lower scores (Hindman, 1989, p. 82).

There is some research on victims to support what offenders contend: Vulnerable children may be more often targeted by sex offenders. Retrospective studies of adult females have confirmed that as a group, they had few friends as children (Finkelhor, 1984; Fromuth, 1983; Peters, 1984), although, as Finkelhor points out (Finkelhor & Baron, 1986), it is impossible to know from retrospective studies whether the social isolation preceded the abuse —and thus may have been a factor in the sex offender's selection process—or whether it followed the abuse and was a result of it (Finkelhor, 1984).

Relationship With Parents

Likewise, a number of studies have found that living apart from biological mothers or fathers increased the likelihood of sexual abuse (Finkelhor, 1984; Herman, 1981). In some studies, this finding was dramatic. In the Finkelhor study, it was the strongest risk factor identified, resulting in a threefold risk of sexual abuse for those girls who grew up without their biological mother. Several studies identified separation from the father as a risk factor

(Finkelhor, 1984; Miller, 1976; Peters, 1984; Russell, 1986). Bagley and Ramsay (1986) found that separation from either parent was a risk factor, and Miller (1976) found that separation from both parents was likewise so.

In addition to parental absence, maternal illness or unavailability appears to be a risk factor (Finkelhor, 1984; Herman, 1981). Specifically, physical illness, alcoholism, depression, and psychosis have been implicated.

A poor relationship with the mother has consistently discriminated victims from nonvictims. Five studies (Bagley & Ramsay, 1986; Finkelhor, 1984; Landis, 1956; Miller, 1976; Peters, 1984) found that victims were less close to their mothers than were nonvictims. However, whereas some of these studies (Bagley & Ramsay, 1986) found mothers of victims to be more often harsh, punitive, and cold, other studies simply found more distance between mother and daughter (Peters, 1984). Again, it is impossible to determine whether the distance preceded or followed the sexual abuse. The dynamics of incest in particular are such that daughters might well feel isolated and estranged from their mothers. Finally, a number of studies have found that conflict between parents was a marker for sexual abuse (Finkelhor, 1984; Fromuth, 1983; Gruber & Jones, 1983; Landis, 1956; Peters, 1984).

Rapists and Target Selection

Rapists also select victims based on a mix of opportunity, specific characteristics, and on consideration of their chances of getting caught. For cruising rapists and for burglar/rapists, the primary consideration is often simply who crosses their path at a convenient time in an opportunistic place. Even when rapists are selecting for specific characteristics, those characteristics are often projected onto the victim. Rapists frequently talk of "uppity women" or "bitches," that is, characteristics they project onto women on the basis of the way the women walk or the expression on their faces. Fremont (1975) reported one rapist saying, " 'I considered her snobbish and phony. . . . I forced myself to do it to prove a point to her, to prove that she wasn't as big as she thought she was' " (p. 253). Likewise, rapists may attribute to the victims their own sexual desires. Groth (1979) quoted one rapist as saying:

> I would fantasize about confronting a girl with a weapon, a knife or a gun, and that she would tell me that I didn't need it and that she wanted me, and that she wanted me sexually. She would say, "No, you don't need it, you don't need a gun, you don't need any of this, you're enough." (p. 26)

The decision to rape is so much an internal one, based on anger or power needs, that rapists frequently do not recognize their victims in court.

Summary

After offenders experience high-risk factors, they select a victim. Child molesters are often specific in their choice of victim, targeting children of a particular age, sex, build, or characteristic (e.g., hair color or athletic ability). For many rapists, opportunity and calculations of the chances of getting caught are more important than any victim characteristic. One rapist said about assaulting a coworker at work that he took a "calculated risk" that she was the sort of person who would not report it.

Planning and Deviant Fantasy

Although deviant fantasy can occur at any point in the offense cycle, it tends to follow covert behavior and precede overt behavior, that is, masturbatory fantasy may precede intent, but often follows SUDs. The offender who knows from the start he is planning a sexual assault may begin the cycle with masturbatory fantasy, frequently to previous victims, whereas the offender who is hiding from himself his true motivation is more likely to engage in sexual fantasy during or after target selection.

Likewise, planning may occur earlier in the cycle as well if the offender begins his attempts to gain access to potential victims by mapping out a strategy. However, the fine-tuning of the plan must still await the specific selection of a target, and must take into account current situational factors. The care and thoughtfulness that go into planning the approach to a particular child is suggested by these words, written by an incarcerated intra- and extrafamilial offender who reoffended almost immediately after release, that is, shortly after writing this description:

> Now, you must realize that none of my victims are strangers. I know them and their families well because I have been stalking the potential victim for quite some time. They are usually members of my church . . . friends from work . . . or friends from the neighborhood. While stalking the victims, I was learning their interests, needs, and weaknesses. It is very easy for a child molester to pick up on needs of love and affection. . . . CHILD MOLESTERS ARE VERY PROFESSIONAL AT WHAT THEY DO!!!

Sex offender planning may be active or passive. Active planning consists of developing a plan for manipulating or coercing the intended victim into sexual activity, whereas passive planning does the same while continuing the charade that the offender has some other purpose in mind. In the latter, the strategy is often developed in the form of a thinking error. For example, Pithers et al. (1988) describes the offender who targeted a child in a park after noticing he had been left out of other children's games. " 'Poor kid, he looks as lonely as I feel,' Jim says with a sigh, 'Maybe I should go talk to him' " (p. 156). Although Jim may protest to himself as well as to others that he was merely trying to help the "poor kid," in fact, his self-talk describes his method of obtaining access. He will approach the child as a friend who understands what it is like to feel down and left out of things. He may well "victim stance" with the child, that is, cast himself in the role of victim, describing his own problems (selectively) and engaging the child's sympathy. He will certainly offer emotional support, and soon the "poor kid" is likely to have a lot more problems than he did before Jim decided to help him.

Summary

Planning is an integral part of the deviant cycle, although it may occur at different points for offenders who admit they are going to commit an offense and offenders who lie to themselves about it. For the former, planning may occur at the very beginning of the cycle as they set out to obtain access to children. For offenders who use SUDs, planning may take a more passive form and is more likely to occur after target selection.

Grooming or Force

Force

The next step in the process is engaging the intended victim, and either manipulating or coercing him or her into sexual activity. Although some violent offenders may do no grooming whatsoever (attacking the victim suddenly with no preamble), most will groom the child to the extent of persuading him to enter a van, or the adult to the point of opening the door to a stranger or persuading her to go out on a date with him:

> Primarily it was knocking on their door, or quite often finding somebody sunbathing in their yard or whatever. Approaching them or either knocking on their door, saying I have an emergency situation, car trouble, or child that is ill, or whatever. . . . Get confidence. . . . The more need to get someone in confidence.
>
> (rapist of 28 women)

Thus violent offenders often combine grooming and violence. Why use violence at all with children when it is clear that young children are trusting and gullible and can be manipulated into sexual activity? Why use violence at all with adults when it is clear that rapists typically have access to consenting sex and are frequently married (Abel & Rouleau, 1990; Groth, 1979; Groth & Burgess, 1977; Kanin, 1985)? Because some offenders are sexually aroused by violence, some even by violence without a sexual component.

That violence is a sexual turn-on for some men has been repeatedly shown in plethysmograph studies, although results vary slightly. Quinsey, Chaplin, and Upfold (1984) found that rapists were more sexually aroused than were controls by descriptions of rape, and less aroused by scenarios of consenting sex. By way of contrast, three other studies have found that rapists were equally aroused by rape and by consenting sex (Abel et al., 1977; Barbaree et al., 1979; Quinsey & Chaplin, 1984). Controls in these three studies, as in the study by Quinsey et al. (1984), were more aroused by consenting sex than by rape.[1]

In addition, Barbaree et al. (1979) found that nonrapists had even less arousal to nonsexual violence—that is, violence without any sexual content whatsoever—than they did to rape, whereas rapists did not show significantly less arousal even to the nonsexual assault scenarios than they did to consenting sex and rape scenarios (although there was a trend: $p < .10$). Quinsey et al. (1984) established that rapists responded specifically to descriptions of nonsexual violence to females (and not to males), whereas controls showed little arousal to nonsexual violence to either sex. (Sex was not varied in the Barbaree et al. study because the victims were all female.)

The degree of arousal to nonsexual violence to females has been found to correlate with the degree of damage that rapists inflicted on their victims during the actual rapes (Abel et al., 1977; Abel, Becker, Blanchard, & Djenderedjian, 1978; Quinsey et al., 1984). Indeed, in Abel's research (Abel et al., 1978), those men who had committed sadistic acts could be identified in the laboratory by their high degree of sexual arousal to nonsexual violence. By contrast, controls were found by Quinsey and Chaplin (1984) to respond sexually least of all when victim suffering was made explicit, although victim suffering did not decrease rapists' arousal.

Maletzky (1991) obtained similar results. Fifty-five rapists, whose rapes were not unusually violent, were compared with 25 rapists whose rapes were extremely so. The less aggressive group was markedly aroused by the consenting sexual scenes, and less so as the content became more aggressive. The extremely aggressive group showed the opposite pattern: They became more sexually aroused as the aggression increased, and 9 of them had erections in reaction to scenes with no sexual component.

Barbaree et al. (1979) argue that these types of findings suggest that rapists are simply aroused by sexual stimuli. It is not that their arousal is increased, it is just not decreased by violence.

However, that does not address the number of rapists who are sexually aroused by pure violence toward women, without a sexual component. Barbaree and Quinsey both believe that such sex offenders are expecting sexual elements in the story (Barbaree, 1990; Quinsey et al., 1984) and are sexually aroused in anticipation, rather than being sexually aroused by violence toward women per se. Quinsey infers this because his research established that rapists were aroused only by nonsexual violence to women, but not to men.

That men who respond sexually to nonsexual violence constitute a particularly dangerous subgroup of offenders—a subgroup aroused by violence and not just by anticipated sexuality—is evidenced by later research by Rice, Harris, and Quinsey (1990). They found that the degree of psychopathy and sexual arousal to nonsexual violence predicted recidivism at least as well as an array of demographic, psychiatric, and historical variables.

In addition, the fact is that rapists in the real world are not passively consuming stories being read to them; they are *inflicting* the violence themselves and therefore are in control of the degree of brutality involved in the rapes. If some rapists were not aroused by violence, then why would they choose to employ gratuitous degrees of extreme violence on their victims? The fact remains that a percentage of rapists inflict extensive damage on their victims, far beyond what is necessary to subdue them, exercise power and control over them, or humiliate them. The "anticipated sexuality" explanation for arousal to violence in the laboratory fails to explain rapist behavior in the real world.

Svalastoga (1962) found that in 21% of his sample of 141 rapes, the rapist beat or kicked the woman and "interfered with respiration"[2] in another 20%. Wright (1980) found that 14% of the victims in his sample of rapes ($N = 255$) were severely beaten, 16% were choked, and 2% were stabbed.

Although some authors attribute gratuitous violence simply to an expression of anger (Groth, 1979), that explanation does not address the fact that such men appear to target women exclusively for their outbursts. An alternative explanation is suggested by the plethysmograph data. Simply put, men use gratuitous violence while raping women because it is sexually arousing to them.

As Herman (1990) has noted, "The fact that victims loathe being assaulted should not obscure the fact that offenders enjoy assaulting them" (p. 182).

Similar results have been found in studies of child molesters (Abel, Becker, Murphy, & Flanagan, 1981; Avery-Clark & Laws, 1984; Quinsey & Chaplin, 1988). In fact, Abel et al. (1981) found that six out of eight female-oriented pedophiles had more sexual arousal to descriptions of violent sex with children than to scenes of manipulated sex with children. The clinical histories of these men were consistent with their plethysmograph interests and suggested sadistic interests. For example, one had shot off a teenage girl's arm with a high-powered rifle for the sexual thrill it gave him. Sexual arousal to coercive sex with children has been shown to correlate with victim damage (Avery-Clark & Laws, 1984; Quinsey & Chaplin, 1988). There was little sexual response in these studies to descriptions of pure nonsexual violence toward children.

Studies differ markedly as to the number of child molesters who actually use the threat of force, force itself, or excessive force with their victims. Christiansen and Blake (1990) found that 45% of their sample of incest offenders used force or the threat of force, according to their victims (although less than one fourth of the offenders admitted it); Russell (1984) reported that 41% of the incestuous offenders in her study used force, according to their victims. The fact that the Russell study and the Christiansen and Blake study obtained similar results is interesting, given that the rates of force are so high in both. It is surprising that incest offenders would use force so frequently, given that they already have power and control over their victims by virtue of the relationship.

Moreover, most of the force described in a subsequent analysis of Russell's data (Russell, 1986) was minimal. Twenty-nine percent of the victims received mild levels of physical force, such as pinning or pushing, whereas only 2% of the victims were hit or slapped and only 1% were beaten. Although a comparable breakdown was not available in the Christiansen and Blake (1990) study, the examples used to illustrate force by no means involved minimal force: " 'He would beat me up and feel my breasts at the same time.' " " 'My father would hit me hard and throw me up against a wall. He dislocated my jaw once, and put me in the hospital' " (p. 96). Feltman (1985) also found force to be a significant factor in incestuous abuse: 19% of female incest victims had been beaten, threatened with a weapon, or abused with a weapon.

Christie, Marshall, and Lanthier (1979) studied child molesters in general and found that 58% used excessive force, as compared to 71% of rapists. Surprisingly, more child molesters inflicted noticeable injury on their victims than did rapists (42% vs. 39%). A lower figure was found by Gebhard et al. (1965), who determined that 12.2% of female-oriented pedophiles (incest and extrafamilial) used significant aggression during their contacts with children. The Gebhard et al. results, however, may be contaminated by the fact that they relied solely on the self-report of offenders, whereas Christie et al. relied not only on offender self-report but on arrest records, presentencing reports, transcripts of testimony, and medical records from victim exams.

Also relying on police reports, De Francis (1969) found that 50% of 250 child victims of sex offenders reported being coerced, and an additional 10% reported being threatened. Coercion included being held down, being struck repeatedly with a hand or fist, or being shaken violently. Children were also frequently told offenders would hurt, kill, or maim them, or harm or kill their families.

It must be pointed out, however, that cases that result in police involvement may be somewhat different from cases that do not. Physical coercion, particularly if it leads to victim damage, may influence the family to go to the police or influence the authorities to prosecute the case. However, it does not necessarily influence children to disclose more often. Sauzier (1989) found that children who had been subjected to intercourse with aggression were among the least likely to report. The majority never disclosed directly. The abuse was discovered accidentally, by medical evidence, for example, or sexualized behavior by the child.

Summary. Victims are either manipulated or coerced into sexual activity. Those offenders who use coercion against children or adults frequently use more force than necessary to accomplish a specific sexual goal. Such child molesters and rapists have been shown repeatedly by plethysmograph studies to be aroused by sexual violence. A subgroup of rapists appear to be aroused by nonsexual violence toward women, and that subgroup appears to inflict more damage than other groups.

Grooming

Grooming appears nearly universal, either in place of or in addition to coercion as a technique for gaining sexual access to children. The establishment (and eventual betrayal) of affection and trust occupies a central role in the child molester's interactions with children.

> I would single a kid out and begin bestowing small simple favors on them, such as taking them out to lunch at McDonald's once in a while when we would be involved in sports or something. I would wind up with one particular kid that I would wine and dine. Or even give small gifts to, and one of the things that I would caution kids about is that any coach or anybody that says well, I'm doing this for you special and we need to keep this from other kids, don't say anything, they need to start being concerned about where this is headed. But mainly showing favoritism, beginning to cultivate the friendship with them, and I would say to any adult, and I did this, any adult that moves down to a child's level to become their buddy, about just what they're involved in, their little silly romances and whatever, that to me is an an abnormal thing for an adult. When an adult does that, I think that's a danger sign they need to watch. That should not be of interest to the adult.
>
> (extrafamilial offender/coach/minister)

The grooming process itself often seems similar from offender to offender, largely because it takes little to discover that emotional seduction is the most effective way to manipulate children.

> First of all, I spot a potential victim. As I stated earlier, he must meet certain criteria. If he passes the criteria I've established, then I begin my game. I start out by saying something to him in a way to make him feel good about himself (e.g., "Hey buddy,

how's it going? It sure is good to see you. I've been thinking about you a lot lately. I think you're one of the neatest guys I know. You're more mature than most kids your age."). He usually responds positively. I then put my arm around his shoulder. If the boy flinches away, I write him off as a potential victim because I know I am wasting my time. But if he accepts my "innocent hug," I continue by offering to take him somewhere (e.g., "Hey, I've been looking for someone to go to the ballgame with me this weekend. How would you like to go? I've got an extra ticket and no one to go with. We could go to the game together. Then on the way home we could stop for some pizza or hamburgers. What do you say?"). If the boy responds positively to the physical contact, he inevitably responds positively to the offer of a ball game and pizza. He usually gets excited that I'm showing an interest in him. If he says he wants to go, I will tell him that we need to ask his parents. . . . Together the boy and I go to the parent . . . usually the mother. (Most of my victims had no father, but if he did, I did not want to give the impression that I was substituting the father's role. However, if the boy did not have a father at home, I went out of my way to give that impression.) Usually it was no problem obtaining permission to take the boy out. My "family grooming techniques" were as simple as having built the reputation of a good Christian who loves kids. With the boy at my side excitedly pleading with his mother to let him go, I almost always got permission to take him.

I rarely molested a boy the first time out. I tried to show him the best time of his life. I continued playing games with the boy, such as hugging and light wrestling to see how he responded. If he was uncomfortable in any way to my touching, I left him alone to seek out a more responsive potential victim. (Let me say here that my success rate up to this point was about 80%.)

I showered potential victims with small gifts. I might stop off unexpectedly somewhere and get a bite to eat, or I might unexpectedly stop at a bowling alley so we could bowl a few games. Kids really enjoyed the unexpected extras I showered them with. My purpose in the small gifts was to win the child's trust. It was my way of winning his love and eventually his affection. Boys loved to go to the arcades, Go-Cart tracks, and Putt-Putt golf courses. They usually enjoyed going to movies, but most of all, they enjoyed the special attention they were getting from me.

When there was no doubt that the boy liked me more than anyone else in the world, I began telling off-color jokes. This was a measuring device of his sexual knowledge. When I told a few dirty jokes, the boy would in turn tell me one that he knew. If he laughed at my jokes, I would then tell one a little more vulgar. If it ever got to where he didn't understand the joke, I would explain it to him. Sometimes I would touch the boy in the genital area to explain the joke. If the boy had an erection, I knew he was ready. I could tell by his eagerness to hear another joke and by his erection whether or not he would be responsive to my overall plan.

Finally I was able to get the boy to spend the night with me. After getting him to my house, I would run around in my underwear. I usually suggested he do the same since it was "just us guys." Before long, we would start wrestling around or telling dirty jokes. It usually didn't take much to convince the boy to sleep in the bed with me. Sometimes I massaged him and worked my way down to the genital area. But if I got him to sleep in my bed, I *always* succeeded in molesting him. The greatest challenge was getting permission for him to sleep over at my house.

(intra- and extrafamilial
offender of up to 100 victims)

The cleverness (and the tenacity) of offenders in setting up grooming is illustrated by the above offender's course upon release from prison. He moved to a new city and walked into a church off the street. He asked the minister if the church accepted "ex-cons." The minister responded that they did if the ex-con were truly repentant. He responded that he had been in prison for passing a "cold check," and that he had paid his debt and was ready to turn over a new leaf. He suggested that the minister call his former prison to verify what he was saying. "When I was in prison," he said, "I had this favorite hymn, and I told myself when I got out of prison that whichever church was playing that hymn, it would be a sign from God that that was the church for me. And father, your church was playing that hymn."

The minister did nothing immediately, but when the offender became active in youth activities, he did call the prison to inquire. The prison chaplain was new, and unfortunately had not known the offender. He told the minister he was vaguely aware that the man had been an inmate but was not sure why, and unfortunately neglected to get the minister's name or the name of his church. The story eventually reached the head of the treatment program, but nothing was known except the name of the small city the offender was in. The treatment program head contacted the local police and sent them a training film that the offender had made in prison (and for which he had signed a release permitting distribution) that described his grooming techniques. Motivated by the tape, the police searched and eventually found not one, but two churches whose ministers had been told, "When I was in prison, I had this favorite hymn. . . ." In one of those churches, he had already sent the minister's son a letter telling him what a good Christian boy he thought he was.

Warner-Kearney (1987) found that 90% of incestuous fathers admitted that they deliberately tried to build trust with their intended victims. Seventy-three percent of the offenders felt that the trust was "important" in that it decreased the chance of exposure.

To further reduce the risk of exposure, many offenders follow a slow progression in which most of the time is spent gaining the child's and the family's trust. One incest offender, a minister who molested his grandchildren, explained the necessity for a slow progression as follows:

> It was working step by step and progressively bolder, and probably if I had came right out and laid my granddaughter on the bed and undressed her and had oral sexual contact with her right now, she would have probably left the room screaming, left the house screaming.
>
> (intrafamilial offender)

The necessity for a long period of grooming occasionally saves some children from child molestation when their acquaintance with the offender is too brief for his particular grooming pattern. The following offender sadistically raped his own children while choking them, but molested few of the foster children in his care:

> I didn't have any attraction to the girls and, but a lot of, I didn't really have a lot of problems with the boys because of the fact that most of them were not there long enough. It would take me a good year a lot of times to get to know them really, really well before I would entrust them to get to do anything with them, and to me, I had to build up a really strong bond of trust between myself and that person before I would ever have any sexual contact with them.
>
> (intra- and extrafamilial sadistic offender)

However, grooming can be much briefer and can play on the child's curiosity or use enticements:

> How I met the child was, I had a little boat and we lived across the street from a canal. And instead of trying to cart the boat back and forth every day when I got finished with it, I found a family that had a dock that they weren't using, and they allowed me to park it there. And they had a son who was my victim. And I forget, not exactly sure, I believe I had some pornography magazines in the boat and took him for a ride down the canal. . . . He asked me about the books and I said well, sure, go ahead, take a look at them. And then we, I went into explaining the erection and so forth, and experimenting on him and showing him how to get an erection, masturbating him. And that's how that curiosity, I played on that curiosity role a lot.
>
> (intra- and extrafamilial offender)

This was the first victim for this offender, who was an adolescent at the time. He was arrested for it, but "did not receive any treatment of any sort. It was more of a slap on the wrist type thing and we'll just forget about it. You forget about it, we'll forget about it and that's what it was." He went on to molest "numerous" other children who were total strangers to him.

As I look back on it, I can see that I groomed 90 percent of my victims. I waited for them. It was obvious they were going to come out. They would be passing by and I would have something that I thought possibly they would like to see, or play with, or willing to, and I set myself, set them up. . . . Say hi and then entice them with something.

Later, I had abused a number of other children, picking them up in parks, playground, public swimming pools, with enticements of money or rides or just anything that was going on during the time, took them to the park, and I would entice them with these things. . . . Most of them were just one night, one time thing. Never saw them again.

(intra- and extrafamilial offender)

Eventually he moved on to his own children. The access, he said, was easier. With incest, moreover, there is the opportunity for prolonged grooming. The following offender had intercourse with all three of his daughters, one of them over a period of 6 years. He molested two of them concurrently.

With the oldest daughter, it began for us by being alone at home, and at this time I was smoking pot, and it began by me turning her on to smoking pot, and this is something that I used with all three of them. Not knowing at the time it was a pattern, but this is what it was. After a while of this, this playing, I became like their dealer, their supplier, their sugar daddy in all three instances. They would come home from school and look to see if I had something rolled up. With the oldest, that was all that was involved there in the sense of that because we would sit around, again, on the bed watching TV, smoking joints, listening to some music, and the petting began from that.

The first thing that we did was we smoked pot. Then I would do things like leave a Penthouse or something, you know, one of those type of magazines laying around. In other words, introduce them to pornography. And then there was suggestions and things like that. . . . Generally, you know, I made them feel good. Told them how pretty they were, you know, things like this, and petted around on them, more so nonverbal communication than just saying, hey, let's do this.

I would ask them, Do you mind if I do this? Is it okay in doing this? Are you okay? In other words, here am I the adult saying to them, I'm asking for your approval. I'm asking for your okay. Is it okay that I do this? Again, asking the child to give consent for something that I already knew was not okay.

(intrafamilial offender)

Although the above victims were teenagers, the grooming process is similar regardless of age. One offender described how he enticed his 2-year-old daughter to suck his penis: "Well, I told her things like this is what mommy does and why don't you try it this way and sort of coached her along on what to do." Grooming, moreover, is not limited to victims.

In the meantime, you're grooming the family. You portray yourself as a church leader or a music teacher or whatever, whatever it takes to make that family think you're okay. You show that child, you show the parents that you're really interested in that kid. And you just trick the family into believing that you are the most trustworthy person in the world. Every one of my victims, their families just totally offered, they thought that there was nobody for their kids than me and they trusted me wholeheartedly with their children.

(intra- and extrafamilial child molester)

Indeed, this offender was correct. Even after he admitted to child molestation, many families of the children with whom he had had contact refused to allow the police to interview their children, and some wrote him in prison.

Implications for Survivors

The slow progression of abuse in many cases presents difficulties when the victim discloses before the offender has fully achieved his sexual goals. Juries often appear reluctant to convict a man for touching a child's vaginal or penile area over the clothes. Practically speaking, the failure to convict often means that the offender reunites with the family. With such a compulsive behavior, it is not to be expected that many offenders will learn their lesson from such a close call. (Indeed, even offenders who are jailed repeatedly do not learn their lesson.) However, many victims do learn their lesson and never disclose again. The relatively low rates of reoffenses for incest offenders compared to extrafamilial offenders (Maletzky, 1991) may indicate that those offenders reoffend less, or it may indicate that reunited victims disclose less.

Certainly, disclosures of grooming techniques that fall short of breaking any laws are often minimized by adults to whom the child turns. In one school, 10 girls—the entire complement of girls in a fifth-grade class—reported inappropriate touching by the male teacher: stroking their thighs, standing much too close, snapping girls' bras, and so forth. School officials minimized the offenses and refused even to reprimand the teacher. The superintendent of schools admitted to me that he did not even know exactly what the girls were claiming. He could not ask them directly, he said, because the subject was sufficiently delicate that interviewing them might be harmful. Of course, those same girls continued in that teacher's class, which was not considered harmful.

Because sex offenders groom for such a long period of time, the child is in a catch-22. Disclosing early—ideal in terms of preventing more extensive abuse—may in fact backfire and accomplish nothing except arousing the offender's ire. Disclosing later means more trauma. By the time the teenage children of the sadistic rapist/choker disclosed, they had much to tell and extensive physical and psychological trauma to prove it.

Grooming presents enormous difficulties for survivors. At the heart of it lies the engagement, manipulation, and betrayal of the child's trust. The depth of the betrayal is often much worse than the formal relationship with the offender would suggest because he has used that formal relationship as a springboard to emotionally seduce the youngster in a much deeper way. The relationship with the offender is often not just a relationship, but a relationship of persuasive warmth. Children are in every case hungry for love, but offenders sometimes choose children who are starving for it.

Difficulties with trust and intimacy are repeatedly found to be sequelae of sexual abuse (Browne & Finkelhor, 1986a). Survivors often find themselves suspicious of anyone seeking a close relationship. Safety lies not in holding but in holding off.

I once saw a man on emergency who was paranoid. He presented at the emergency room as a homeless man passing through town who wanted to find some sort of shelter from the cold New England night. His paranoia emerged full blown when the emergency room staff—noticing his obvious malnutrition—offered him an ice cream bar. He ate it, but immediately began to ruminate about it. It tasted funny, he said. What was in it? Maybe something was in it. He thought somebody had put something in it.

Given his type of mental illness, I did not send him to the local church group that operated a shelter; I did not know how he would react if he thought people were poisoning him. The local police, however, agreed that he could spend the night in jail if he wished. (He, of course, refused treatment or an inpatient stay and did not meet criteria for involuntary commitment.) He seemed reluctant to go to jail, and at first I thought it was because it was jail—I would have been reluctant, too—but it was, I found, the fear the police would make him eat breakfast. He would only go when I promised him he would not have to eat breakfast.

Imagine needing something as badly as people need food, and imagine feeling that the food would poison you. Imagine further that you felt that way because it really happened. Imagine someone laid out a feast, someone you know well and who, you think, loves you, certainly someone whom you love. The feast is extravagant, beautifully presented, but has been deliberately poisoned. You might well find eating to be a somewhat tenuous experience after that. Such is the dilemma of intimacy for many adult survivors.

Summary

Grooming is ubiquitous in child sexual abuse cases. At the heart of it lies the emotional seduction and betrayal of the child's trust. A time-consuming operation, offenders often groom children for months, and occasionally years, before they sexually abuse them. The slow progression of grooming often produces a catch-22 for disclosures: If the disclosure is early enough, the offender often has not broken the law, or has broken it minimally. Later disclosures concern behavior more difficult to minimize, but it produces more negative sequelae for survivors. The betrayal of intimacy, particularly, leaves a painful residue with a long half-life.

Offense

After all of the preceding parts of the cycle are completed, the perpetrator commits the sexual offense. The type of offense is often not static, but changes over time. Thus sexual offending is frequently a progressive disorder, and offenses grow more intrusive as time goes on.

> For a long time, back when I was 20 or so, it was just more or less a touch thing. I wanted to make them feel good. It really wasn't, it was sexual arousal to me but I didn't ask them to do anything to me in return. Usually, once I got sexually aroused and made them feel good, I would go off in private and masturbate, or leave them for the sexual arousement on my own. Then in later years, it increased, you know, and I got, I let it get sexually aroused, I would ask them to do the same things to me that I would do with them. And then again, for a long period of time, it only involved oral sex and touching. And then later, through the years, in the later years, why, it progressed where, you know, I went in and sodomized a few of these kids.
>
> (intra- and extrafamilial child
> molester of 30 children)

The escalation may include the type of offense, the type of victim, or both.

Interviewer: *Supposing that you hadn't been caught for this offense, that your granddaughter had not told, do you think that you would have escalated . . . what might have happened next?*

Offender: *I could foresee a continuation, a stepped up continuation because that's the way that it had progressed up to that point, and I don't have any reason to believe that it would have changed because it seemed to be a* *progressive thing. . . . I would probably have gotten more bold with the older children, who would have been able to accommodate sexual intercourse.*

Interviewer: *When you say with the older children, what children did you mean?*

Offender: *With older children in general.*

(intrafamilial offender of 2 granddaughters)

Sexually deviant behavior can begin when the offender is quite young, and escalate over the course of many years.

Interviewer: *And when you began your Peeping Tom behavior, how old were you then?*

Offender: *I'd be guessing, but I know I was very young. I would say 11 at least.*

Interviewer: *And how frequently did you look in a window?*

Offender: *Well, of course that was situational. It depended on the weather. It was mostly in summer when school was out. And it was quite frequent through that period of time through the summer when school was out. And I can even remember thinking that there was, must be, I must be a freak or odd even as a child at that time because my friends, kids I played with, weren't interested in going with me. . . . So it was on my own. But I couldn't understand why I needed to do that and they didn't. . . . That [referring to rape] didn't start until I was around 26, 27 years old. I can recall before that occurred, before the assaults occurred, I can recall having fantasies of coming home from work, because I worked different shifts and she would be asleep. I can recall having fantasies of—I didn't call it rape in my mind because it was my wife—but force and making my wife have sex with me and not being able to stop me. . . . And I can recall even waking up in my sleep, having sex with my wife, while she was still asleep, and right prior to that me having a dream about forcing someone to have sex, a woman to have sex with me but not recognizing who it was. A faceless person in a dream. . . . It was a faceless person in the dream, but when I come out of the dream I would be having sex with Joan.*

(rapist of 28 women)

The escalation is sometimes driven by a need for more excitement once the offender habituates to less intrusive sexual offending. Frequently, the progression is from hands-off to hands-on offenses.

Rapist 1: *I mean, it's like, the rape was four years away from the divorce, and in those four years were a hundred orgasms outside of a window watching people make love, watching women take their clothes off, watching women take a bath.*

[Here he described the first time he crossed over from voyeurism to rape.] *I wanted that excitement, you know. There's this one situation where this woman had fallen asleep on the couch, and the TV was on but the shows have gone off. There was just fuzz, and she had on a little negligee, and there was a very beautiful woman like Playboy and, you know, I'm looking in there, and lots of time it's a hurried, rush situation, I'm just going to catch a glimpse, let's get off here. But this is, I've got all night. She's fallen asleep, and so my fantasies were allowed to go wild and I wanted more. I wanted some excitement, and there was some urgency there and there was a lot of feeling and there was some anger there, and I wanted to take a cigarette—I smoke cigarettes—and drop a cigarette in on her. Do something. Get some feeling there. Get something going. I wanted to really, I think sexual drive was involved in feeling a lot of this, but there's definitely some anger coming out there, you know, and something that wants to complete this, this fantasy, this act, this whole thing, to get more to it, to get this excitement thing, you know.*

So I'm going to go inside. I'll just go inside. I didn't have a mask. I didn't have gloves. I didn't have a weapon. I didn't have a plan, like I'm going to do sexual intercourse, anal intercourse, oral intercourse. You know, I didn't have any plan. You know, I had these fantasies about having sex with her, you know, about sexual intercourse, but I didn't have it all put together in some plan. I just had all this energy, and I just went to another window and opened it and went in and told her, woke her up.

First I turned off the TV. I didn't know what to do. I should have left the TV on so I could see what was going on, but I didn't know what to do. I turned off the TV, woke her up, and I said I'm just going to have sex with you. She's going, what do you want. And starting to scream, you know. And I'm being real nice. You know, I'm just going to have sex with you, like. And then she says, well, no. And then I grabbed her by the throat and I said I'm going to rape you, and she realized the anger and violence, that the possibility was there, and then she said all right. Just don't hurt my child. See, her child was sleeping in the other room and that was, like, I

never intended to hurt your child, but I know I could manipulate you with
that and that was, like, information stored.

I wanted her to perform oral sodomy on me and she started, she was
crying a little bit and that kind of—but she did that and I got so excited I
kind of—but she did that and I got so excited I was just like going to come
within one second and I didn't want to.

Rapist 2: *Was rage on your mind? When you wanted her to perform oral sex*
I felt just now when you said that she started crying, I felt a whole lot of
rage. I did. I think I would have been if I wanted it I wanted it and damn
her crying, she was going to do it.

Rapist 1: *Yeah, I didn't quit because she was crying. I quit because it would be*
over for me and I wanted it to last. I wanted to do something else.

(voyeur/rapist)

That offenses change over time was confirmed by Abel and his colleagues. Abel et al. (1985) found that less than half of rapists (44%) began their sexually deviant careers by raping. More than one fourth (26%) began with child molestation, whereas 9% began with voyeurism and 8% began with exhibitionism. By contrast, 75% of child molesters began with child molestation, although 13% began with exhibitionism, 3% with voyeurism, and 3% with rape.

It makes intuitive sense that rapists would less often begin with rape than child molesters would begin with child molestation. Many sex offenders develop their deviant pattern and commit their first offenses during adolescence (see Chapter 1, "Age of Onset"). It takes far more aggressiveness to sexually assault an adult than it does to peep, expose oneself, or molest a child. Many adolescents begin committing offenses while baby-sitting. It appears to be relatively easy to take advantage of small, naive children who have been told to "do what the baby-sitter says." It is considerably less so to assault someone who is roughly the same size and likely to fight back.

The issue often arises as to whether hands-off offenders— exhibitionists and voyeurs, for example—are dangerous in the sense of being or becoming physically assaultive as well. Some correlation between the hands-off and hands-on offenses has been consistently noted (Abel et al., 1988; Freund, 1990; Gebhard et al., 1965; Grassberger, 1964; Yalom, 1960).

However, the question cannot be answered simply by noting co-occurrence or by looking at the number of rapists who are also exhibitionists or voyeurs. The latter figure may have no correlation with the number of exhibitionists or voyeurs who become rapists. As has been often noted, it may well be that the overwhelming majority of heroin users have also used marijuana, but that does not say anything about the percentage of marijuana users who also use heroin.

At least four studies have specifically looked at the percentage of exhibitionists who were also rapists. Gebhard et al. (1965) found that 10% of exhibitionists also committed rape, whereas Grassberger (1964) found 12%. More recently, Freund (1990) found that 15% of exhibitionists and 19% of voyeurs were rapists, whereas Abel et al. (1988) found that 25% of exhibitionists and 37% of voyeurs were rapists. Freund, however, noted that the Abel data were more likely to be accurate in this instance than his own, given the differences in confidentiality afforded clients in the two studies. The results of the assessments in the Freund study were accessible to treatment personnel and/or the courts, whereas Abel et al. had a Federal Certificate of Confidentiality that protected the data from involvement in the legal system. (The Abel et al. study had a number of other confidentiality safeguards as well; see Chapter 1.) Without such safeguards, Freund (1990) felt that "harshly punishable activities or propensities to carry out such activities will be underreported" (p. 200). Thus as many as 25% of exhibitionists and 37% of Peeping Toms may be, or at some point may become, rapists—unfortunately, not an insignificant number.

Summary

Sexual offenses often change over time, frequently from less intrusive to more intrusive. Sex offenders often begin their deviant careers quite young, and escalation may occur over the course of a number of years. The change often occurs as the offender habituates himself to less intrusive sexual offending and escalates the type of activity, type of victim, or the situation in search of increased excitement. As many as one fourth of exhibitionists and more than one third of voyeurs may eventually become rapists.

Maintaining Secrecy

To avoid the legal and social consequences of their behavior, sex offenders must keep the child from disclosing the abuse. They maintain secrecy in a variety of ways: threats, promises, bribes, but most commonly, by exploiting the child's caring.

> I instilled in them the kind of hurt that would be involved to my wife, to all of us, how much it would hurt my wife if it became known. You know what I think I counted on the most—this is going to sound strange—I counted on them loving me enough to not tell.
>
> (intrafamilial offender with all three daughters)

Offenders will maintain that secrecy is not just in their best interests, but that they are concerned about the best interests of the family and even the child.

> I said if anything ever happens, I'll have to kill myself because I don't want your mother to go through this trial. And I said I don't want you to have to face this either.
>
> (sadistic offender who sodomized his two boys while strangling them)

Some offenders rely exclusively on trust and rarely even discuss secrecy with the child. They rely on the child not only to keep the secret but even to function as an early warning device for the suspicions of others.

Interviewer: *How did you keep your victims from telling?*

Offender: *Well, first of all, I've won all their trust. They think I'm the greatest thing that ever lived because I'm so nice to them and I'm so kind and so, you know, there's just nobody better to that person than me. . . . If it came down to, you know, if it came down to, I have a, this is our little secret, then it would come down to that, but it didn't have to usually come down to that.*

Interviewer: *But you did speak that in some cases?*

Offender: *In some cases you had to. Some cases you could almost tell that the child was really uncomfortable and was really nervous, and in a case like that, you would have to say, you know, this is our secret, and we would reward that child with special gifts or whatever it was, whatever it took to keep the guy's mouth shut.*

    If a family becomes suspicious, well, they're not really going to bring it to me, they're going to bring it to the kid first and the kid—I've got the kid so well-groomed that the kid's going to come to me and say, well, my mom asked me if you've ever tried to do anything to me or anything like that. Well, then I begin working on the family, still being kind of nice to them but maybe backing off of that child just enough until the parents' suspicion gets back down again. Maybe I'm not with them as much. I won't maybe have as much physical contact. I won't put my arm around the child as much. I'll do whatever it takes to convince that family that there's not a problem.

(extrafamilial offender/youth choir leader)

The manipulation of trust is such a powerful device that offenders frequently see no need to threaten.

> I think people have a misconception about this. Just the fact that you are a popular, well-known, well-liked-by-kids adult is enough. You don't have to threaten kids. Oh, they would have done anything to please me, because they liked me.
>
> (extrafamilial offender/minister)

Those that do threaten children may use either psychological or physical threats.

Offender: *He at that time was only 7. . . . And I would fondle him, and at first I'm not sure whether I masturbated in front of him or not. I know after a period of time I did. And then after that my daughter, my stepdaughter, reached approximately 6 or 7 years old. And I was still molesting my stepson. And I had shown, I was starting to use pornography with my* *stepson. And I wanted to let him experience intercourse so I showed him how to penetrate his sister. And they did that while I masturbated.*

Interviewer: *How during this would you keep the secret, keep them from talking about what was happening, what would you do there?*

Offender: *I would, I believe I would say that this is just going to be our secret. . . . But at a later time, they, I used threats. I said all right. If you tell, you're going to get in trouble. They're going to take you away from your family. They're going to throw you in jail. You'll never see each other again. The whole family will end up in jail, not just me. . . . Well, they, of course, became very uncomfortable with it. They did not want to do it. They would not tell me, they would flat tell me no and then I would force them. I would say, well, you can't leave this house or you wouldn't get your dinner or we will not go to the show or you will stay in your room for the next two weeks if you don't do it. And I would threaten them with, you know, confinement. Imprisonment.*

(intra- and extrafamilial child molester)

However, not all offenders threaten or bribe children. Some simply assume the child will not tell or will not be believed if he or she does.

For years, I really didn't feel threatened as far as the legal issues because I've never, what few children that have told on me is really, there's been a couple of children that's told on me for sexual involvements. And it never turned into nothing. The parents refused to believe them and everything, but most children were willing to keep it quiet anyways. They were my friends and they cared about me, too, and they didn't want nobody getting upset and they didn't want nobody getting mad, and they already had enough confusion in their life as it was, and they didn't want to add to that confusion by bringing up something like that.

(extrafamilial child molester of 30 children)

Finally, some offenders believe that discussing disclosure will tip off a very young child that the behavior is wrong. Such offenders have usually gone to some trouble to reassure the child that the behavior is normal, "what mommy does," or "what other little girls/boys do with their daddies," or even "what mommy wants you to do." Thus they say nothing about secrecy.

> I never mentioned to her that I didn't want her to tell. I don't know, I guess maybe if I told her not to, then I would have thought that she would have been, wait a minute, this is supposed to be a secret, I've got to tell it. If it's a secret, I've got to tell somebody. So I never went about telling her not to tell her mother or whatever.
>
> (intrafamilial offender of 2-year-old daughter)

In addition to threatening, bribing, or assuming silence, many offenders take evasive action as well.

Offender: *Most of them I would assume that I just figured that they wouldn't say anything about it, you know, and I would stay away from the park for a week, two weeks, and then might go back and select myself another victim.*

Interviewer: *Just swear off in between?*

Offender: *Yes. Yes.*

Interviewer: *For fear of being caught?*

Offender: *For fear of being caught and then coming back and pointing the finger.*

Interviewer: *And then what would happen?*

Offender: *I would crawl into a cubbyhole. And just stay out of sight. . . . Stay at home. Be extra, work extra hard at my homework. Bring my grades up. I always had good grades.*

Interviewer: *At age?*

Offender: *14.*

> (intra- and extrafamilial offender
> describing stranger molestations)

Evasive action may be more than avoiding the specific spots where they molested children. They may leave their jobs or even the area.

Generally, after I'd had sex with a boy and everything, I would always feel guilty afterwards, and I would do things, I would, a lot of times I'd move out of state, I'd move to different towns and, you know, I've made it. I just completely quit associating with the whole family at times, you know, to keep from going back and being involved with this boy anymore. . . . And sometimes within, during the next six months, you know, I'd usually find another victim.

(extrafamilial offender)

Summary

Sex offenders manipulate children into silence in a variety of ways: by bribes, threats, and exploiting trust. They often try to convince the child that secrecy is best not only for the offender, but for the child and his family as well. Manipulation is a sufficiently powerful device that offenders do not need to threaten children. Those who do threaten children may use physical or psychological threats.

At the other extreme, some offenders do not even discuss disclosure because they assume the child either will not tell or will not be credible. Particularly with young children, offenders may not discuss disclosure because they do not want the child to know there is anything inappropriate about the behavior.

Finally, some offenders do not rely solely on the silence of the child but take evasive action as well. Evasive action may be as simple as avoiding the scene of the molestation or as extensive as leaving a job or the entire state.

Guilt, Remorse, and Shame

Sex offenders are frequently distressed following disclosure. Depression is common and suicide is sometimes a risk. However, naive family and friends (and sometimes even therapists) may assume that remorse will prevent relapse, an assumption made particularly when shame over disclosure is misread as guilt over the behavior.

I have lost my job and probably one of my professions. I have a criminal record I must live with for the rest of my life. I have to live every day with what I've done.

(intrafamilial offender)

This offender was clearly distressed, but note that each sentence began with "I." He was lamenting the consequences of disclosure, not the harmfulness of abuse. In fact, distress over the former is more common than concern over the latter. Bernard (1975), as noted in Chapter 1, found that 90% of pedophiles in a pedophilic organization had no desire to reduce or eliminate their attraction to children. Likewise, Ageton (1983) found that only 14% of adolescent sex offenders felt guilt over their behavior. As Herman (1992) has noted, "Genuine contrition in a perpetrator is a rare miracle" (p. 190). There is, in fact, a wide range of reactions in sex offenders to issues of guilt and remorse.

Interviewer: *Did this [molesting children] cause you some conflict inside?*
Offender: *Yes, it did.*
Interviewer: *You know, gosh, here I am.*
Offender: *Why am I doing this? Asking myself am I a homosexual? And I kept on telling myself no, I'm not. And that question continued in my mind up until the time I was an adult. Through marriages. And in between marriages. And I've experienced homosexual activity. And I didn't enjoy it. So I said no, I'm not a homosexual.*

(intra- and extrafamilial sadistic offender)

This sex offender did not even understand the question. His egocentricity and narcissism prevented him from realizing that the interviewer was asking whether he felt badly about his treatment of the children. The offender's answer, that he worried about being gay, illustrates his total lack of empathy. By way of contrast, the following incarcerated offender felt his prison sentence of 20 years was "reasonable" given his molestation of his grandchildren.

I felt tremendously guilty and sorrowful for my actions, and being a devout Christian, it was really added to the stress, because I now not only felt guilty about what I was doing to my victims and to myself, but also what I was doing to God, which was a new factor and added to the stress.

Prison to me had been a . . . I don't really know the term to apply to it. But it's been a godsend, I think. I may not feel that way had my victims not been so close to me. I hope that I would feel that way. But I can't speculate about something that never did take place. But those kids mean a lot to me. And my daughters, my family means a lot to me. And this has given me a way to make some amends.

(intrafamilial offender/minister)

The process of separating genuine contrition from public shame is complicated by the fact that many offenders see apologetic behavior as mitigating their culpability. By "showing the jugular," as it were, they attempt to undermine others' anger and blunt retaliatory aggression.

When attempting to determine whether or not the sexually aggressive behavior is truly egodystonic—that is, whether the offender is ambivalent or conflicted about molesting children—or whether the offender is simply victim stancing, it is useful to note whether there is evidence of contrition before disclosure.

A charismatic minister molested another minister's daughter while watching a ball game at the girl's house. He left the other adults to go to the bathroom but walked into the young adolescent's room instead, fondled her breasts while (he thought) she slept, then masturbated to ejaculation over her. The daughter told her father several days later, and he confronted his fellow minister (and best friend), revealing in the process the fact that he was planning to report the abuse to the authorities. The molester then checked into a psychiatric inpatient facility, saying that he was having a "nervous breakdown" to which he attributed the molestation. However, the nervous breakdown did not appear at the time of the assault nor in the interim between assault and disclosure. Up until the day he checked into the hospital, the minister appeared to be functioning perfectly normally to those around him.

Some offenders, however, do have histories suggestive of guilt over the behavior. One offender had moved in and out of his home for years, telling his wife each time simply that he could not stay there. He threatened suicide, became extremely depressed, and was bitterly self-critical. His wife thought he was having an affair, but never suspected he was molesting their daughter.

Another offender had tried in multiple ways to obtain information and help:

Offender: *I was seeking professional help all the time. And I was trying to talk to my parents about this thing. I was trying to think, to talk to my brothers about this. I tried to talk to a minister once and this guy, he was a friend of mine. And I mentioned, you know, the fact that somebody else had made a statement about the possibility of me having sex with children. And this guy laughs, you know, and he said, you know, I could never believe anything like that about you. And I don't know actual, exact words and everything, but he thought it was the silliest thing he'd ever heard, and here I was trying to tell the guy that I was . . .*

Interviewer: *You were involved with children?*

Offender: *Yes. And he was my friend and he was a minister. And I didn't know who else to go to at the time and I was trying to talk to him. And I don't believe, I don't know what kind of effect it would have had on him if I'd actually told him that I was sexually abusing children.*

Interviewer: *So it sounds like you tried to go for help, too. But you weren't finding any?*

Offender: *I didn't have no idea where to look. I didn't have any kind of information. I spent hours in libraries throughout. I mean over and over and over and I'd look in libraries and just for information, addresses about people you could talk to about sex issues and things like that. I didn't just sit around until I abused kids and let it happen again and it was no big deal. It was a big deal to me.*

(extrafamilial offender of 30 boys)

When there is evidence of guilt over the behavior, it is easy to misread its significance. Both offenders cited above continued to molest for many years despite their discomfort with it. The incest offender continued for a 5-year period and only stopped when he was caught. The extrafamilial offender molested for more than a decade, ceasing to do so only when he was arrested and incarcerated. The following offender, who also never stopped molesting his grandchildren until he was caught, was constantly remorseful.

Offender: *What would you do afterwards?*

Interviewer: *Cry. Pray. Ask for forgiveness. And not only ask for forgiveness from God, but I'd ask for forgiveness from my granddaughters, too, because it was, there was a lot of pain involved. It would have been a simple thing if I hadn't have been closely related to the victims.*

(intrafamilial offender/minister)

Guilt, then, is no more effective in controlling the abusive behavior than hangover guilt is in stopping alcoholism. There are alcoholics who swear with every hangover that they will never drink again, and sex offenders who apologize after every molestation, but continue to molest.

However, guilt is relevant to motivation for treatment. Offenders who believe that "this behavior isn't immoral, you know, it's just illegal," as one offender said to me, have only the threat of incarceration as a motivation for treatment. In those circumstances, they may focus their energies on getting away with molesting rather than controlling it. The former will keep them out of jail as surely as the latter. The offender who is upset by his behavior has more motivation to control it.

Summary

Although perturbation and distress are common in offenders after disclosure, these reactions are often more related to shame over disclosure than to guilt over the behavior. There is, in fact, a wide range of reactions in sex offenders to their behavior—from sincere contrition to psychopathic indifference. Even when guilt and remorse are present, however, they are often ineffective in controlling the behavior. Although guilt may distress, dismay, and even torture the offender, the only behavioral result may be a pattern of offending and apologizing repeatedly, or offending intermittently when attempts at control fail.

Thinking Errors

In 1961, Samuel Yochelson began his study of the criminal mind. Overextended in private practice, with little time for writing or reflection, he decided at age 55 to make an abrupt change in his professional focus and enter a field of which he knew nothing, and of which he was convinced no one else knew a great deal either. In this way, he hoped to make more of a contribution to society than he felt private practice allowed (Yochelson & Samenow, 1976, p. 2).

He began by applying the same psychoanalytic concepts to his work with criminals that had been useful to him with noncriminals, but after several years pronounced his work a total failure. The treatment group he ran had begun operating as a gang, with some members working together in an elaborate check-writing scheme, and others cooperating to steal and fence booty. Samenow joined Yochelson as he began to reorganize his theory and his thinking. Rather than imposing a theory on the data, they elected to derive a theory from their observations of the criminal mind.

The work proved exceedingly fruitful, and from it arose the concept of criminal thinking errors, that is, the notion that criminals are characterized not by distortions in their affect but by errors in their thinking patterns. Yochelson and Samenow noted rapid affective shifts in criminals, often from extreme sentimentality to overt brutality, and decided that "feelings were an epiphenomenon of thought. They could be changed by substituting different thinking processes" (Yochelson & Samenow, 1976, p. 33). Although Yochelson and Samenow concentrated on criminals in general, their work on thinking errors, in particular, has been widely used by experts in sex offender treatment (Jenkins-Hall, 1989; Knopp, 1984; Murphy, 1990).

Yochelson and Samenow defined thinking errors as "mental processes required by the criminal to live his kind of life"

(Yochelson & Samenow, 1976, p. 359). They commented primarily on process thinking errors, which they termed "automatic errors of thinking." Among these they included (a) "I can't," (b) victim stancing, (c) lack of time perspective, (d) failure to put oneself in another's position, (e) failure to consider injury to others, (f) ownership, and (g) superoptimism.

"I can't" is the tendency of criminals to disguise "won't" behind "can't" when refusing to do things they do not want to do. They "can't" resist impulses; do their homework assignments; give up cigarettes, alcohol, or drugs; stay away from children; quit seeing a new girlfriend (with small children); leave Big Brothers, Boy Scouts, the church youth group; or talk about why not.

"I can't" is often part of victim stancing, the claim (and often the belief) that they are the real victims. They are abusing because they were abused. They are abusing because their families, bosses, or society has treated them poorly. One offender who raped a hitchhiking girl and cut off her hands felt he had been victimized by her because it was her fault he did those things to her.

Another who had killed another man angrily protested at a parole hearing that he was simply a victim of the incompetence of the system. The other man, he claimed, had committed many crimes for which he should have been incarcerated. Had this other man been incarcerated, he would not have been out on the streets for the killer to stab.

In a victim apology session, an adolescent offender tried to tell his two 6- and 7-year-old victims that he (the offender) was frightened that he would run into them (because he was under a court order to stay away) and how difficult it was to live with such fear.

Lack of time perspective, or "instancy," is simply the failure of offenders to take into account the future consequences of present behavior. However, it is not true that offenders live totally in the present because many sex offenders are quite cunning about gaining access to high-risk situations, and selecting and then grooming a child, all of which take considerable planning and require considerable time. The seeming lack of time perspective is perhaps more fairly related to the superoptimism of the criminal —that he will not get caught or punished—than it is to a true inability to appreciate the future consequences of present behavior. When asked whether he worried about getting caught, one offender said,

> Never. Never dreamed. Never gave that a thought. Never worried about it. I never worried about what would happen. I always thought that I could handle anything. If anything could come out, if anything came out, I would take care of it and it would be no problem and we'd settle it, you know, behind closed doors, and I'm sure that was a false assurance because of my position, and I was well-liked in the community by everyone. Was Mr. Nice Guy. Everybody liked me, so I thought, well, shoot, I could handle that.
>
> (extrafamilial offender undetected for 20 years)

Offenders both fail to put themselves in others' shoes and fail to consider injury to others. The phenomenon is aptly illustrated by the story of the female thief who stole, she said, because she needed the money. "Would it be OK for someone to steal from you," her therapist asked, "if they needed the money?"

"Oh no," she replied, "because I need the money."

The failure to appreciate injury to others is interwoven with the concept of ownership or entitlement. If the offender wants sex with a child or with an unwilling adult, it is his right to have it. Neither is treated as a separate human with rights. If they refuse the offender what he wants, they may find they have evoked considerable anger because he is "entitled" to it. The sex offender below was describing his thought processes just before he entered a window and raped a woman he was voyeuristically watching.

Rapist 1: *I need this. You know, I need to get off. I need some sex. I need a release. I need some relief.*

Rapist 2: *Now she's posing. What about she's posing. She wants—*

Rapist 1: *I can't control myself. I need this, and once I do this, I'll be okay. I mean, it's like, let me just get this out of the way and then I can go on with my life or with whatever I wanted to do, and it was exciting, very, very exciting, secretive. It had an allure to it, it was very powerful.*

Whereas Yochelson and Samenow concentrated on process thinking errors, other authors have reported on content thinking errors (Abel et al., 1984; Jenkins-Hall, 1989; Murphy, 1990), such as specific beliefs that the sex offender uses to justify and rationalize his behavior. Blaming the victim is frequent.

> And I did very well until I had a foster son who had, was very street-wise, and recognized the fact that I was gay and got me going a little bit playing around, and once I started, I couldn't stop again.
>
>   (sadistic offender who molested students
>   he taught, boys from the community,
>   foster children, and his own children)

Likewise, reframing the abuse as somehow helpful to the child is popular.

> I didn't really plan to do it again. . . . When she woke up, she started crying for her mother and I got to thinking, well, she was interested in this, it kept her attention for a little while a couple of days ago, I'll just, in order to get her to stop crying, then I'll let her do the same thing again. So in my deranged mind, I was thinking I was doing something to help her, but when I was actually trying to help myself.
>
>   (intrafamilial offender of 2-year-old daughter)

Frequently offenders use palliative comparisons to minimize their behavior.

> With me, I've never struck a woman. I've never hit one and it's kind of weird, I don't even believe in it. It's repulsive to me that guys can beat up women. It bothers me greatly. I've had friends who burglarized houses that had a woman home and they nearly beat the woman half to death. I've never done that. And like I said, at the time when I raped, I was kind of thinking, well, hey, this isn't as bad as me beating her up. . . . I just raped her. At that time, I didn't feel that there was that much as I've learned to the violation.
>
>   (rapist/burglar)

Thinking errors cannot be placed at any particular point on the deviant cycle because they permeate every stage. Sex offenders make them while making SUDs ("That's all behind me now, so there's no reason I can't go back to being a camp counselor."); staying in high-risk situations ("Why should I leave the pick-up game just because a little kid starts playing? Nothing can happen out in public like this."); targeting a victim ("That poor child, he looks as lonely as I feel."); planning the offense ("Lisa and I should spend more time together. We can do that while her mother is shopping."); committing the offense ("It doesn't hurt to look. She'll never even know I was there."); and even afterwards ("I'll never be stupid enough to do that again.").

Summary

Thinking errors are used by sex offenders to justify and minimize their behaviors. Process thinking errors include (a) "I can't," (b) victim stancing, (c) lack of time perspective, (d) failure to put oneself in another's position, (e) failure to consider injury to others, (f) ownership, and (g) superoptimism. Content thinking errors include self-statements that blame the victim for the abuse, reframe the abuse, or use palliative comparisons. Thinking errors cannot be placed at any particular stage in the cycle because they permeate every stage.

Discussion and Implications
for Clinicians and Survivors

The notion that sex offenses are isolated events with no past and no future allows the offender to escape responsibility for obtaining appropriate treatment and for making certain lifestyle changes that would reduce the possibility of relapse. If a sexual offense is simply "an irrational 2 minutes" of a man's life, there is no reason for, or point to, treatment. Vague notions that the victim somehow provoked the offense or that family dynamics and stress somehow took away the offender's ability to make choices regarding his behavior likewise deflect responsibility.

The reality is far different from the myth. The actual offense is merely the weed that appears above the surface; it is supported by a vast network of roots—thinking errors, deviant arousal patterns, SUDs, planning and grooming activities, target selection, techniques for maintaining secrecy—all of which ensure that other weeds will pop up, regardless, in other places.

Although the actual offenses obviously affect victims, it is less often recognized that the more hidden parts of the cycle—the grooming, the subterfuge and deception, the methods of maintaining secrecy—all have an impact as well. To understand the sequelae of sexual assault, one must understand how each of these is processed and internalized by the survivor.

The clinician who treats survivors should be well-versed in the dynamics of sexual assault. It is important to be able to replace the confused reasoning of the child or adult survivor who has internalized the thinking errors of the offender with accurate knowledge and information. In fact, the 4-year-old did not "provoke" the sexual molestation by emerging from the bathroom nude. On the contrary, the offender may well have removed the towels to force him to do so. In fact, the offender who told his daughter it was her "job" to take care of daddy sexually because mom (according to the offender) was not, was not telling her the truth, as the survivor believes, but was merely grooming her.

In addition, adult survivors must make decisions about the probability that their offender will molest other children, and therefore whether or not to protect their children and other child relatives from him. Doing so is often highly disruptive to the family. Given what is at stake, adult survivors are not content with a simple "yes, he is dangerous" from their therapist, but understandably need to know enough about sexual assault to make the decision for themselves.

Finally, therapists who treat adult survivors frequently treat spouses of sex offenders as well. Decisions about supervised and unsupervised visitation, about whether and when to reunify the family, and about warning signs of potential relapse all require the spouse to be well-versed in the dynamics of sexual abuse. Even child victims can be taught the warning signs of imminent relapse so that they may notify a parent, therapist, or other adult while the offender is still in the grooming stage.

Although learning how sex offenders think and how they behave is disheartening and dismaying, nevertheless, the best protection against sexual abuse is understanding it. Sex offenders get away with far too much, far too often because the average layperson and far too many clinicians do not know enough about sexual assault to avoid being conned. Sexual abuse is not an accident. It does not "just happen." It is not typically an impulsive act. It is a series of interlinking thoughts, feelings, and behaviors that are highly compulsive. It will not go away on its own. It is not easy to change, and it can never be cured, only controlled.

Notes

1. Controls were all nonrapists, but in the Abel et al. (1977) study, they were sex offenders with other paraphilias.

2. Presumably, this means strangled or choked.

3

Sadistic Versus Nonsadistic Offenders and Their Effects on Victims

Sadistic Offenders

Of the different typologies for classifying offenders, the division of the subgroupings into sadistic and nonsadistic has the most salience for understanding victims because of the dramatic difference in the victim's experience. Sadistic offenders have been discussed extensively in regard to rape/murder (Holmes & De Burger, 1988; Leyton, 1986; Ressler, Burgess, & Douglas, 1988; Ressler, Burgess, Douglas, Hartman, & D'Agostino, 1986; Rule, 1980; Wilson & Seaman, 1992), but less has been written about chronic sadistic abuse, and still less about chronic sadistic abuse of children.

Langevin (1990) defines sadism as "a sexual anomaly whereby an individual derives sexual gratification from the power and control over his victim, from their fear, terror, humiliation, and degradation, as well as from their injury and death" (p. 106). The gist of this definition—that sadists derive sexual pleasure from inflicting pain—appears to be universally accepted.

Examples of sadistic behavior are scattered throughout the sexual abuse literature:

- a man shot off a teenage girl's arm for the sexual thrill it gave him (Abel et al., 1981, p. 133)
- a rapist of 13-year-old girls preferred to rape them anally on cement floors so that the rapes would be more painful (Abel et al., 1981, p. 133)
- a rapist of over 100 women bit their breasts, burned them with cigarettes, beat them with belts and switches, pulled out pubic hair, and shoved poles into their vaginas (Abel et al., 1977)
- a father used lit candles to cauterize the cuts he inflicted on his daughter's vagina and around her nipples (Fine, 1990, p. 168)
- a serial killer would smother his wife with a plastic bag until she passed out and then would have sex with her. He beat her with belts and burned her with cigarettes (Groth, 1979)
- a father who knew his 9-year-old daughter was afraid of the dark tied her to a tree in the woods and allowed different cronies to come out of the woods and rape her during the night (Gelinas, 1992)

Approximately 2% to 5% of sex offenders are sadists (Langevin, 1990). Both Groth (1979) and Abel et al. (1987) found that 5% of their samples of incarcerated and outpatient sex offenders were in that category. Abel et al.'s 28 sadists averaged 29 acts with 5 victims for a total of 3,800 acts with 132 victims. In an earlier publication with an overlapping sample, Abel et al. (1985) differentiated types of sex offenders. Six percent of child molesters, 11% of rapists, 11% of voyeurs, 11% of frotteurs, and 4% of exhibitionists had committed sadistic acts (Abel et al., 1988). Freund (1990) found rates that were generally similar. In his sample of 440 sex offenders, 4% of voyeurs, 6% of exhibitionists, 9% of frotteurs, and 16% of rapists were sadists.

However, higher figures have been found. Thirty-one percent of Marques et al. (1989) sample of incarcerated offenders were sadists, as were an astonishing 45% of Langevin's (1990) small sample of 20 sex offenders.

Sadists appear to have different patterns of sexual arousal than do other sex offenders and controls. As noted earlier, rapists often have sexual arousal to both consenting and forced sex, but not to depictions of physical violence without a sexual component. Sadists, by contrast, are often not aroused at all by consenting sex, but may be particularly aroused by nonsexual assaults (Abel et al., 1981). Abel describes one such offender who had 17% of full erection to descriptions of consenting sex, 61% to descriptions of rape, and 79% to depictions of pure violence without a sexual component (Abel et al., 1977). Groth (1979) describes a serial killer who claims to have never had a consenting sexual fantasy.

Fortunately, sadists infrequently target children. In a study by Freund (1990), 87% of his sample targeted adults, 9% targeted adolescents and adults, 2% targeted adolescents alone, and 2% targeted children and adults or children, adolescents, and adults. When they do victimize children, sadists may choose them either because they prefer prepubescent targets, or as part of their general callousness toward all life. For example, Groth (1979) quotes a serial killer as saying:

> The picture in my mind was one of torturing a victim with everything from matches and cigarette butts to a propane torch, electrical stimulation, needles, and so forth. . . . The first victims were female, because I had an impulse to rape and hurt. The last three were female for rape reasons, but with more emphasis on hurting and humiliation. . . . And, on a few occasions, there have been concepts of taking a "dry run" or a practice run using a small child as victim, male or female. (p. 56)

This callousness would meet the most conservative definitions of evil. Simply put, it is monstrous and inhumane—one wishes inhuman—and to the nonsadistic, incomprehensible. DeYoung (1982) describes a sadist who attacked an 11-year-old girl, raped her, bound her hands and feet, tied a rope around her neck, and dragged her across an open field until she lost consciousness, at which point he left, thinking she was dead. When asked what he had felt like at the time, he said, "Like Superman—strong, invincible and horny, too!" (p. 125).

Likewise, Joseph Kallinger, the serial killer, tortured his own son to death. As his son lay dying, with his final breath, he said, "Daddy, please help me," at which point Joseph Kallinger reached orgasm (Norris, 1988, p. 32). It will be difficult for the nonsadistic to read those lines; it was difficult for me to write them. It is important that we both understand it was not difficult for Joseph Kallinger to enact them.

Sadists are a sufficiently distinct subgrouping of sex offenders that most major typologies have included them (Gebhard et al., 1965; Guttmacher & Weihofen, 1952; Knight & Prentky, 1990; Lanning, 1987; Prentky & Knight, 1991; Rada, 1978). Knight and Prentky (1990) included them in their classification of both child molesters and rapists in the most empirically based typology to date. Their division of rapists included "opportunistic," "pervasively angry," "vindictive," and "sexual," the last further divided into sadistic and not sadistic. Thus sadists are one of the few categories of rapists whom Knight and Prentky consider to be motivated by sexual arousal. Of course, the sexual arousal involved—to violence, pain, humiliation, and suffering—is by no means normal.

Generally, sadists can be distinguished from other sex offenders by the degree of injury they inflict on victims, although that distinction is by no means an infallible guide. Knight and Prentky (1990) found what they term "muted" sadists among both rapists and child molesters: offenders who had sadistic fantasies, but who had not injured their victims severely. Although this group had not acted on its fantasies—at least for the charged offense—it is unclear whether this is a stable group over time. Many sex offenders report that their fantasies often lead their behavior. Over time, both fantasies and behavior escalate.

In addition, other types of offenders can also cause severe injuries. Pervasively angry rapists were distinguished by Prentky and Knight (1991) from vindictive rapists on the basis of the specificity of their attacks. Pervasively angry offenders seem to be, as the name implies, mad at everyone, and they have a history of physically assaulting men as well as sexually assaulting women. Vindictive rapists, by contrast, only attack women: Their anger is specifically misogynistic.

Both, however, use gratuitous violence, that is, violence in excess of what is needed to accomplish rape. At their worst, angry rapists can batter women to death, not because they derive sexual pleasure from their victim's pain, but because they are discharging anger. They rationalize their attacks as "just desserts" and have a litany of complaints against all women, or particular categories of women, such as women they believe "look all stuck up."

But although the injuries may be severe in both cases, the nature of the assault, motivation, affect, and thinking patterns differ between angry offenders and sadists. First of all, the sadist is not angry. Groth (1979) quotes a sadist, for instance, who said, "At no point during the incident was I aware of any anger towards the victim, although I now recognize a resentment or jealousy of girls" (p. 45). One sadistic killer would tell his victims prior to his assaults:

> "First I'm going to torture you in the most horrible and painful manner I can think of. Then I'm going to abuse you sexually in the most degrading way I possibly can think of. Then I'll kill you in the slowest and most painful way I can conceive. . . . Do you have any questions?" (Heilbroner, 1993, p. 147)

The sadist slowly tortures; the angry rapist explodes.

Surprisingly, some commonsense differences turn out to be myths. Sadists are so severely disturbed that a history of childhood antisocial behavior is often assumed. However, Rosenberg, Knight, Prentky, and Lee (1988) found that sadists were less antisocial and impulsive as children and adolescents than were other rapists.

However, this does not necessarily mean that the sadist was a normal child. The sadism may not have progressed past the fantasy stage during childhood, or perhaps the sadist was sufficiently secretive that he did not get caught. True sadists appear to have an encapsulated disorder and may not have a general history of acting-out behavior. Other signs of disturbance thus may not be present. Heilbroner (1993) quotes Hazelwood describing some sadist killers as " 'three-piece-suit-offenders.' " " 'One was a churchman, another worked as a high-level executive for a Midwest chain. One guy was an ex-cop.' " Some of the worst, he noted, were " 'pillars of the community' " (p. 148).

Although the disorder may be encapsulated and hidden, it is apparently both extensive and intensive. Sadists in Rosenberg et al.'s study engaged more often in other paraphilias than did other rapists and had more rapid reoffense rates (Knight & Prentky, 1990).

Chronic Sadistic Abuse

Although sadists who kill generate the most publicity, many sadists torture but do not destroy their victims. Of those who target children, clinical experience suggests that they are frequently in-home offenders, given that it is considerably more difficult to maintain sadistic control of a child over time from a more distant leverage point.

There is some research in support of this clinical experience. Prentky, Burgess, and Carter (1986) found that sadists more frequently offended against family and friends (19%) than did other rapists (3% to 8%). Of course, this sample included primarily men who attacked adults; thus the percentage of child-oriented sadists who attacked family and friends was not clear. Becker and Coleman (1988) found that 4% of their sample of incest offenders were sadists. The following case is an example of chronic incestuous sadism:

> Julie, a 32-year-old therapist, asked to be put on my waiting list, saying that time was not a factor because she had "some issues" but nothing pressing. Several months later, when I called to set an appointment, she reported that she had been released from an inpatient unit less than 2 weeks previously. The unexpected hospitalization had occurred because of an acute-onset psychotic episode with paranoid features. The episode was triggered by memories of her father torturing all of the five children in the family over most of their childhoods.
>
> Furthermore, several siblings had had acute psychotic episodes over the years in which they told similar tales of torture. In between psychotic episodes, each child had lost the memories and did not believe the other siblings' stories. At the time

Julie emerged from the hospital, two of her siblings had recovered parts of their memories while in nonpsychotic states, and Julie was able to compare notes to some extent.

Prior to recall, one of Julie's sisters had moved in with her parents and left her 4-year-old child alone with her father. Julie's mother had literally moved out into the garage apartment, giving the child's grandfather free access to her. The child eventually reported sexual abuse, triggering her mother's memories of her own abuse. She confronted her father, telling him if he did not plead guilty, she would rally all her siblings to testify about the ongoing sadistic abuse throughout their childhoods. The father pleaded guilty to that one victim and was sent to jail.

No doubt, had the jury heard the full story, her father would have stayed behind bars far longer than he did. Julie reported that he would bring in a tray of instruments to torture her and make her pick which one he would use. She was never able to describe all the instruments, but did speak of his use of a pencil point on the clitoris to inflict pain.

She remembered her mother holding her hands while her father tortured her, and became enraged when I asked if she was holding her hands to comfort her, as Julie implied, or holding her down. How could I say such a thing, she screamed. How could I even imply her mother would hold her down?—thus revealing the benign transformation she had made to find comfort in the midst of torture. In fact, Julie's mother would often initiate the episodes with Julie, coming into her room to tie her up and "prepare" her. Julie would often beg and sob, "I'm not ready, Mom. I don't have time. I haven't had enough time. Not today, Mom. I need more time." Julie was referring to her conscious attempts to "get away," to enter a state of consciousness where she was not present. Her mother would routinely strip her from the waist and tie her legs apart. Julie would beg to have her hands free, "I won't do anything with them. I promise I won't. Just don't tie them." On occasion, her mother would hold them rather than tie them.

Julie's father would often gather all the children in the family and make them pick which child would go first. In addition to torturing the children, he made them perform sex acts on each other and played humiliation games in which he would put individual children on a leash and make them act like dogs. Julie said it was easier to be the dog than to watch her siblings be so humiliated. He once made her mother go outside on a leash pretending to be a dog at Halloween, and caused a considerable uproar in the neighborhood—Halloween not being a sufficient cover to hide the sadistic nature of the act. The police were called, as they had been on more than one occasion.

Julie and her siblings were too afraid to talk to the police, and she remembers vividly a pair of policemen who knew something was very wrong. The older policeman said to the younger, "They won't tell us anything; there's nothing we can do." Julie watched the policemen leave with her face pressed against the windowpane. She remembers the younger officer turning and looking back at the house before getting in the car, no doubt seeing Julie with her face against the glass.

Julie states that her mother also had sex with her when the father was not present. This continued well into her teenage years. Her mother defended the abuse by saying that because no pain was involved, there was nothing wrong with it. At one point, while being molested by her father, Julie opened the door to her bedroom and found her mother on the other side, listening and breathing hard in a state, she believed, of sexual arousal. At another time, she remembers coming out of the room where her father was molesting her and begging her mother to intervene. Her mother sent her back, saying, "Your father's too weird. You're just going to have to deal with him yourself."

Her mother was also tortured by her father. Julie has a particularly strong memory of her mother staggering out of the bedroom one morning with her arms tied to a broom stick across her shoulders in the position of a cross. There were brooches stuck through her mother's breasts, and her mother was pale and bleeding and "looked horrible." Her father also prostituted her mother, and her mother would beg not to have to go on the street again.

Sex rings were part of her father's repertoire during the children's preschool years. Bringing a child was the price of entry and he brought his own children to trade for access to others'.

In addition, Julie was aware of violent, extrafamilial molesting. She opened a closet door in her own home one day and found an elementary school-age Hispanic child tied to a chair and gagged.

It has become fashionable not to believe any reports of abuse not admitted by an offender or proved with corroborative evidence. In this case, skeptics will claim that the offender admitted under pressure (how many offenders admit otherwise?) and point out that there is no corroborative evidence. Some will discount the sisters' memories.

However, as the therapist in this case, I would point out that the initial deterioration and flood of memories occurred prior to my client entering therapy. Neither hypnosis nor drugs were ever used to assist memory, nor were any special techniques used. The focus of therapy was not on reclaiming memory, but on maintaining stability as the memories surfaced. Far from my suggesting abuse, I was unprepared for the sadistic nature of the abuse, and was surprised and shocked by it.

None of the descriptions of abuse were of events that could not have happened. There was never any evidence of cult activity (although there was mention of a pornography ring). There were no ritualistic elements. The descriptions were of sadism, pure and simple, and there was little difference in the tales of my client and the writings of the Marquis de Sade.

Goodwin (1993) has noted that some of what is termed "ritual abuse" could be more accurately termed sadistic abuse. She notes that the Marquis de Sade included in his descriptions of sadistic acts:

> locking in cages, threatening with death, burying in coffins, holding under water, threatening with weapons, drugging and bleeding, tying upside down and burning, wearing of robes and costumes, staging of mock marriages, defecating and urinating on victims, killing of animals, having victims witness torture, having them witness homicides, pouring or drinking of blood, and taking victims to churches and cemeteries. (Goodwin, 1994, pp. 483-484)

These acts, Goodwin notes, are among the 600 different types of sadistic acts the marquis described in the book, and they are 15 of the 16 types of acts that are routinely described by adult survivors in accounts of "ritual abuse" (Goodwin, 1994). The only one missing is photography, which had not been invented in 1789. However, an equivalent was described: peepholes and stages where observers could watch the abusive activities.

Although some members of the public, and even of the profession, appear to have difficulty believing that such evil exists in the world, in fact, those who work with sex offenders and listen to their stories have no trouble believing it at all. I have on tape an interview with an incarcerated sadist in which he matter-of-factly describes dressing his own boys in Boy Scout uniforms and suffocating them while he sodomized them. He was caught when he planned the murder of a real estate agent he had invited to the house. He thought he had his two teenage boys—who by then had endured years of sadistic abuse—so much under his control that they would help him with the murder. His plan was to overpower the agent, tie him up, rape, torture, and kill him.

The sadist was furious when the boys instead turned him in; he insisted the whole thing had been a fantasy. It was ridiculous for them to assume, he said, that he was serious. "They have no idea," he explained, "how much mess it would make." How long, he was asked, would it have taken before he would have been ready to act on the fantasy? "About 2 years," he said casually. "In about 2 years I would have been ready."

Immediately after the taping, the sadist called his lawyer, who advised him to withdraw permission for the tape to be used for training purposes. Consequently, I have never been able to share the tape with anyone. I keep it, though. I expect it to be subpoenaed someday as evidence in the sentencing phase of a murder trial.

Thinking Errors of Sadistic and Nonsadistic Offenders

The difference between angry and sadistic rapists may be blurred by the degree of physical damage that both may inflict.

However, the differences between the "garden-variety," grooming child molester and the sadistic child molester are quite clear. Grooming offenders are "turned off" by the presence of pain; they do not intentionally inflict physical suffering. Typically, they do not use physical violence of any sort, preferring instead to manipulate children into sexual activity through cycles of trust and betrayal.

Nonsadistic offenders engage in a variety of creative thinking errors, the effect of which appears to be to mask from themselves the child's aversiveness to the behavior and to rationalize their own involvement. Indeed, I have known novice clinicians to wonder if such offenders were psychotic, given the lack of reality testing implicit in their projections:

> She was acting just like a little whore. She got out of the bathtub and ran around the house nude.
>
> (molester of a 4-year-old)

> She knew just what she wanted and how to get it.
>
> (offender who taught a 2-year-old
> that she would not be fed unless
> she performed fellatio on him first)

> I admit to incest, but I'm not a child molester. Incest was something we did as a family.
>
> (father of 13 children by his three daughters)

Although such thinking errors constitute a considerable barrier to treatment and act as releasers for sexually deviant impulses, their prosocial aspects should not be ignored. Simply put, the typical child molester wants to believe that children desire sex with him because he is not sadistic. Recognizing the child's aversiveness would be a "turn-off," that is, would decrease his arousal rather than increase it and would induce conflict between his desire for sex with children and his capacity for empathy.

One incarcerated offender described how he had molested all three of his daughters using seduction and photography as his tools. He would buy fancy lingerie for his teenage daughters and ask them to pose in it for photographs. He escalated this hands-off molesting carefully and slowly over time, and even "asked" permission before he did anything new. He praised his daughters and told them how beautiful they were. He was careful to minimize physical discomfort.

The result, he admitted, was that the eldest daughter, now in her 20s, was still in denial, still defending her "love affair" with her father. She was currently married to a man almost 20 years older than she and was highly symptomatic.

The offender was so skilled at manipulating his daughter that she never understood she had been victimized. The lack of physical violence, the illusion of consent, the subtlety of the coercion— all furthered the thinking error that the offender was not doing anything harmful. This illusion was necessary, not only to prevent activation of his conscience (which might well have made it more difficult for him to offend) but to protect his sexual arousal as well.

Such offenders often do have a capacity for empathy that can be seen in other areas where they are not blinded by their own desires. This capacity and its emergence in nonsexual areas is one factor in the refusal of family, friends, and acquaintances to believe that such a man could be a child molester. Because they themselves do not have thinking errors around children and sex, they cannot understand how a man they consider kind and empathic could have sex with a child.

In trying to make sense of offenders' simultaneous capacity for empathy with others and their lack of it with their victims, I once hypothesized that molesters could cognitively take the perspective of the child—because offenders frequently appear to know children well enough to manipulate them—but would not feel for them emotionally. In this view, they are capable of perspective-taking but not of empathic concern.

In investigating this empirically, my colleagues and I discovered that there was a link—but in the opposite direction (Salter, Kairys, & Richardson, 1990). Empathic concern did not differ between sex offenders and a matched sample of nonoffenders, but perspective-taking did. In other words, even individuals with a capacity for empathy were unaffected by the pain of others if they did not take the others' point of view and correctly identify the feelings. Without accurate perspective-taking, empathic concern is as useless as a smoke detector with a working siren but a broken sensor.

By contrast, the sadistic offender does not distort the child's point of view. Gelinas (1992) described one such offender who saw that the child was mentally escaping the molestation by gazing out of the window. He shut the curtains. In that act, he revealed both that he knew the child's experience was aversive and that he was capable of determining even subtle ways the child had of relieving her pain. The act tellingly indicated that his goal was to increase suffering, not pretend it was not there.

Sadistic offenders have thinking errors, but the nature of sadism is such that denial of victim suffering is not one of them. Instead, sadists will sometimes project onto victims their own sense of being sick, perverted, or evil. Sadistic incest offenders—a small minority of incest offenders, to be sure—seem prone to fusion and enmeshment with their child victims. They may rail at the child that she is disgusting, sick, or has no capacity to love. One offender repeatedly told his small daughter that she was too egocentric ever to have children. Another told his child that she did not feel things, she just pretended to. His daughter was continually finding, rescuing, and nurturing hurt animals and had no understanding as to why her father insisted she did not care about them.

Victim's Perspective: Nonsadistic Offenders and Emotional Invisibility

A child molested by a grooming offender, that is, a nonsadistic offender who uses manipulation rather than violence, has an experience of emotional invisibility. Her reactions are misread by the offender to suit his own needs. Thus she is not "known" by him in the same way that a child molested by a sadistic offender is "known." Her true feelings are invisible to the former even as they are carefully monitored by the latter.

The nonsadistic offender is not accurate in assessing the victim's reactions, and offers to her an image of herself that has little authenticity. However, children's beliefs about who they are and what they feel are influenced dramatically by feedback from the environment, and eventually, the offender's projections onto the child are internalized by her, creating shame, confusion, and conflict. Who he says she is is a person no one would want to be. This false (but internalized) self-image often emerges during the course of treatment as a distinct voice, or strain, within the survivor that is consistently self-punitive and self-critical. The internalized offender's voice typically embodies three beliefs: that the child is worthless, enjoyed the abuse, and is responsible for it.

The Child Is Worthless

Even in the absence of verbal abuse, this message is communicated by the offender's willingness to use the child for his own needs in disregard of the child's experience. The survivor often emerges with a belief that her needs, wishes, and desires do not matter. She often struggles with codependency as she takes responsibility for other people's affect but seems to be unaware of her own. After all, has she not been taught that she is responsible for the offender's sexual interest in her? It is a small step to see herself as responsible for everyone's affective response to her.

In addition, many offenders are openly emotionally abusive. One incestuous father called his daughter "cunt," "whore," and "bitch" each time he raped her. Less dramatic, but no less harmful, is the constant criticism to which many offenders subject their victims. Eventually, the victim may conclude that nothing she does is ever right. One offender wanted his daughter to speak with a phony "upper-class" accent, and corrected her each time she lapsed into her normal voice.

Because of either implicit or explicit messages, the victim is likely to emerge from sexual abuse with the belief that she is unimportant, worthless, possibly even bad. What happened to her, therefore, was not very important. Probably, she thinks, she deserved what she got.

The extreme forms of a negative self-image—the sense of being horrible, of being slime, of being disgusting—are more typical of survivors of sadistic, rather than nonsadistic, abuse. Sadistic offenders sometimes project onto their victims their own, and unfortunately accurate, sense of being evil.

The Child Enjoyed the Abuse

The issue of physical responsiveness is particularly shame-based for victims. Because the grooming offender is trying to justify his behavior by blaming the victim, it is often important to him that the child respond physically. He will often stroke the child's clitoris or penis in order to induce arousal, while telling the child that she or he wants him to do this.

The child is faced with a conflict that, however he resolves it, is likely to leave sequelae. If his body responds to the abuse, he will find it difficult to resist the offender's interpretation of that response: that he wants the abuse to occur, that he is enjoying it, and that his "wanting it" was the reason it occurred in the first place. He is unlikely to report the abuse for fear the offender will tell about his physical responsiveness, possibly even his orgasms, and therefore his "role" in the abuse.

This pairing of an emotionally aversive experience and sexual pleasure is confusing to a child and is likely to make it more difficult for him to develop a healthy adult sexuality. Sexual arousal during sexual abuse is one way that survivors become alienated from their own bodies; many see it as a form of self-betrayal. They become angry and distrustful of their own sexual response, and thereafter, sexual arousal itself becomes aversive. This is particularly so when the early pairing of sexual abuse and sexual arousal has resulted in a disordered arousal pattern. The survivor may be sexually aroused by memories of the abuse or by fantasies of similarly humiliating and/or frightening situations.

Because the child has no concept of a healthy sexuality, and no sense of her own rights or own worth, she may find herself later in emotionally abusive or battering sexual relationships. The situation will be used by the internalized offender to reinforce the view that she is bad.

On the other hand, if the child successfully numbs her body and does not respond physically, she has developed a capacity for dissociation that may make it more difficult for her to respond sexually in adult relationships. This may be a global impairment, and any sexual activity may result in an immediate numbing, or it may also be selective and may be triggered by certain sexual positions or verbal exchanges.

Oral sex, for example, is particularly aversive for children, and many adult survivors not only fail to enjoy oral sex, they dissociate when it begins and remain dissociated throughout the remainder of the sexual encounter. For many, the missionary position triggers aversive memories of a male who may have weighed four times their body weight taking their breath away by lying on top of them. Later, they find themselves frightened or gasping for breath whenever they try the missionary position.

That adult survivors frequently have long-standing sexual problems is well-documented in the literature (Becker, Skinner, Abel, & Cichon, 1986; Becker, Skinner, Abel, & Treacy, 1982; Briere & Runtz, 1987; Finkelhor, 1979; Herman, 1981; Jehu & Gazan, 1983; Maltz, 1988; Maltz & Holman, 1987; Meiselman, 1978; Tsai, Feldman-Summers, & Edgar, 1979). Sexual problems are so common that at one point, I had treated no adult survivors in years who did not have them. I was surprised, then, when a survivor with an unusually violent and sexually abusive father denied having any problems. Eventually, in therapy, she described her sex life in more detail. Unaccountably, she found herself crying whenever she had intercourse. She would lie under her husband passively, uninvolved either sexually or emotionally, while tears ran down her cheeks, and both she and her husband pretended not to notice.

The Child Is Responsible for the Abuse

The child has responsibility for the occurrence of the abuse, either because she "wanted" the abuse to happen or because the offender could not possibly (supposedly) resist her potent sexuality. As evidence of this claim, offenders will cite (a) the child's physical responsiveness, particularly if the offender manipulated the child to orgasm (see above); (b) the child's natural tendency to freeze during the initial abusive episodes, and therefore the lack of a violent response on the child's part; and (c) the child's habituation to the abuse over time (Summit, 1983). This latter, the capacity for accommodation that is part of the human species' evolutionary viability, is misread by the offender and fed back to the child as justification for the abuse.

Offenders frequently justify their behavior long after the fact by saying that the victim "didn't say no," to which Eliana Gil appropriately responds, "tell me how she said yes" (E. Gil, personal communication, October 19, 1994). The assumption that children will resist the abuse, preferably violently, is based both on a misunderstanding of children and an underestimation of the skillfulness of offenders. To respond violently, children must first of all view the episode as inappropriate sexual contact, about which the majority of victims may not even have heard. It may be years before the child puts words to the experience. This vulnerability is compounded by the fact that the offender is almost inevitably in a position of power with regard to the child, that is, a position in which he can and does define the child's reality.

Much has been written about the power differential between victim and offender, but the effect of that power differential does not extend just to habits of compliance, but to the definition of reality. Often the child has developed considerable trust in the offender and accepts the offender's behavior as appropriate. An implicit statement that the behavior is appropriate is made simply by the fact that the offender is engaging in it.

In addition, offenders frequently show the child pictures of other adults and/or children engaging in sexual activity, and/or verbally reassure the child, "This is what little girls do with their daddies." Controlling the child's reality is the most insidious way that offenders compel compliance.

To say that the child does not necessarily have the tools to define the experience as abusive is not to say the child does not define it as aversive. Aversiveness does not automatically equal abusiveness for the child. Children go through a variety of aversive experiences, from rectal thermometers to shots to stitches, and sometimes to surgery, which they intensively dislike but that the adult world reinforces as appropriate and insists that the child tolerate.

In addition, the child's difficulties in defining reality are compounded in many cases by the slow and insidious progression of abuse. Offenders rarely begin with full intercourse, but work from appropriate to inappropriate touching in such a gradual way that the child is never sure where the line was crossed. Even in the teenage years, he may be afraid to confront marginal behavior for fear of being accused of having a dirty mind. By the time the behavior is clearly inappropriate, the child may fear being compromised, that is, having to answer the question of why he let it get that far.

Children do not always protest the abuse because (a) the offender has won their trust and they want to please him, (b) they are afraid of being punished or hurt if they disobey, (c) both, or (d) they have dissociated. Although it appears more common for familial offenders to trade on trust, they may also trade on fear. Extrafamilial offenders may use either.

The child does not know (and the offender will not admit) any of the above. Instead, the child internalizes the offender's belief system that he is worthless, he wanted the abuse, and he is responsible for it. He is often left with an inaccurate and distorted picture of the abuse and of himself. Typically, this picture will be internalized so deeply that the adult survivor, looking rationally at the situation, will say that he does not believe it was his fault, while wondering nevertheless why he feels so guilty and so worthless. Indeed, the adult does not believe that he is responsible, but the child within him does.

Victim's Perspective: Sadistic
Offenders and Emotional Visibility

The nonsadistic offender's victim has the task in therapy of removing a borrowed self-image: of finding and countering the internalized offender's voice, easing the shame and self-doubt that the offender's accusations engendered, and learning to hear the less derivative parts of himself. However, at least he does not have a terror per se of emotional visibility, that is, of having his thoughts and feelings known by others. Often confused, self-critical, hopeless, and at war internally, he is frequently relieved by the emotional visibility engendered by effective therapy. Because he was abused while being emotionally invisible, safety, for the victim of nonsadistic abuse, lies in emotional visibility. He may respond so positively to emotional visibility within therapy that issues of dependency are created. Therapy may be the only place he feels like himself, free at least for a time of the crippling, internal critic that haunts him.

However, for the sadistic offender's victim, emotional visibility holds no solace. He was known by the offender, and the offender used the child's thoughts, feelings, and wishes to hurt him. Any expression of caring or interest in anything was dangerous because it could be attacked to hurt him. High levels of potentially decompensating anxiety may be generated by the "being known" quality of therapy that is all the more debilitating for the client because of the confusion for both client and therapist that accompanies the deterioration.

Why is this client decompensating? Therapy seems to be going well. Together the therapist and client are uncovering hidden feelings, motivations, wishes, and thoughts. The client's experience is becoming increasingly clear to both. In the therapy, the client is becoming more and more who he really is. Subterfuge and camouflage are less and less evident. So why is the client getting worse? If it is puzzling and worrisome to the therapist, it is horribly disappointing and frightening to the client.

The child's fear of being known will make this and any other sort of intimacy a perilous and anxiety-ridden venture. Therapy for survivors of sadistic abuse must proceed slowly, with constant focus on the client's reactions to the therapist knowing him. The therapist cannot take any sort of trust for granted, and must not accept superficial reassurance too easily if the client is also decompensating. Although logically, the client may not distrust the therapist, action always tells the tale better than words. When a client's actions and words differ, the therapist is well-advised to shut her ears.

Implicit and Explicit Denial

Although victims of nonsadistic and sadistic abuse face different issues with regard to emotional visibility, they face similar issues with regard to the visibility of the abuse in the world at large. The offender may deny the victim's experience of the abuse, or may acknowledge it by using it to inflict further pain during the episodes, but at least he admits that the episodes occurred. This does not stand without exception; there have been offenders who entered the child's room at night in the dark, never spoke, and never admitted by word or deed at any other time the existence of the abuse. More typically, the offender speaks during the abuse, and frequently before and afterwards, in an attempt to groom, persuade, instruct, bribe, and/or threaten.

Much of the literature has focused on whether or not the nonoffending spouse knew the abuse was occurring. It most certainly matters in retrospect: A survivor whose mother did not know may feel unprotected, but not necessarily unloved. An unknowing parent also will find it easier to side with the adult survivor rather than the perpetrator. The adult survivor can have a "lights-on" experience of visibility with her parent that can be highly therapeutic. Confronting a colluding spouse, however, is in effect confronting an offender, and that spouse must move considerably further in her own healing to admit and take responsibility for that behavior.

At the time, however, it mattered little to the child whether the spouse did or did not know. The child's experience was invisibility in either case. Either the spouse knew about the abuse and covered it up (explicit denial), or she did not know and therefore could not validate the child's reality (implicit denial).

Regardless, for the child, the experience was similar. Rape in the night was followed by breakfast with family who acted (albeit for different reasons) as though nothing had happened. Upon leaving the house, she faced an entire world of implicit denial. Everyone—teachers, friends, coaches—all acted as though nothing had happened. Such a child was faced with a disquieting choice: Side with the shared reality; repress, or at less suppress as deeply as possible, the abuse, and tell herself that nothing happened; or cling to her reality at the expense of a consensual world. The secret burdened her, made her feel isolated and alone, and different from her friends.

It is easy to underestimate the isolating effect of implicit denial, but few adults would be comfortable in a situation in which they saw an object—a table, for example—that others did not see. Moreover, if they had never seen a table before, their ability to define it, to understand its meaning and its purpose, would be severely limited. Were a single person to walk in the room who also saw the table, that person would play an enormous role in defining it. His attitude toward the table would be absorbed, his descriptions adopted, his definitions accepted. The question, then, of why the victim internalizes the perpetrator's attitudes, beliefs, and cognitive distortions so readily is simply answered. There is no competition. Everyone else is acting as though the abuse never happened.

Denial and Supervised Visitation

The effect of implicit denial is one reason that supervised visitation with nonadmitting offenders can be so detrimental to children. Those who favor such visits often point to the fact that because the visit is supervised, offenders cannot physically traumatize the child. Actually, this may or may not be true, depending on the degree of vigilance of the supervisor. It has happened on occasion that persons chosen to supervise were friends and/or relatives of the offender and did not believe he was guilty. Therefore, they saw no difficulty in leaving the child alone with the offender while answering the phone, hanging out the laundry, or even running to the store.

Even when the supervisor stays physically present during the entire visit, he may or may not be aware of thinking errors by which offenders manipulate children. The offender may victim stance: for example, talk about how terrible his life has been since he had to move out of the home, how much he misses his children, and so forth. He may attempt to drive a wedge between the nonoffending spouse and child, saying, for example, that he cannot come home because his wife does not trust him. If he has been prevented from saying directly that he may go to jail if she continues to disclose the abuse, he may allude darkly to not knowing whether he will see his daughter again. One nonoffending, but denying spouse was prevented from threatening the child in front of the supervisor, but was allowed to take the child to the bathroom. In the bathroom, she immediately began to tell the child that, if she continued to disclose, her dad would go to jail and the family would have no way to support themselves.

In addition, even if the supervisor has been trained to recognize thinking errors and is comfortable intervening, he may not know certain idiosyncratic words, gestures, or objects that have special meaning for the child. One offender put Xs and Os on letters to the child, which he had previously told her did not mean hugs and kisses but symbolized oral sex instead. Hindman once worked with an offender who repeatedly clicked a fountain pen around the house whenever he wanted to intimidate his young victim. He even took the pen to a clarification session. Only later was it discovered that it was the same pen with which he molested the child (J. Hindman, personal communication, October 17, 1994).

Still, if none of the above occurs, the offender, by denying the abuse, is once again denying the child's reality and contributing to the child's self-doubt and fears that he is crazy. By not acknowledging the abuse, the offender is forcing the victim to choose, once more, between his caring for the offender (which would incline him to deny his own experience and echo the reality on which the offender is insisting) or standing by his own experience (with all the isolation and loss of a consensual reality that that stance implies).

In the therapeutic tension between client and therapist, therapists often simply try to "take away" the client's sense of responsibility for the abuse. "It's not your fault," the therapist tells the client repeatedly, and is puzzled by the client's tenacious sense of responsibility. "It didn't make you different from the rest of humankind," the therapist says, and is puzzled by the client's sense of isolation and difference. The fact is that from the therapist's point of view, the client is not responsible for any of the abuse or its sequelae. Unfortunately, the client's abusive history makes her no different from one third of other American women (Finkelhor, 1986; Russell, 1984; Salter, 1992; Wyatt, 1985).

However, from the client's point of view, she may have participated in deception at least, even if she holds herself accountable for nothing else. She had an experience that did isolate her from the world as others knew it. It most certainly did make her feel different.

This point came home to me most painfully on a recent visit to my childhood home. I ran into my best friend in childhood, Gracie, who was also back visiting. "You've played prominently in my therapy this year," Gracie told me. "Why?" I said, surprised. "Because," she said, "I was sexually abused as a child and couldn't tell you. I remember once in fourth grade, we were walking down the sidewalk together and you said, 'Being best friends means you don't have secrets from each other.' I said, 'I don't have any secrets from you.' It was the first time I lied, and the beginning of seeing myself as someone deceptive."

Only three other people knew of the abuse, she told me: her husband, her therapist, and her priest. "Why me?" I wondered. "I've seen this woman casually a couple of times in 25 years. Surely there must be other people closer to her than I?" But then it was obvious. I was the one person she had to tell, and she was not really telling me at all. She was telling her best friend in fourth grade. She was redoing. She was refusing to see herself as someone deceptive.

Therapy and Adult Survivors

The task for the adult survivor of nonsadistic abuse is to remove a borrowed self-image; she must challenge and shake a shame-based view that she is someone who actually wanted her father/brother/mother to have sex with her, and solicited, initiated, and enjoyed it. That does not turn out to be as simple as having a therapist tell her it is not her fault. Telling a client that the sexual abuse is not her fault will speak only to the conscious mind, which is likely to "know better" anyway. It is a feeling, a sense of guilt, and not a rational thought process that causes the adult survivor to believe that the abuse is indeed her fault. Arguing with her will simply cause the belief to go underground. The essence of therapy is affective change, and affective change cannot be dictated.

For the victim of sadistic abuse, the task is to learn that safety does not lie in deception, in hiding one's true feelings, and to appreciate that there can be benevolence in the face of vulnerability. The endless quest for emotional invisibility on the part of the sadistic abuse survivor can mimic alexithymia in its extreme form. Certainly, fear of emotional visibility is a factor in many survivors' difficulties with marriages and partnerships, because there can be no intimacy when one partner remains emotionally opaque.

The task for the therapist is to facilitate this process, beginning with an affectively appropriate therapeutic stance. Therapy must indeed embody benevolence in the face of vulnerability. The therapist must be a "compassionate presence" in the Buddhist sense. Such a presence ultimately will be internalized by the client into a "loving kindness to the self." Clients do not expect their revelations to be met with benevolence or compassion, nor do they come to therapy with "loving kindness toward the self." Rather, they come with the internalized voice of the offender—a hostile and distorted critic defining their self-image—and often with the rage that was too dangerous to turn toward the offender, turned toward themselves. Their unconscious learning has been that vulnerability will be met with projection, codependency, and sexual exploitation. Much has been written about "therapeutic neutrality," but if strictly translated, that neutrality could be construed as the necessity of maintaining an indifferent stance toward pain. Indifference to pain is simply reabuse.

Empathy, however, is not a benign drug. For some adult survivors, life has held precious little of it, and they have learned to adapt, much as dwellers in the desert do, to a sparse environment. The therapist who floods her client with an unreserved empathy, without regard to her client's capacity to absorb it, without consideration of the effects of it, can be thought of as acting in a profoundly unempathic way. The question may be raised whether she is acting according to what her client needs or according to what she needs. Those of us in the helping professions are usually well aware of the countertransference characteristics of anger. The narcissistic aspects of empathy are less often emphasized, yet clearly, among the reasons people become therapists is the desire to see themselves as caring, supportive, warm, and empathic people.

The client who finds herself in the presence of a therapist who offers massive dosages of empathy without regard to her needs may find that the warmth itself triggers an old, primitive hunger for the parent she never had. The session is over all too soon. The 50-minute vial of sweet, clear water makes the desert seem moribund by comparison: The outside world is dimmed and gray; no one there has quite the same capacity to make her feel precious and to feel heard. Soon, she finds it is too long to wait until the next week for another vial of life-giving water. She calls for an appointment in between. The water is just as sweet, and just as short-acting. She is beginning to gain a sense of herself in therapy as someone who has been hurt, not as someone who is perverted, weird, and deserving of blame and censure. She finds that by calling the therapist in between sessions, she can get a shorter, but still intense hit of life-giving water. But by now, she is beginning to get angry. Why is her therapist so withholding? She feels she has to beg, to apologize for something that should be her due. If the therapist cares, can't she see how important this is? Before long, the client is calling several times a day, and in the middle of the night. By now, the client has a diagnosis of "borderline personality disorder" and an angry, increasingly self-protective therapist. Empathy was the drug, and we were the pushers. To complain of our client's addiction, therefore, has a particular irony.

Summary

Approximately 2% to 5% of sex offenders are sexually aroused by their victim's pain, suffering, humiliation, and fear, and thus can be considered sadistic. Sadists tend to be less sexually aroused by consenting sex than are other sex offenders, and more aroused by nonsexual violence. They are a sufficiently valid and reliable subgrouping of sex offenders that they appear in most major typologies.

Sadists can be reliably distinguished from other sex offenders by the degree of injury that they inflict on victims. This distinction is not absolute because angry offenders also gratuitously injure victims. Although both may inflict severe injury, angry sex offenders and sadists differ in their affect, the specifics of the assaults, their motivation, and their thinking patterns.

More has been written about sadistic killers than chronic sadistic offenders. Notwithstanding, the latter are likely far more numerous, and more often assault their own families.

Sadists, unlike grooming offenders, do not make thinking errors around victim suffering. They are well aware that their victims are in pain. Nonsadistic offenders, by contrast, project onto their victims their own sexual arousal. Because they are not aroused by pain and suffering, they fantasize that the child is a willing partner because they need her or him to be so. The thinking errors that sadistic offenders do make often involve projecting onto the child their own sense of internal evil. Thus they justify their assaults by telling themselves that the child deserves to suffer. Some offenders who molest high numbers of victims have generic thinking errors for the entire category of "child." "I think young girls and boys are meant to be sex slaves or sex play things for adults," one offender wrote to another.

Because sadistic offenders know the child's emotional reactions and use them as a guide to increase suffering, adult survivors of sadistic abuse are often terrified by emotional visibility. They resist intimacy—not because they fear betrayal, as the survivor of nonsadistic abuse does—but because they fear that their vulnerability will be used to hurt them.

Survivors of nonsadistic abuse find solace in emotional visibility, and they fear emotional invisibility because their abuse occurred under conditions in which their emotional reactions were ignored and denied.

Although survivors may have different issues regarding emotional visibility, they have similar reactions to the visibility of abuse in the world. They may or may not have suffered from the explicit denial of those around them (the refusal to believe the abuse in the face of disclosure or other evidence), but inevitably they suffered the effects of implicit denial (the fact that many people who knew them did not know the abuse was occurring). Implicit denial makes the survivor feel isolated and different.

The preceding discussion has major implications for therapy. The survivor of sadistic abuse, particularly, will find the "being known" quality of therapy to be frightening. At least some unexplained cases of decompensation in therapy result from this dynamic.

4

Apology and Forgiveness in the Context of the Cycles of Adult Male Sex Offenders Who Abuse Children

Hilary Eldridge

Jenny Still

The offender's apology to the person he has sexually abused is often seen as an important part of the survivor's process of healing and moving forward. Although the notion of apology can be very helpful, there is much that can go wrong to turn the experience of receiving an apology into further abuse. The aim in this chapter is to explore the purpose of apology and how its success or failure is linked not only to the survivor's healing process, but also to the agendas of the various parties and to the offender's cycle as well. We will explore specific examples of apologies that reabuse and will suggest ground rules to increase the chances of a positive outcome for the survivor.

Questions appropriately asked about apologies might include the following: What is the purpose of the apology? Whom is it for? Who does, or should, initiate it? When is it real, and how does the survivor recognize whether or not it is real? When, if at all, should it take place? What is the effect on survivors and on their relationships with others, such as the offender, nonoffending parent, and significant others?

The entire question of forgiveness is frequently linked with the offender's apology. For many families, once the offender has apologized, he has "done all he can do" and the survivor is then under pressure to forgive him. This expectation, however, raises questions. Does an apology imply forgiveness, or is it about letting go? Is forgiveness an issue? If so, whose issue: the offender's, the survivor's, or the therapist's? Our belief is that apology and forgiveness are two separate issues, and we will address them as such.

What Constitutes an Apology and What Is Its Intended Effect?

A real apology is usually seen to be an admission by the offender that he was responsible for the abuse and that he regrets his actions. It should be a genuine and explicit statement in which the offender says, in effect, "I was responsible for abusing you and for setting the scene in which I abused you. I was wrong and I'm sorry." It should include a recognition of the preconditions to abuse (Finkelhor, 1984), and the offender should be able to admit his intent and the devious ways in which he overcame external inhibitors, such as other family members, as well as the victim's resistance. The apology should also be genuine and not just an academic exercise.

The apology should be for the survivor's well-being, not just a device to make the offender feel better. If it is truly for the survivor, then care needs to be taken that there are no hidden messages within it that enable the offender to maintain power and control.

Therapists, nonoffending parents, child and adult survivors of sexual abuse, and, in fact, some offenders, too, have hopes for the outcome of apologies. Some of these hopes are very positive and could assist the healing process. How realistic such hopes are will depend partly on the nature of the offender's cycle and how much real change he has made. The impact, too, is dependent on how much progress the survivor and other family members have made.

Hopes Often Expressed by Adult
Survivors and Child Survivors of Abuse

Both adult and child survivors of sexual abuse may be in a position of either wanting an apology themselves or having someone else want that apology for them. The agenda and the impact may be different if the apology takes place in childhood or adulthood; developmental stages and time distance from the abuse have an effect on efficacy. However, hopes can be quite similar. Child survivors sometimes hope:

"I'll feel better if he says he's sorry."

"It'll mean I was right to tell."

"It'll show me that his treatment is working."

"It'll show me he's taking responsibility."

Some unrealistic or unproductive agendas may include:

"I still feel it's my fault: Perhaps he'll help me see that it wasn't." (It is dangerous to rely on the offender to do this. Even if he's well-intentioned, this statement implies his control over the survivor.)

"It'll show me I haven't lost him: I've lost everyone else." (And maybe that is because the offender drove a wedge between the victim and everyone else.)

"He was closer to me than anyone else. Maybe we can still be like that." (And maybe that is what the offender wants.)

"It'll show he's forgiven me for telling." (Offenders shift blame onto their victims, and hence survivors may have agendas linked to being forgiven themselves.)

"It will help my relationship with my brother, sister, etc." (Offenders manipulate family dynamics to isolate their victims;

hence the survivor may be going ahead with the apology meeting for the sake of other siblings who may still blame the victim for the loss of their father.)

"Other people will like me more if I forgive him." (Again, the victim is doing it for someone else.)

The hopes of adult survivors of child sexual abuse are often very similar and reflect a desire for the offender to accept responsibility in a way that facilitates a letting-go process for the survivor. Some unproductive agendas, similar to those described above, may be the following:

"It'll help my relationship with my partner." (The survivor is doing it for someone else.)

"It'll reconcile me to my family." (And maybe it will not.)

"Maybe he (they) will forgive me for telling at last." (Who needs forgiving?)

Hopes Often Expressed by Offenders

Offenders sometimes do have positive agendas regarding apologies. These can include positive wishes for the survivor and productive agendas for themselves, too.

"It'll make him or her feel better."

"It'll help him or her see that I was responsible."

"It'll mean I can begin to forgive myself a bit and move forward in therapy."

However, offenders sometimes have agendas that have nothing to do with genuine apology. Some unproductive agendas may include:

"It'll make it OK." (And it certainly will not.)

"I'll find a way to show her who's in control. Then maybe she'll keep quiet about the other stuff." (!)

"It'll mean he or she (the victim/other people) will forgive me." (And maybe he or she does not want to.)

"It'll mean that the court will be lenient when they see I said I was sorry." (And maybe the court should not be.)

"My partner, mother, brother, sister, will think I won't do it again, and that will make it harder for me to be caught next time." (!)

"Once I've said sorry, that will make sure I never do it again." (Is it really that easy?)

Hopes Often Expressed by Therapists

How realistic are the hopes of therapists may depend on their knowledge of offenders. Hopes often include:

"It'll give the message to the survivor 'you're not to blame.' "

"It'll show him or her that the offender takes the responsibility."

The therapist sometimes has personal agendas. For example, the survivor's therapist may feel very angry with the offender and feel he "deserves" to apologize; on the other hand, the therapist may believe that growth can come only from forgiveness. Some unproductive agendas may include:

"Whatever he says will be wrong. He won't mean a word of it." (Maybe he will, maybe he will not.)

"He ought to do it; it's the least he can do." (When did "ought to" produce a real apology?)

"He or she (the survivor) should have a chance to forgive him."
(Maybe that is not what the survivor wants.)

Are Positive Outcomes Realistic
in the Context of Offending Cycles?

Apology takes place not only in the context of the survival process but also in the context of the offending cycle within which the victim was abused. The nature of the offending cycle has consequent problems for victims that affect the likelihood of a positive outcome from an apology. Decisions about apology must take into account not only the survivor's healing process, but also the offender's change process. As therapists, we often ask why survivors say:

"I don't believe it was abuse. Leave me alone."

"It was my fault. I seduced him."

"If I don't forgive him, I must be bad."

"He still loves me."

"It was all my mother's fault."

"He'll never forgive me for telling."

The answer to why the survivor might hold those beliefs may lie in the cycles of the offenders. Knowledge of offending cycles provides us with the key to some of the missing information that explains why survivors sometimes fight to hold on to dysfunctional beliefs. In manipulating their victims, offenders may provide a distorted framework for identification of self-worth that they then validate. Hence, the survivor's sense of self-worth may be linked to the offender's belief system. A therapist who challenges the survivor's beliefs without knowledge of how these have been brought about is bound to meet with a fight.

In deciding whether an apology is going to be helpful, the offender's cycle and its possible effects on the survivor have to be considered. The offender's beliefs and manipulative tactics may be present whether the medium for the apology is face-to-face, taped, or written. Offenders can perpetuate the thinking errors they implanted during the abuse by feeding them into a so-called apology. Although a general discussion of the deviant cycle can be found in Chapter 2, this chapter will focus on certain aspects of the deviant cycle that have important implications for apology sessions.

Belief Systems Producing Continuous or Inhibited Cycles

Sex offending cycles are driven by thinking errors, and the child who is abused has those thinking errors transmitted to him or her throughout the cycle. The offender holds beliefs that give him permission to offend by legitimizing, excusing, minimizing, or justifying the behavior, or blaming someone else for it. The strength of the offender's thinking errors may determine whether his cycle is continuous or inhibited, which in turn has an impact on the child who is being abused.

Continuous Cycles

Offenders with continuous cycles have a belief system that legitimizes their behavior to the point where the cycle is only interrupted by their perceived risk of being caught. For example, a fixated pedophile who believes sexual abuse is not abuse at all, but an expression of love, may convince himself that he is really helping or "loving" children. A man who believes that postpubertal girls are generally provocative and "ask for it" may persuade himself that they deserve or want "it."

Breaks in the offending cycles of such offenders will only occur if they discover they have made a targeting error, that is, the child they have chosen may tell and is therefore too risky to pursue. In this case, they may target another child or children. Such offenders have an essentially continuous cycle, uninterrupted by worries about the way their behavior harms either their own self-image or the victim.

These offenders have extremely distorted beliefs about their offending behavior, and they delude themselves about the victim's behavior, interpreting it in ways that support their own beliefs. However, they do not delude themselves about the process by which they come to offend. When detected, they may lie to the police and the courts, pretending that their offending "just happened once." Nevertheless, they do not lie to themselves about the premeditated and deliberate nature of their offending because they believe that right is really on their side.

Implications for Survivors and for Apology

For continuous cycle offenders, the behavior is only a secret because the law is wrong—hence "we" will get into serious trouble if "we" are found out. If the offender is a pedophile operating with other pedophiles, this notion may be reinforced through fear of retribution from the "ring." Pedophiles with this type of cycle can be very effective in persuading the children they abuse to their point of view.

It is rare for this type of offender to make a nonabusive apology. Either he has not changed his core beliefs, and may use the opportunity to further manipulate the victim, or he may have changed so dramatically that he runs the risk of destroying the victim's sense of self-worth—self-worth that may have been based on the belief that the offender loved the child.

One offender, Bob, had a continuous cycle. He told himself that abuse happened to him as a child and that he enjoyed it. In therapy, he successfully broke his old thinking patterns, and when asked what he would say to one of his many victims if he now had the chance, he wrote the following:

Jon,
   I am writing this letter to you to let you know the facts of what I did to you. What I wanted from you was your young body to satisfy my lust. I did not love you. I only gave you toys so you

would not tell about what I was doing to you, and to make you think good things of me. It is not your fault what has happened. I touched your private parts and that is all I ever wanted to do to you. Adults who really love children do not do that kind of thing.

You may remember the days out I took you on and said I enjoyed those days. I did not enjoy those days with you I only wanted to see you so I could abuse you. Your parents love you and want you to grow up to be a good person and not to be the same as me. You are a very good boy and no different from any-one else.

Given that Bob carefully chose children who had a difficult relationship with their parents, and then went out of his way to make those children believe that he was the person who really loved them, such an apology could destroy the children's sense of self-esteem and self-worth at a stroke. It is possible that this re-alization could be a beginning, a means of letting go and moving on for the survivor, but the possible effect of such an apology—particularly on a child—would need to be anticipated and worked through in the context of ongoing therapy. The happy ending Bob fondly envisaged for such children with their parents may not be possible, either.

The greatest risk, however, would be that the survivors met with Bob and could not accept the incongruity between Bob's words and the feelings they had about him. Hence they may beg Bob to retract, and he might just do so, thereby validating their self-worth and confirming the thinking errors that this was about "love," not abuse. All the previous grooming could then fall back into place.

Most abusers with continuous cycles do not progress as well as Bob. They have too much to lose in terms of their own view of themselves if they change. They may pay lip service to therapy and their so-called apology letters may be full of hidden contra-dictory messages.

For example, Andrew, a pedophile with a similar, if rather more bullying, offending pattern to Bob, was asked to write out what he would like to say to his victim if given the opportunity. He wrote the following:

> My dear Joe,
>   I am finding it very hard to say my true feelings and to say that I'm sorry for the things that I did to you [suggests he is under duress, that is, that this is not what I really feel]. You showed me love and happiness in the times that we had together. The friendship and love from me was and still is absolutely true [I loved you suggests I still do]. I am sorry because I abused my position as a friend who you trusted and treated as an uncle. When I touched you on your private parts, your penis, your bottom, this was wrong and I am truly sorry for what I have done [reabuse through detailed reference to what he did]. Now you must forget me and start afresh [paradoxical suggestion here: how can they forget someone who loved them so much?].

Inhibited Cycles

In some cycles, the offender's beliefs are not so secure; internal inhibitors operate to break the cycle. The length of the breaks will depend on the strength of the internal inhibitors, the strength of the distorted thinking that legitimizes offending, and the strength of the deviant arousal or desire to offend.

Some offenders have quite lengthy periods when their cycles are inhibited and they do not offend. However, they still indulge in thoughts that legitimize offending, and they may still fantasize about abuse, thereby strengthening the desire to reoffend.

Offenders with inhibited cycles do question their behavior. They question whether it is perverted, and they worry about the way it reflects on them. They may also recognize that it hurts the victim. They feel bad about their behavior and seek to relieve themselves of this burden by shifting the blame. They make the abuse "our guilty secret," and emphasize that it is the victim's fault, and possibly also the victim's mother's fault, and "therefore not mine." They may seek an excuse to offend. They may make a whole series of seemingly unimportant decisions (Jenkins-Hall & Marlatt, 1989) that will help create the opportunity to carry out the secretly desired behavior. This process enables them to avoid facing the pain and responsibility of recognizing that they planned to reoffend.

Some offenders may break through their internal inhibitors by indulging in self-fulfilling prophecies that lead them to feel sorry for themselves and entitled to comfort. An offender, for example, whose self-image is poor (either due to past experiences, or to his identification of himself as a pervert) may expect other people to realize he is "no good" and to reject him. He sees rejection even if it is not there by seeing and hearing selectively. He may then behave in ways that create rejection. Hence he eventually sees that the world is against him, and this provides an excuse to seek comfort in his own distorted beliefs. He may fantasize increasingly about children, using as justification the belief that only children love and understand him, whereas the adult world does not.

An offender who perceives rejection may indulge in revenge-type fantasies about attacking and hurting others because he feels attacked and hurt. Sometimes, fantasies may include distorted "love" and revenge components. Therefore, offenders who tell themselves they love children may also be motivated by anger.

As well as blaming the victim, such offenders often blame the nonabusing parent for rejecting them and thereby "causing" the abuse. Essentially, the offender is interpreting external events and the behavior of others in a distorted way, thus providing himself with a distorted rationale to do what he wants to do: Reoffend.

Implications for Survivors and for Apology

Children who are abused by offenders who have inhibited cycles may be exposed to the offender's self-delusory and blame-shifting tactics that not only prevent disclosure, but make the offender feel better, too. They are also negatively affected by the process through which the offender provides himself with another excuse to offend. In apologies, offenders with this type of cycle often say "sorry" and then imply in subtle ways that it was really someone else's fault.

Hugh, for example, recognized that it was wrong to abuse children, and he needed to provide himself with an excuse and someone to blame. He set his wife up to reject him. He made sexual approaches to her in unreasonable ways at inappropriate times to make sure she would reject him. Then he could blame her and say, "If only she was better sexually, I wouldn't have to turn to children. It's all her fault." Sally and Sarah, who were abused by Hugh when they were 7 and 9 years of age, respectively, were encouraged to believe that they were being abused because "Mummy doesn't love Daddy enough"; hence, they were clear it was her fault.

Hugh set up the circumstances to make it appear as if the child, rather than he, initiated the behavior. He planted pornographic videotapes in a place where his children were sure to find them. He made the tapes particularly attractive by leaving them with blank labels. He spied on the children each time they looked at tapes to see if they had found them. Eventually, when he "accidentally" caught them watching the pornographic tapes, he told them off. He used the tapes as a means of introducing the children to sex, at the same time warning them that he was doing them a favor by keeping it secret that they had watched forbidden tapes.

Hugh pushed away his sense of guilt by deluding himself that it was all Sally and Sarah's fault, because if they had not found the pornographic videos, he would never have abused them. (He conveniently "forgot" that he put the tapes there to be found.) This thinking error was easy to implant in Sally and Sarah because they knew that they had found the pornographic videotapes and that Hugh had told them it was all their fault. If they had not found the tapes, he would never have abused them. They may carry that thinking error into adult life until they see the way they were groomed by Hugh.

A therapist working with Sally and Sarah without actual knowledge of Hugh's strategies would have to make an assumption of highly manipulative tactics and then help them turn around all their beliefs about who had done what, where, and how. Without this, Hugh could rely on the thinking errors he had implanted in his children and reaffirm these in an "apology" meeting. For example, "I'm so sorry—if only you'd never found those tapes!"

The Senses Cycle
and Affective Flashbacks

Sights, sounds, smells, and tastes often trigger survivors into affective flashbacks (see Chapter 5). These flashbacks are difficult to deal with because they are not processed cognitively and, as such, provide enormous opportunity for offenders to reassert control and thereby reabuse.

One man always wore a particular pair of shorts for offending purposes. Another invariably used a particular type of soap for washing both his nieces and himself before he abused them. Then he gave them strawberry milk shakes. Some offenders have special messages that say to the child "It's time." One man, for example, would leave an unlit cigarette on the edge of a table. Another would just look at the door and raise an eyebrow to indicate to his son, "Get upstairs."

The implication of sensory messages for apology meetings is enormous. The survivor may not have a cognitive memory of the messages and their meanings, and if the offender—on purpose or unwittingly—gives that message during the meeting, the survivor may have to grapple with feelings that appear to come from nowhere. The sight of the shorts, the smell of the soap, the mention of the strawberry milk shakes, the recognition of the "look" or the symbol may trigger a set of complex and often frightening feelings.

The offender may deliberately use the old messages to create that effect and to exert control, just as he did during the time of the abuse. When asked what they would say to their victims if given an opportunity, two offenders of different religious persuasions, both of whom were the religious teachers of the children they abused, used a preaching tone in a videotaped exercise. Both had used this in their grooming and could reestablish control by using it again.

One of the worst outcomes in an apology meeting is for the offender to give a hidden message that the therapists present know nothing about, and that the survivor can neither process nor communicate. This exactly replicates the abuse scenario—the survivor is a child trying to ask for help but doesn't have the words, and no one hears.

Themes Commonly Found in Apology Statements That Feed Into Thinking Errors Implanted by the Offender During the Abuse

The following themes can appear in the apologies of both badly and well-motivated offenders. It is only offenders who have carefully thought out their apologies or those who have developed considerable victim empathy—as opposed to simple victim awareness—who manage to avoid them.

Long-Term Control: Offender Belief in the Permanently Damaged Victim. Sex offending is mostly about power and control, and the notion of the victim's survival or escape from the offender's control is alien to offender thinking.

Long-Term Control: Offender Pride in His Ability to Control. Offenders in the early stages of therapy (and those who do not progress) often take pride in how clever they were to manipulate everyone.

Explicit Descriptions of the Abuse. Some offenders deliberately do this in order to reabuse. Others do it because they are at a point in therapy where they are being asked to stop distancing themselves from their offending and to be more explicit. They may not have reached a point where they recognize how this will affect the survivor.

Paradoxical Statements. Most offenders say, "You must feel awful," "You must not feel guilty and responsible." There is an implication that the survivor ought to feel awful and guilty and responsible.

Extra Burdens. Many offenders cannot resist laying extra burdens on the survivor. The main burden is, "Please forgive me."

I'm Sorry, BUT . . . Many apology statements start well and then move into excusing the offender, and minimizing and justifying the behavior. These statements manage to imply that not too much harm was done, really. The offender has suffered much more than the child, and so on.

The Double Message. This implies that it was the child's fault, really. "You weren't responsible—but you were."

The Textbook Approach. Offenders in therapy who are developing victim awareness may become clearer about the possible effects of abuse on children. They put this into an apology. Is it really in the survivor's interests to hear about the possible sequelae of sexual abuse from their abuser?

These themes can be found either separately or in combination in the following letters. They were prepared by offenders in therapy who were asked what they would say to their victims in a letter if they had the opportunity. Even though some of the offenders were making progress and wrote well-intentioned letters, the letters all contained thinking errors used during the abuse. None of the letters could have been appropriately seen by the survivor in question without risk of reabuse.

Example 1

An offender who abused his niece, Sally, is doing well in therapy, has an inhibited cycle, and has always recognized harm done. However, he implies permanent damage and continued control. This implication will hurt Sally regardless of whether or not the offender is well-intentioned. He wrote:

> Dear Sally,
>   I am going to explain to you what I've done to you [control], so you don't feel ashamed of yourself or guilty [paradox: suggests she might do so]. When I put my hands on your body and between your legs this was very wrong of me [reabuse through

explicit reference to what he did]. You felt that you had to allow me to do it. You were thinking that whatever I did or told you was right. It was wrong of me to make you think this. It was my fault that I did these terrible things to you. Do not blame yourself because how could you know what I was doing to you was wrong [paradox again]. You were at an age where you did not know what I was doing. I took advantage of your innocence. I have hurt your feelings and your mind and what I have taken cannot be replaced [permanently damaged victim: message, your mind is not your own]. Please forgive me for what I have done to you [another burden]. I am very sorry.

Example 2

An offender who abused his nephew has an inhibited cycle and is making progress, but is still very much into power games. He gives a good explanation of how he set things up, but what are the implications of that? Is such frankness empowering for the victim or bragging on the offender's part? Is he not saying "Look how powerful I was?"

Dear Matthew,
    You are sadly the victim I have created. I manipulated the situation in a very crafty way [pride in ability to control]. This caused you to touch my private parts: which was very wrong of me. I want you to know you were not to blame, it was my fault [paradox]. It was my idea that we should play that game. I should not have asked you to participate. When you did participate you thought it was good fun [I'm sorry, BUT . . .]. I knew you thought this and I encouraged you to touch my private parts. I took advantage of your childhood to have sex. I should have known better and set an example. I'm very sorry—please forgive me [extra burden].

Example 3

One offender, who abused the son of friends, at the time of writing the following statement had shown some word change, that is, he had learned to parrot the "correct" point of view. However, he had a continuous cycle and maintained strong underlying pedophilic beliefs that children could consent. He wrote:

Dear Johnny,

I hope you will not tear this letter up, but spare a few minutes to read what I have to say [control]. I know now that I've caused you and your family much distress. You must feel guilty and ashamed for what I have done. I want you to realize you have no cause to feel guilty or bad [massive paradox]. In no way were you to blame. I was responsible for it all. I hope your parents will accept this and understand that it was not your fault [further paradox implying that the victim's parents blame the victim]. I'm sorry for all the distress I must have caused you and the trouble you must have gone through from your parents and friends [further paradox, implying that the boy's friends blame him, too]. There is no way I can make amends. I can only express my deepest regret and ask your forgiveness [extra burden].

Example 4

An offender who abused his stepdaughter has an inhibited cycle, is progressing in treatment, and recognizes harm done. Nevertheless, he cannot resist advocating for his own interests, exercising continued control, and unloading a huge burden on the victim.

My dear Angela,

I know that I have hurt you and caused you much suffering. I have broken the trust that you had in me and I have used my position as a father to take advantage of you instead of taking care of you. I realize the extent of the damage I have done to you and I can never make up for it. You should not feel guilty about anything: You are blameless and innocent. I am the only one responsible. I am the only one to blame.

I am now begging you to forgive me for all harm that I have done to you. I have asked for forgiveness from God and I am now asking for yours. We all have to appear in front of God and I do not wish to appear in front of him without your forgiveness. I know that it can be very difficult for you to forgive me and I pray God to enlighten your heart with his mercy. May he who is our maker bestow his security and his protection on you. May he shower his choicest blessings on you. May he who is most compassionate guide you in his right path. May he who is the sustainer give you the best of this world and the best of the hereafter [extra burden! She now has responsibility for the offender's immortal soul. If she does not forgive him, does that mean she has not taken "God's right path?" What are the implications for her in the hereafter?].

Example 5

An offender who abused a neighbor's daughter is at a stage in therapy where he is himself struggling with contradictory thoughts. This is evident in the letter. On one hand, he tries to take responsibility, and on the other, falls back onto his victim-blaming tactics.

Dear Caroline,
   I've written this letter to say I'm truly sorry for the damage I have done to you and for taking advantage of you. I would like to tell you that I have abused other little girls in the past and thought nothing of it. Now I have realized the damage I have caused to them and you. I would like to tell you that you were not to blame and not to feel guilty and to watch for other abusers, and not to give in to them [double message: says she was not to blame and then implies she gave in to him]. And if it happens to your friends, please tell them to be aware and take every step you or your friends can to stop them from doing it to other children [extra burden: now she and her friends have to stop other offenders from offending]. I know how you feel against me but I'm aware now not to reoffend again because I've learnt to control myself more against girls around your age [double message: suggests she is the predator, not him].

Example 6

Another offender, who is struggling with his own pro- and antioffending beliefs, pays lip service to responsibility and then rapidly minimizes his offending.

Dear Paul,

I am writing to you to apologize for what I did to you. I know you did not understand at the time, but by now you must be fully aware of people with sexual problems such as mine [I'm sorry, BUT . . . I've got sexual problems]. I did this to you hoping that no harm will come to you at a later stage in your life. I don't want you to take any blame yourself for what happened. I am the guilty person. I hope you've settled down and put this past experience well behind you. If anyone touches you on your private parts in the future you must tell your parents before things get worse like you experienced with me, but you were young and did not expect anything to happen [double message: you should have told your parents and that would have stopped me]. What I have done to you I have done to other children as well, and when I was a little boy I had to go through the same experience myself [I'm sorry BUT . . . implication, it was because I was a victim, or perhaps there is a more sinister message, "it's normal really." The next sentence suggests this too.].

I know that society does not tolerate this sort of nonsense, but you do meet people like me from time to time and you must be aware of that. As a result of what I've done to you and my own children I have been living in hell. I had my children put in care, my wife almost left me so I have been in a terrible state of mind. Do not blame yourself [huge double message: Do not blame yourself, you have only wrecked my life.]. I am being punished for my sexual pleasures [I'm sorry BUT . . . implies they were pleasures, not offenses, hence who's in the wrong here?]. I am having treatment so I am hoping that at the end I will be a better person.

Example 7

Here is an offender with an inhibited cycle who abused a boy he knew through school. He is making huge strides in victim awareness and is developing empathy. The letter is appropriate in parts, but sometimes sounds like a textbook on child abuse. He is describing to the victim all the things that might go wrong for the victim in the future. Is this helpful?

Dear Robert,

I feel that a letter to you saying I'm sorry could not make you feel better about the way I abused you. I am doing the only thing I can do which is to take treatment so there will be a greater chance there will be no future victims. I made a special effort to be close to you and then I abused you. If I could not get to abuse you, I would have moved on to abuse another boy. I hope you get the treatment you'll need because of the effects of what I did to you, all of which may not be seen now [the textbook approach: suggests to the victim that there may be more problems in store for him in later life]. I hope you know you were in no way to blame and I was responsible for totally wrecking your childhood [power issue: maybe Robert's childhood was not totally wrecked]. I hope what I've done to you won't totally dominate the rest of your life, and you're able to lead a life you feel is worthwhile [paradoxical implication of long-term control].

The offender in Example 7 quickly recognized what was wrong with his letter and repeatedly struggled to improve it. The outcome of his struggle was that he realized that any attempt to initiate apology would be controlling and thereby a reabuse of the victim. He felt that the best thing he could do for the victim was to get out of his life.

If the request for apology comes from the survivor, and if the request is in the context of the ongoing therapy of both survivor and offender, then often it can be helpful. Realistically, though, apologies usually contain the kind of themes described in the letters above or are so well-rehearsed that they present the offender in a light that bears no relation to the reality. A survivor who receives a very well-rehearsed apology may be misled into believing that the offender has changed much more than he actually has. The ultimate paradox here would be when the offender presented himself so perfectly that the victim felt more guilty, because after all, how could such a "good" man be responsible for the abuse?

Should Apology Be Linked to Forgiveness?

In the *Oxford Dictionary*, the definition of "forgive" is "to let off, to pardon." Apology is often seen as a precursor to forgiveness, and it is a societal norm to say "That's OK" when someone says "I'm sorry."

We have already seen that, in their attempts to apologize, most offenders also ask for forgiveness. Although the offender might feel good about being forgiven, when is forgiveness actually helpful to the survivor?

Survivors have myriad reasons for wanting to forgive the offender. Forgiveness is sometimes seen as a means of coming to terms with the past and healing torn relationships. Likewise, survivors may wish to forgive as a means of gaining an inner peace. They may wish to let go of feelings of anger, rage, and rejection. They may want an outcome compatible with religious beliefs, or to hold on to positive qualities about the offender, who may be a close relative. In some cases, forgiveness may be a step toward family reconstruction. In others, it may be a means of evicting the offender from their lives—an ending and a moving on.

However, there are problems inherent in linking notions of apology with forgiveness, one of which is that many offenders foist their agenda of forgiveness onto the survivor regardless of the survivor's own wishes or interests. In considering whether forgiveness will be helpful or not for the survivor, the following questions should be asked.

What or Whom Are We Talking About Forgiving?

Forgive the behavior? Forgive the person? If you, as the survivor, forgive the behavior, what are the implications for you about your own behavior at the time of the offending? If you, as the survivor, forgive the person, and that person is your father, then does that have more positive implications for your own self-image? Is it possible to separate forgiveness of the behavior from forgiveness of the person?

If it is a person you are forgiving, is it the offender? If it is the offender, this forgiveness must be seen in the context of who the offender is and what kind of grooming he has used. Is it the non-abusing parent? Is it easier to forgive the offender if you are still left with someone else to blame, such as the nonabusing parent? Does this situation feed into the offender's beliefs and grooming tactics, his shifting of blame from him to his spouse? Does forgiving the offender at the expense of the nonabusing parent perpetuate the tensions in family relationships that the offender set up?

For Whom Is the Apology?

When forgiveness is offered by the victim not so much for his or her own purposes but to appease others or to ameliorate the family situation, it may be counterproductive. Someone who has been abused within the family, for example, may want to forgive because he or she hopes it will improve his or her relationship with his or her nonabusing parent. This happens frequently when the parent is still struggling with her own feelings about a relative or partner offender. A nonabusing parent may still be making decisions about whom to "support." The survivor thinks, "It will make it easier if I forgive him. Then my mother can (a) accept him back because there is still a part of her that wants to do this, (b) let him go and support me, or (c) try to work it out together. She wants both of us—the offender and me."

Forgiving an offender because he wants or needs the forgiveness is even more harmful for the survivor. When is healing for the survivor ever about servicing the offender's needs?

Forgiveness may help with these aims, but survivors who forgive with these goals in mind may get trapped into a forgiveness for which they are not ready and do not really feel. In the end, they may have even more hostile feelings against the nonabusing parent, such as, "I had to 'forgive' him because of her."

Sometimes people want to forgive in order to get along better with their siblings; they do not want the siblings to have to make a choice between the offender and the victim. If the offender's grooming or "set-up" of the family is still working—with or without his presence—siblings may blame the survivor more than the offender. The survivor may think, "If I accept the apology and forgive him, I'll keep the family together." Forgiveness in this instance would continue the offender's control of the family and be dysfunctional to the healing process.

There are layers of complexity with which to struggle if forgiveness is to have a positive rather than a negative effect on healing, and healing is, after all, the main consideration. Healing is about moving on and letting go, and that may be very different from forgiveness. Real care should be taken that forgiveness is not simply a continuation of offender grooming but is instead a liberation from that grooming. Adult survivor therapy that is informed by knowledge of offenders—and, if possible, of that particular offender—should help the survivor work out the nature of that liberation. Bass and Davis (1993) suggest, "Eventually you will have to come to some sort of a resolution in your feelings about the abuser so you can move on. Whether or not this resolution includes forgiveness is a personal matter" (p. 53). Sgroi and Sargent (1993) concur: "Forgiveness should not be viewed as the sine qua non of coming to terms with the relationship with the abuser" (p. 31).

Most offenders try to ask for forgiveness regardless of whether the survivor wants to give it. It is important for the therapist and survivor not to allow the offender to dictate the agenda for the survivor. It is our belief that an appropriate apology can take place without forgiveness. The survivor's needs may require hearing the offender accept responsibility, and then moving on and letting go—not forgiving him.

When Is an Apology Real and What Can Be Done to Increase the Chances of a Positive Outcome for the Adult Survivor?

Sex offenders are expert at manipulating people in order to justify their abuse to themselves and to others, as well as to maintain control and protect secret wishes and plans. Offenders often apologize in order to minimize the abuse, be forgiven, and assuage any guilt. Likewise, they may want to gain sympathy from other family members or to appear remorseful in the eyes of a

court, and thereby get a lesser sentence. They may want to maintain power and set up a scenario that facilitates reabuse.

How does the survivor know that the apology is more than
just another lie? This is an area in which an awareness of the
change process that takes place for offenders in therapy is helpful.
When an offender is in sex offender therapy, it is crucial that the
opinion of his therapist regarding his progress—or the lack of it—
should be sought by the survivor's therapist before an apology
meeting is considered.

The first question must be: Is an effective apology a realistic
possibility with this particular offender? Is he capable of making a
reasonable attempt at it, or will he simply use it to reabuse? Bass
and Davis (1993) note, "Survivors often waste precious energy hoping to get people in their lives to change, apologize, or take responsibility. For the most part, these wishes are fantasies" (p. 66).

For an apology meeting to be nonabusive to the survivor, the
offender must have made considerable progress in his change
process. He needs to have demonstrated change at a behavioral
as well as thought and belief level, and to have done sufficient
work to ensure he does not begin using old manipulative tactics.
Both survivor and offender need to have reached a point where
they recognize how grooming has taken place in the past and
could be attempted again.

Timing in the Context of
the Offender's Change Process

The change process is not linear (Eldridge, in press). At times,
progress seems rapid, but newborn thinking is fragile and painful, and the offender may slip back into comfortable old ideas before taking the next step forward. This slipping is very common
in the early stages of therapy. Also, in the early stages, the offender may want to apologize, but the kind of apology given reveals the fragility of change. The offender's words and deport-
ment may seem incongruent—he may say some of the "right"
things, but then slide in a look or a comment that shows he has no
real victim empathy.

Offenders often want to apologize so that they can be forgiven, and they will try to send deeply inappropriate letters to their victims. Word and thought change unaccompanied by feeling and belief change can result in a very abusive apology. Hence apology should rarely be considered in the early stages of therapy.

If the offender progresses well, feeling, belief, and behavior change begin to fall in line with word and thought change, and there can be scope for a reasonable attempt at nonabusive apology. A good sign of progress happens when the offender stops wanting to apologize without the survivor requesting the apology. Such an offender may realize that the best he can do for the survivor is to do what he or she wants, even if that means keeping out of his or her life altogether. Matching the action to the expressed intention speaks much louder than mere words.

The catch-22 of apology is that the offender may regroom, because grooming is part of how he still interacts with people: It is the only behavior he knows. If, on the other hand, he tries to be different and to apologize as the person he has become rather than the abuser he was, the victim will still remember him as he was and will not understand he has changed, even if he has. An apology that appears so out of character with how the child knew him earlier could be bewildering and reinforce the belief in the survivor, "It must have been my fault, because he seems like an OK guy who would have accepted it if I'd only said 'No.' "

Suggestions for Apology Sessions

There is a risk that an apology by the offender may tap into the same feelings that the survivor experienced during grooming, that is, of being manipulated, controlled, and conditioned. The survivor may have a sense of powerlessness in the face of the offender's persuasiveness, whether he persuades through violence, anger, intimidation, or seduction tactics. This sense, in turn, may tap into any number of feelings in the survivor, varying from "I want 'nice daddy' back" (and this can be an issue whatever the age of the survivor) to feelings of helplessness.

In preparing for an apology, the survivor needs to have identified and be prepared for the offender's manipulative tactics with planned coping mechanisms. Working with a therapist to profile the offender who abused them and understand what manipulative tactics he used can be a very empowering experience for many survivors.

The survivor may want information and explanation—not just an apology. In reabusive apology sessions, the offender says how sorry he is and then goes into explanations that place the responsibility on the victim and other family members—on everyone except himself.

One way of avoiding this scenario is for the survivor to make a list of questions he or she wants the offender to answer. The offender then answers these by letter. (The letter should be sent by the offender's therapist—thus allowing it to be vetted and, in addition, protecting the survivor from having the offender know her address.) This places the survivor in control from the beginning and avoids the survivor actually seeing the offender again if he or she doesn't want to. If, on receipt of the reply, the survivor wants to take things a step further, he or she then asks for further explanations. The offender replies on audio- or videotape. The survivor watches the tape with the therapist. The two together then analyze what has been said and how it has been presented, and together they identify anything that had a particular effect on the survivor. Changes in the survivor's feelings should be analyzed: What are they about, and how can the survivor empower him or herself?

It is only after this step has been taken that consideration is given to the possibility of a meeting. It may be sufficient for the survivor to read the letter or watch the tape, possibly monitoring it for the use of negative themes described earlier in this chapter. The survivor may recognize that the offender has not changed much and that precious energy is being wasted. He or she may feel it is time to stop hoping for the impossible and to move on. Once grooming is understood and the offender is seen in the light of that knowledge, it may be that the victim's memories of "nice daddy" or "fond uncle" cannot be separated from that person's abusive side. The two sides may not, in fact, have been separate.

The warm memories that the survivor has of being loved by the offender as a child may be reinterpreted by the adult eye as memories of being groomed, rather than cherished. A whole new and positive therapy agenda not based on false hopes may now be set. In these circumstances, some survivors feel that they do not wish to meet with the offender. Others may feel that they still want a chance to express their feelings in a face-to-face meeting with the offender before moving on.

In other situations, where the offender has progressed well and is a close family member, then the survivor may want to consider a meeting, having first worked out how to handle any attempts at regrooming or shifting responsibility. If that meeting goes well, the survivor may think it is realistic to see if there is scope for more contact, and possibly some healing of the relationship. Whatever decision is made, the survivor must be the one to make it.

For adult survivors who may not have seen the abuser for a long time and have a memory, distorted by time, of what the offender was like, seeing the offender on videotape may inform them whether or not they wish to take another step. It will also help the survivor see—and hence plan how to deal with—the offender's grooming strategies. Some offenders, for example, seek to give an underlying message of threat. Others seek to make their victims feel sorry for them and may even cry on the tape. It may be easier to gain perspective on such tactics without the offender in the room.

Where meetings do take place between the offender and survivor, it is helpful to have not only the survivor's therapist present, but also the offender's therapist. The latter is likely to have a thorough knowledge of the offender's grooming tactics and may be able to intervene appropriately to support the survivor. Both therapists need to be clear that they are there to support the survivor. The risk of affective flashbacks should be recognized and planned for so that the survivor has a means of communicating distress to his or her therapist. An advance plan for dealing with such a communication at the time, and analyzing it after the event, needs to be worked out between the survivor and therapist. Finally, the survivor must feel empowered to stop the session at any point.

Conclusions and Ground Rules

Helpful ground rules for an apology session dictate that it occurs:

- When the apology is wanted by the survivor for the survivor.
- When the offender is capable of it and is reasonably motivated. Not all offenders do well in therapy and reach a point where they genuinely regret their actions.
- When it is nonabusive and does not set up a scenario for further abuse.
- When it does not tap back into grooming or offending behavior.
- When it is empowering for the survivor.
- If the survivor is in control of the session at all times.

Apology can be a positive experience for survivors as long as the survivor wishes it and that wish is realistic. It needs to take place in the knowledge of the offender's cycle and the extent to which he has changed. The decision about whether it is accompanied by forgiveness or not is a personal one for the survivor to make freely.

If the process arouses anxiety in the therapist or survivor, then maybe the following questions should be asked: What do we hope to achieve by doing this, and is it achievable? Is this the best way of doing it? Are there better ways in which our objectives can be met in therapy? Perhaps the moral is, if in doubt, then place valuable energy in more productive areas.

If there is any doubt about the above conditions being met, then, in our view, apology can be a dangerous course of action. It may feed into the offender's desire to continue controlling and manipulating, and may be damaging to the survivor's healing process. Although some offenders can change and do have genuinely positive agendas, some do not and will inadvertently or even willfully reabuse under the guise of an apology.

5

Footprints on the Heart
Effects of Child Sexual Abuse on Emotions

What does sexual abuse do to people? Far from an academic concern, this is a burning issue for clinicians concerned about what to do on Monday morning. We cannot treat what we cannot see, and all too often, we cannot see what we do not know to look for. Unfortunately, clients do not necessarily report or even know how child sexual abuse has affected them. The connection between the insult and the sequelae is obscured by the distance in time between the two, and the chronic nature of the abuse and the sequelae may mean that the client may never remember having felt differently. Her negative affect and self-critical cognitive style, her difficulties with intimacy and with sex, she may simply attribute, for example, to her core "badness."

Whereas the effects of child sexual abuse may be so pervasive as to be elusive, the sequelae of rape, by contrast, are more readily apparent. Rape shatters assumptions previously held and changes attitudes and beliefs profoundly; it can induce sudden-onset anxiety, depression, phobias, and posttraumatic stress disorder (PTSD) in such a dramatic way that identification of sequelae is rarely difficult. It is always easier to see the effects of a lightning strike than the malformations caused by drought.

But the clinician who eagerly picks up the literature on child sexual abuse may be frustrated by its lack of tie-in with clinical practice. Studies employing symptom checklists abound, but little in the literature suggests how those symptoms may be ameliorated by which specific techniques in therapy. With a few notable exceptions (Briere, 1989, 1992a; Herman, 1992; Putnam, 1989), the literature on effects is specific but not tied to treatment, and the literature on treatment is general and not tied to effects.

Finally, the literature on effects has grown so voluminous that reading it is equivalent to trying to move a 200-pound piece of round sculpture. It is hard to find purchase. Like the blind man and the elephant, the reader circles the field. Ah, yes, PTSD. Some studies find it is the major sequela of childhood sexual abuse, but no, it does not seem to account for the cognitive changes in belief systems. What about those survivors who do not have it but who are nevertheless significantly affected? Intimacy, sex, and other interpersonal problems—the reader continues to circle —symptom studies of anxiety, depression, and dissociation— wondering just how it all fits together.

Prospective studies find that symptoms change over time. At one age, internalizing symptoms may dominate, and at another, externalizing ones (Friedrich, 1988). What does that mean? Summaries of studies—potential life rafts for those drowning in single-study articles—often catalogue studies (Beitchman et al., 1992; Browne & Finkelhor, 1986a), but only a few (e.g., Finkelhor, 1988) make sense of the diverse findings, and fewer still (Briere, 1989, 1992a) explain their relevance for treatment. It is an easy literature for collectors, a difficult one for meaning-makers.

This chapter will attempt to take a tour around the elephant, while trying to nudge him into a slightly different posture. I begin by looking at the history of child sexual abuse research on sequelae, and document the denial and minimization prevalent in early studies. I then describe affective symptoms associated with child sexual abuse, particularly depression, anxiety, and PTSD, as well as raise questions about the role that revictimization plays in the generation of affective symptoms. Finally, I address the question of the specific links between child sexual abuse and affective symptoms. Why are adult survivors so often anxious and depressed? What needs to be known about the links between childhood trauma and later affective symptoms in order to treat those symptoms?

Later chapters will discuss cognitive sequelae and false solutions: methods of avoiding or medicating pain. Thus I attempt to provide a roadmap to the existing literature while reorganizing it into a scheme that can be used directly in the treatment process.

Historical Perspective

Although there may have been a "steady flow of publications over the last thirty years or so" on the sequelae of child sexual abuse (Conte & Schuerman, 1987, p. 380), that steady flow has been dwarfed in the past 10 to 15 years by a tidal wave of research. Much of this more recent research seems to focus singlemindedly on establishing a simple association between child sexual abuse and long-term psychological sequelae.

"Why?" the reader may ask. Did anyone ever assume that child sexual abuse would be harmless? Well, actually, yes. A number of older studies did. The belief that child sexual abuse was not traumatic was entwined with the belief that it was, in actuality, not a trauma visited on the child but a form of acting out by the child, which Bender and Blau (1937) termed "sex delinquency" (p. 511).

In keeping with this point of view, Weiss, Rogers, Darwin, and Dutton (1955) described a victim who was 5 years old when her stepfather began molesting her and 7 years old when he began having intercourse with her. They described him as "rough and abusive" (p. 16) and noted that he threatened to beat the child if she told. Even so, she told repeatedly to a disbelieving mother. Nevertheless, Weiss et al. discuss "specific factors in Dorothy's development" that "have to be considered in order to account for her sexual activities" (p. 18). They argue that Dorothy's jealousy of her mother, her hostility toward her mother, and her sense of rejection were important causal factors in the abuse. They note that the mother's jealousy of the child and her conflicting attitudes toward her "hampered the development of a stable conscience in the child" (p. 19). By contrast, "a detailed discussion of the offender is not relevant" (p. 18).

Likewise, when describing an obvious pedophilic ploy on the part of an adult sex offender, Bender and Blau (1937) blamed the victim instead of the pedophile:

> The most recent experience was with a 40-year-old married salesman who was in the habit of watching the boys at play. One day the man was accidentally struck on the thigh and lowered his trousers to examine the injury; the boy expressed an interest in his genitals and the man invited him to sex play. . . . There is no doubt that the boy was the seducer of the adult in this case. (pp. 509-510)

There is every reason to doubt that the boy was the seducer of the man in this case or any other. It seems that it was suspiciously easy for the boy to "seduce" a man who hung around the playground and who just happened to find an excuse to expose himself.

In any case, Bender and Blau (1937) dismiss the effects of external trauma by noting that psychoanalytic theory emphasizes the importance of internal impulse regulation over external trauma in the genesis of psychological damage:

> The experience of the child in its sex relationship with adults does not seem always to have a traumatic effect. Psychic trauma, according to Freudian definition, is an experience which represents an offensive impulse coming from within; it is internal experience rather than external events which prove repulsive and require repression. In our cases, the experience seems to satisfy instinctual drives and any contrary urges (training, moral and ethical ideas, etc.) are probably suppressed by the unique mutual alliance of child and adult. . . . The experience offers an opportunity for the child to test out in reality . . . an infantile fantasy; it probably finds the consequences less severe, and in fact actually gratifying to a pleasure sense. *The emotional balance is thus in favor of contentment* [italics added]. (p. 516)

With such theory in place, it would be difficult indeed to appreciate the harmfulness of child sexual abuse, and so it was.

Sloane and Karpinski (1942) stated the problem succinctly: "The 'traumatic' aspect furthermore loses some of its significance when it is realized that the child itself often unconsciously desires the sexual activity and becomes a more or less willing partner in the act" (p. 666).

The traumatic aspect lost all of its significance for Bender and Grugett (1952), who concluded that "in contrast to the harsh social taboos surrounding such [pedophilic] relationships, there exists no scientific proof that there are any resulting deleterious effects" (p. 827). In fact, the follow-up information in their study consisted almost entirely of superficial social information, such as whether the subjects were married, whether they were self-sustaining, and whether they had children. Despite the superficiality of the outcome criteria, 5 of the 14 subjects nevertheless had obviously poor adjustment; three of the five were psychotic.

Likewise, Rasmussen (1934) found that 46 of 54 incest victims made a normal adult adjustment. However, "normal" was defined as showing satisfactory citizenship and not being in trouble with the law. The eight children who did have a markedly poor outcome even by such criteria were described by others as having an "independent constitutional predisposition to mental unbalance" (Bender & Blau, 1937, p. 501) operating independently of their sexual victimization.

Other authors who found negative effects also found ways to reassign them to other sources. Rosenfeld (1979) discovered a high incidence of marital problems, sexual dysfunction, and hysterical characterological disturbance among incest victims. Although Rosenfeld himself felt these were related to the sexual abuse, Henderson (1983) wrote that

[Rosenfeld's] data seem to lead with equal validity to a conclusion that one-third of Rosenfeld's patients have a history from childhood of severe hysterical characterological disturbance, showed the usual relationship disturbances that one associates with severe hysterical character difficulties, and incidentally or even expectedly had acted on incestuous object choices in childhood. (p. 38)

An even more extreme position (if that is possible) was taken by Rascovsky and Rascovsky (1950), who argued that the consummation of incestuous fantasies could prevent manic-depressive illness from developing in certain patients. The patients' real problem, they felt, was a "severely frustrated relation with the mother" (p. 46) to which the incest afforded some relief by providing "real, though partial, satisfaction" (p. 46).

At times, this whitewashing of the effects of child sexual abuse required creative interpretations of the data. In a paper titled "Children Not Severely Damaged by Incest With a Parent," Yorukoglu and Kemph (1966) describe two children they felt "were not seriously affected" (p. 123) by incest with an opposite sex parent: 13-year-old Jim and 17-year-old Jean. However, Jim was periodically suicidal and had a history of stealing, fire-setting, and vandalism as well as acting out sexually with peers and exhibiting himself to younger boys. He was generally described as "manipulative and smooth" (Yorukoglu & Kemph, 1966, p. 113). Jean had severe anxiety and would retreat into escapist fantasies.

Yorukoglu and Kemph explain their findings by commenting that it is well-known that oedipal fantasies can produce severe effects. Therefore, oedipal fantasies must be more harmful than incest because these children had suffered incest but had no ill effects. They felt the positive results meant the children must have resolved their oedipal fantasies prior to the beginning of the incest (Yorukoglu & Kemph, 1966, p. 123). De Young (1982) noted that "one may justifiably wonder whether Jim and Jean shared the authors' conclusion that they had not been seriously affected by the incest" (p. 48).

Not every historical figure, however, considered child sexual abuse to be benign. Ferenczi, in particular, wrote with great power of the dynamics of victimization in a paper that continues to enlighten more than half a century after it was written (Ferenczi, 1933/1949). Research by Kaufman, Peck, and Tagiuri (1954) and by Sloane and Karpinski (1942) also found negative sequelae.

Nevertheless, the balance of research was such that by 1965, Gagnon could sum up by noting "the relatively minor effect on adult adjustment (either sexual or nonsexual) that this early sexual experience has" (Gagnon, 1965, p. 177). Brunold (1964) con-curred: "Lasting psychological injury as a result of sexual assaults suffered in infancy is not very common" (p. 8). Some authors continued to suggest that child sexual abuse could, in fact, be positive. In a 1979 conference on child abuse, a West Virginia social work professor announced that incest "may be either a positive, healthy experience or, at worst, neutral and dull" (DeMott, 1980). Prior to 1980, it is fair to conclude that the harmfulness of child sexual abuse was not well-established.

Depression

Modern research in this area began in the 1970s. Research prior to that was often anecdotal and flawed by a host of methodological problems, including a lack of objective measures, inadequate or missing control groups, and inadequate sample size (Mrazek & Mrazek, 1981). Newer research used sounder methodology and far better control groups to look at whether specific symptoms were more common in adult survivors of sexual abuse than in other clinical or nonclinical samples. Depression, anxiety, and PTSD, particularly, were found more often in sexually abused populations.

Of these, depression appears to be found more often in adult survivors of child sexual abuse than any other symptom (Browne & Finkelhor, 1986a, 1986b). For example, Anderson, Yasenik, and Ross (1993) found depressive symptoms in 94.1% of their sample of 51 adult survivors of child sexual abuse, a higher percentage than were found to have dissociative disorders, personality disorders or substance abuse problems. Likewise, Gelinas (1981) stated, "Most incest victims will not request treatment for incest, but for symptoms relating to longstanding depressions" (p. 487). Tables 5.1 and 5.2 list studies of depression in adult survivors of child sexual abuse.

Of the studies employing community samples, 9 of the 13 found higher rates of depression in those subjects who had been sexually abused in childhood. Of the three studies that did not, one study (Murphy et al., 1988) found that only those subjects who had been sexually abused both as children and as adults had more

TABLE 5.1 Community Studies of Depression and Child Sexual Abuse

Study	Sample Size	Sample Type	% Depression in CSA[a] Group	% Depression in Controls
Bagley and Ramsay (1986)	82 csa vs. 285 controls	Random community females	17***	9
Briere and Runtz (1988c)	33 csa vs. 191 controls	College females	Significantly higher scores in csa group on depression subscale of Hopkins Symptom Checklist	
Elliott and Briere (1992)	761 csa vs. 2,072 controls	Professional women	Significantly higher scores in csa group on depression subscale of Trauma Symptom Checklist-40	
Fromuth and Burkhart (1989)	81 csa vs. 501 controls	College males	No difference on Beck Depression Inventory	
Fromuth (1986)	106 csa vs. 376 controls	College females	No difference on Beck Depression Inventory	
Gold et al. (1994)	96 csa vs. 438 controls	College females	No differences between csa group and either nonabused women or women assaulted as adults on Depression subscale of Trauma Symptom Checklist	
Greenwald et al. (1990)	54 csa vs. 54 controls	Community nurses	Csa group significantly higher scores on Depression subscale of Brief Symptom Inventory	

Study	Sample	Population	Findings (CSA)	Controls
Murphy et al. (1988)	120 csa vs. 81 adult sexual abuse victims vs. 184 controls	Random community females	Group victimized both as child and as adult scored higher on Depression subscale of the Derogatis Symptom Checklist 90-R; csa-only group did not	
Peters (1988)	71 csa vs. 48 controls	Random community females	85 in contact*; 59 in noncontact	66
Saunders et al. (1992)	131 csa vs. 260 controls	Random community females	34 noncontact; 46 molestation*; 49 child rape**	28
Saunders et al. (1991)	339 child rape vs. 3,669 controls	Random national community	Child rape group had 2x lifetime risk of major depressive episode and 3x risk of current episode	
Sedney and Brooks (1984)	51 csa vs. 51 controls	College females	65*; 18% hospitalized	43; 4% hospitalized
Stein et al. (1988)	82 csa vs. 2,601 controls	Random community	Lifetime: females only, 22*; Current: all respondents, 13*; 17 female*	6 2 3

a. CSA = child sexual abuse.
*p < .05; **p < .01; ***p < .001.

TABLE 5.2 Clinical Studies of Depression and Child Sexual Abuse

Study	Sample Size	Sample Type	% Depression in CSA[a] Group	% Depression in Controls
Anderson et al. (1993)	51	Clinical	94.1	No controls
Bagley and McDonald (1984)	20 csa vs. 37 other abuse vs. 30 controls	Clinical with community controls	Csa correlated with depression on Depression subscale of Middlesex Hospital Questionnaire	
Bryer et al. (1987)	14 csa only vs. 15 csa and physical vs. 10 physical vs. 27 no abuse	Female psychiatric inpatients	Significantly higher scores on Depression subscale of SCL-90-R	
	14 csa only vs. 14 csa and physical vs. 19 no abuse		Not significantly higher scores on Millon Clinical Multi-axial Inventory	
Gold (1986)	103 csa vs. 88 controls	Clinical and community mixed	Csa group significantly higher scores on Beck Depression Inventory	
Herman (1981)	40 csa vs. 20 controls	Clinical females (incest) vs. outpatients with seductive fathers	60	55
Meiselman (1978)	26 csa vs. 50 controls	Clinical female (incest) vs. outpatient controls	35	23
Tsai et al. (1979)	30 csa vs. 2 control groups of 30	30 clinical vs. 30 csa but nonclinical and 30 nonclinical without csa	Csa group significantly higher scores on MMPI Depression subscale but not elevated in clinical range	

a. CSA = child sexual abuse.

depression than did controls; subjects sexually abused only as children did not. Others (Fromuth, 1986; Fromuth & Burkhart, 1989; Gold, Milan, Mayall, & Johnson, 1994) simply found no differences in the child sexual abuse group and controls. However, Fromuth and Burkhart's sample had a high prevalence of the less intrusive forms of abuse.

Those studies that did find differences in the occurrence of depression often found strong differences. Stein, Golding, Siegel, Burnam, and Sorenson (1988), for example, found three times the lifetime rate of affective disorders in sexually abused women than in controls, and four times the rate of major depressive disorder. The rate of current major depressive disorder was 6.5 times higher in sexually abused women than in controls.

Of the clinical studies, one (Anderson et al., 1993) had no controls. However, the rate of depression in the clinical sample was so high (94%) that it is difficult to imagine a control group that would have had a comparable rate. Of the remaining studies, three (Bagley & McDonald, 1984; Gold, 1986; Tsai et al., 1979) found differences in depression between the child sexual abuse victims and controls, whereas two (Herman, 1981; Meiselman, 1978) did not. Bryer, Nelson, Miller, and Krol (1987) found a difference on one measure and not on another.

Hence clinical studies less often found depression to be correlated with child sexual abuse than did community sample studies. This may be explained by the fact that depression is a symptom that frequently brings individuals into treatment. Thus clinical control samples may have self-selected for high levels of depression.

Noncontact sexual experiences in children (e.g., harassment by an exhibitionist or voyeur) do not necessarily carry the same risk of subsequent depression. Two studies looked at noncontact experiences versus contact experiences and controls (Peters, 1988; Saunders, Villeponteaux, Lipovsky, Kilpatrick, & Veronen, 1992), and both found differences in depression generally between the contact group and nonvictims, but not between noncontact groups and nonvictims. However, one puzzling finding contradicted this general trend. Saunders et al. (1992) found the current risk of depression (depression that was present at the time of the assessment) to be more than 3.5 times higher in the noncontact group than in nonvictims.

Depression is apparently neither late-emerging nor transitory. Lanktree, Briere, and Zaidi (1991) found that their sample of 11 child and adolescent sexual abuse victims were four times as likely to meet the criteria for major depression as 24 outpatient controls (36% vs. 8%). Likewise, Koverola, Pound, Heger, and Lytle (1993) found that two thirds of their sample of 39 6- to 12-year-old girls met *DSM-III-R* criteria for depression. Finally, Dubowitz, Black, Harrington, and Verschoore (1993) demonstrated that depression was stable in their sample of 93 prepubertal children over the 4-month follow-up period, and again, was found more often than in controls.

Although depression may be common in sexual abuse victims, other forms of childhood trauma can apparently produce it as well. Physical abuse survivors show high rates of depression (Briere & Runtz, 1988a; Cole, 1986; Elliott & Briere, 1991a; Henschel, Briere, Magallanes, & Smiljamich, 1990; Runtz, 1987a), as do children of alcoholics (Benson & Heller, 1987; Elliott & Briere, 1991a; Hibbard, 1989; Parker & Harford, 1988) and victims of emotional abuse (Briere & Runtz, 1988a; Henschel et al., 1990; Vissing, Straus, Gelles, & Harrop, 1991).

Hence there can be little doubt that abuse in childhood is associated with depression in both childhood and adulthood. The existence of a correlation, however, does not answer the question of whether the link is causal or associational (Briere, 1992b). Both child sexual abuse and depression, for example, could be related to a third variable, such as family pathology (Peters, 1988). Even if the link is directly causal, the nature of the dynamic is not elucidated by the bare fact of the association. Is depression the result of an altered worldview, of subsequent failures in the development of peer and/or romantic relationships, or of a view of the self as damaged? Is it related to faulty attributions of self-blame and accompanying guilt? Do different factors come into play for different people? The etiology of depression in child sexual abuse victims is important, given that each of the above would necessitate a different focus for treatment, and will be discussed later in this chapter. Simply knowing that the client is depressed is not sufficient to know what to do about it.

Anxiety

Chronic, sometimes severe, anxiety is likewise frequently associated with a history of child sexual abuse. Table 5.3 lists six community studies and Table 5.4 lists three clinical studies of anxiety and child sexual abuse, all of which found a significant relationship. These studies primarily looked at anxiety as a symptom, whereas Stein et al. (1988) and Saunders et al. (1992) both used the more complex criteria specific to diagnosing anxiety disorders.

The results of both approaches were startling. Saunders et al. (Table 5.5) found that victims of childhood rape had 4.5 times the lifetime risk of developing agoraphobia, 7.5 times the risk of developing obsessive-compulsive disorder, and 4.6 times the rate of social phobia as nonabused women. At the time of the assessment (Table 5.6), the abused women had 16 times the rate of agoraphobia, 4 times the rate of panic disorder, 5 times the rate of obsessive-compulsive disorder, and almost 4 times the rate of social phobia as nonabused women.

Likewise, as shown in Table 5.7, Stein et al. (1988) found higher rates of lifetime and current anxiety disorders as well as phobias in the combined pool of male and female subjects and in the female-only group. When pooled, male and female respondents had 2.6 times the lifetime risk of developing an anxiety disorder and were 3.5 times more likely to have such a disorder at the time of the assessment. The pooled subjects had more than twice the lifetime rate of phobias and 10 times the lifetime rate of panic disorder as nonabused subjects. Similarly, female subjects had 2.6 times the lifetime risk of an anxiety disorder and 2.7 times the current risk. Phobias were more than twice as common in the abused group. Interestingly, female subjects were not distinguished by differential rates of lifetime panic disorder, despite the 10-time discrepancy in the pooled subjects.

Beitchman et al. (1992) suggested that high rates of anxiety in child sexual abuse victims might be associated with the use of

TABLE 5.3 Community Studies of Anxiety and Child Sexual Abuse

Community Study	Sample Size	Sample Type	% Anxiety in CSA[a] Group	% Anxiety in Controls
Bagley and Ramsay (1986)	82 csa vs. 285 controls	Random community females	Significantly higher scores in csa group on Anxiety subscale of Middlesex Hospital Questionnaire	
Briere and Runtz (1988b)	33 csa vs. 191 controls	College females	Significantly higher scores in csa group on Anxiety subscale of Hopkins Symptom Checklist	
Fromuth (1986)	106 csa vs. 376 controls	College females	Significantly higher scores in csa group on Phobic Anxiety sub-scale of Hopkins Symptom Checklist (not on Anxiety subscale)	
Gold et al. (1994)	96 csa vs. 438 controls	College females	Significantly higher scores in csa group on Anxiety subscale of Trauma Symptom Checklist (not on Phobic Anxiety subscale)	
Murphy et al. (1988)	120 csa vs. 265 controls	Random community females	Significantly higher scores in csa group on Anxiety subscale of the Derogatis Symptom Checklist 90-R	
Sedney and Brooks (1988)	35 incest vs. 16 extra-familial vs. 51 controls	College females	Significantly more anxiety among incest victims only than among controls	

a. CSA = child sexual abuse.

TABLE 5.4 Clinical Studies of Anxiety

Study	Sample Size	Sample Type	% Anxiety in CSA[a] Group	% Anxiety in Controls
Briere and Runtz (1988b)	67 csa vs. 85 controls	Walk-in crisis clients	Anxiety attacks 54**; Muscle tension 66*	Anxiety attacks 28 Muscle tension 44
Bryer et al. (1987)	14 csa vs. 15 csa and physical abuse vs. 10 physical abuse only vs. 27 no abuse	Female psychiatric inpatients	Significantly higher scores on Anxiety subscales of SCL-90-R and on Millon Clinical Multiaxial Inventory	
Herman and Schatzow (1987)	53	Outpatient clinical	26% had chronic severe anxiety	

a. CSA = child sexual abuse.
*$p < .01$; **$p < .001$.

TABLE 5.5 Lifetime Risk of Anxiety Disorders in Women Sexually
Abused as Children

Diagnosis	Noncontact (N = 35)	Molestation (N = 57)	Rape (N = 39)	Nonvictims (N = 260)
Agoraphobia[a]			18**	4
Obsessive-compulsive disorder		11*	15**	2
Social phobia			23	5

SOURCE: From Saunders et al. (1992). Reprinted by permission of Sage Publications, Inc.
a. Only significant results will be shown.
*$p < .01$; **$p < .001$.

TABLE 5.6 Current Risk of Anxiety Disorders in Women Sexually
Abused as Children

Diagnosis	Noncontact (N = 35)	Molestation (N = 57)	Rape (N = 39)	Nonvictims (N = 260)
Agoraphobia			13***	.8
Panic disorder			8*	2
Obsessive-compulsive disorder		9*	10**	2
Social phobia			15***	4

SOURCE: From Saunders et al. (1992). Reprinted by permission of Sage Publications, Inc.
*$p < .05$; **$p < .01$; ***$p < .001$.

force. In their review, they noted that three out of seven studies of anxiety and child sexual abuse found that force or the threat of force had been common in the original assaults, and that three out of the four remaining studies did not report on force. They conclude that it is unclear whether anxiety symptoms are associated with child sexual abuse per se or with violence.

However, there is little reason to think that the degree of force affects anxiety differentially because each of the studies that Beitchman et al. cite, which found force common (Briere, 1984; Herman & Schatzow, 1987; Murphy et al., 1988), identified other

TABLE 5.7 Lifetime and Current Risk of Anxiety Disorders in Adults Sexually Abused as Children

	All Respondents		Females Only	
Diagnosis	Abused (N = 82)	Nonabused (N = 2,601)	Abused (N = 51)	Nonabused (N = 1,307)
Lifetime				
Anxiety disorders	29*	11	37*	14
Phobia	23*	10	34*	13
Panic disorder	8*	.8		
Current				
Anxiety disorder	21*	6	24*	9

SOURCE: From Stein et al. (1988). Reprinted by permission of Sage Publications, Inc.
*$p < .05$.

symptoms associated with a history of child sexual abuse as well. Violence, certainly, is associated with a poorer psychological outcome in general (Briere & Runtz, 1988c; Schetky, 1990; Wolfe, Sas, & Wekerle, 1994), although it remains to be seen if it is associated with any specific symptom or disorder. If anything, as will be seen, the clearest direct connection between force and sequelae appears to be in the development of PTSD.

Revictimization and Its Relationship to Depression and Anxiety

An interesting question, however, is why any long-term sequelae are associated with a childhood history of sexual assault. Does revictimization as an adult explain later symptoms? Research consistently suggests that adult survivors of child sexual abuse have a high incidence of being revictimized as adults by battery, sexual assault, or both (Briere & Runtz, 1988b; Fromuth, 1986; Herman, 1981; Russell, 1986; Wyatt, Guthrie, & Notgrass, 1992).

Wyatt et al. (1992), for example, found that women sexually abused as children were 2.4 times more likely than controls to be reabused sexually as adults. Russell (1986) found adult incest survivors to have not only far higher rates of victimization through rape or attempted rape since the age of 14 than nonabused women (65% to 36%), but also to have almost three times the rate of victimization through marital rape and to be more than twice as likely to be physically battered. Twenty-eight percent of Herman's (1981) sample of 40 incestuously abused women were battered as adults, compared to none of her sample of 20 women of seductive (but not abusive) fathers. Briere and Runtz (1988b) found that 49% of their sexually abused, emergency walk-in clients had been battered as adults versus 18% of nonabused walk-in clients. Twice as many (18% vs. 8%) had been raped. Schetky (1990), in her review of the research, concluded that roughly half of adult survivors are revictimized in some manner (p. 44).

Apparently, sexual revictimization is more common among survivors of sexual rather than physical abuse. Runtz (1987b) found that almost half (44%) of her sample of adult survivors of childhood sexual abuse were also sexually assaulted as teens or young adults, compared to 20% of adults physically abused in childhood.

Therefore, given the high rates of revictimization in adult survivors, the possibility exists that much of the literature on effects is contaminated by the effects of battering or of adult sexual assault. Some support for this concern can be taken from research by Resnick, Kilpatrick, Dansky, Saunders, and Best (1993), which found that 39% of women who had been physically assaulted at some point in their lives had had PTSD (and 18% had it currently). This was compared to those who had been raped as an adult or child: 32% had a lifetime prevalence of PTSD and 12% had a current prevalence. Clearly, physical assault alone can produce rates of PTSD as high or higher than sexual assault.

Few studies directly compare those survivors sexually abused as children to those abused as adults to still a third group, those abused both as children and adults. One that did (Murphy et al., 1988) found higher rates of somatization, obsessive compulsion, depression, anxiety, and hostility in those women abused as both children and adults over all other groups.

The failure of the adult assault group to have as many symptoms as the multiply abused group suggests that child sexual abuse does have an impact beyond that afforded by the propensity of survivors to be revictimized as adults. In fact, survivors of child and adolescent abuse had a higher prevalence of anxiety symptoms than did nonvictims, whereas survivors of adult sexual assault did not differ from other adults in their levels of anxiety.

This is a surprising finding given that child sexual abuse was often decades distant from the subjects, and adult sexual assault was not only more recent, but by definition always involved violence. Why would individuals sexually abused as children have elevated rates of anxiety, but not individuals sexually abused as adults? It is not possible at present to answer this question definitively, although this finding does suggest that at least some of the symptoms associated with child sexual abuse cannot be explained solely on the basis of adult revictimization.

It is clear, then, that individuals sexually abused as children run a significantly elevated risk of being sexually abused or physically battered as adults. It is also clear that being battered or sexually assaulted only as an adult can lead to psychological symptoms. It is less clear whether symptomatic adults who were sexually abused as children and sexually or physically abused as adults derive their symptoms from the childhood trauma or the more recent adult trauma. Based on current research, the best guess is both. Childhood sexual abuse does appear to have a significant impact on later functioning on its own. Adding adult revictimization only make matters worse.

Etiology of Anxiety and Depression in Adult Survivors of Child Sexual Abuse

The association of anxiety and depression with childhood sexual abuse is not controversial. The occasional study fails to find a relationship with a particular sample on a particular measure, but the overwhelming weight of the evidence is that anxiety and depression may continue decades after the abuse ceased. But why?

This is far less clear. In what manner does sexual abuse in child-hood continue to be present in the survivor's life in a sufficiently vivid manner as to cause ongoing anxiety and depression?

The research literature offers little answer, but clinical experience suggests that anxiety and depression are (a) evoked by affective flashbacks with or without memory of the abuse, (b) secondary to cognitive distortions and internalized perpetrator projections, and/or (c) secondary to current realities (i.e., current revictimization or losses related to the abuse).

Affective Flashbacks

A number of authors (Briere & Runtz, 1993; Eth & Pynoos, 1985; Tsai et al., 1979; van der Kolk, 1987; Wheeler & Berliner, 1988; Wolfe et al., 1994) have noted the extent to which perceptual stimuli (e.g., specific odors, sounds, sights, etc.) can trigger a re-living of the abuse experience, or flashback. Indeed, such triggering is part of the criteria for PTSD listed in *DSM-IV.*

Such flashbacks can occur without conscious memories of the abuse—witness van der Kolk's intriguing case study of a woman who survived the 1942 Coconut Grove fire (van der Kolk, 1987). For decades, she had no memory of the fire, but periodically had psychotic episodes in which she complained that gases were invading her body and electricity was spreading in her body. (Her memories, when they returned, included the room filling up with gas and the fire spreading through the wires.)

She would ask other patients how many lives they had saved from the fire, and once tried to evacuate everyone from the hospital, demanding that the doors be taken off. (The main revolving door at the nightclub got stuck during the fire as people fled and bodies piled up behind it; a second exit was locked.) She was brought to the hospital by the police on several occasions for behavior that included pulling fire alarms in numerous buildings and warning people to get out. Once, she started yelling in a supermarket that gas was coming from the ceiling and would kill everyone. She claimed on one admission to have saved 1,500 lives.

Certainly every clinician who deals with trauma sees clients on occasion who have this type of full-blown sensory flashback,

which includes an active reliving of the experience in an hallu-
cinatory or dissociative manner. However, this extreme form of
flashback is by no means the most common. Far more common is
an affective flashback in which some trigger—an odor similar to
a perpetrator's aftershave lotion, for example—evokes the same
feelings that the client had at the time the abuse occurred (e.g.,
despair, desperation, fear, anxiety, or disgust).

This loop is not cognitively mediated. The client is often not
consciously aware of the trigger, even when she is aware of her
history of abuse. As van der Kolk (1987) notes, survivors have a
tendency to "react to subsequent stress as if it were a recurrence
of the trauma. The patient experiences the emotional intensity of
original trauma without conscious awareness of the historical reference" (p. 7).

Thus the affective flashback is often a sudden, jolting rush of
negative affect that takes the survivor by surprise and that, given
that she is not consciously aware of the trigger, makes no sense. "I
can't understand it," she may say. "I was having a good day. Then
all of a sudden, for no reason, I wanted to die." Careful reconstruction of the circumstances may elicit a trigger—for example,
she passed a 1950s car similar to the one her father drove when he
took her for Sunday drives and molested her—or it may not.

This sequence of events is analogous to an encounter with a
"lava tube," a place down the slope from a live volcano in which
hot lava runs in a current under the surface. When lava hits the
air it becomes gray and asphalt-like and looks like a creeping concrete amoeba. Although the cold gray lava around the tube may
be solid, the thin crust of the lava tube is not and may break
through to the hot lava below under the weight of an unsuspect-
ing tourist—a tourist who has ignored the warning signs (after
all, the cold gray asphalt looks perfectly safe) and has decided to
have his picture taken on a real lava field.

The grisly image is purposeful. The adult survivor may have
a similar experience to the tourist—out for a Sunday stroll, so to
speak, when he feels as though the ground has dropped out from
under him. He becomes emotionally seared without knowing why.

The adult survivor rarely sees the warning signs. A particular
desk that looks like the desk his uncle had in his bedroom, a cer-

tain type of ballpoint pen that looks like the pen her brother used to molest her, the sound of footsteps coming up stairs—all may have sufficient specificity to trigger affective flashbacks. None may register consciously with the client at the time as reminders of the abuse, even for clients fully aware of their history. During these affective flashbacks the survivor stays oriented to the present cognitively, often without even thinking of the abuse. Thus life is confusing to the adult survivor, to say the least, and her first complaint upon entering therapy is often that she thinks she is crazy.

Triggers for Affective Flashbacks

Not all triggers are highly specific. Certain categories of behaviors, situations, or people often function as affective triggers. Sexual encounters are possibly the most common triggers because they represent the single situation most like the original trauma. Silver, Boon, and Stones (1983) found that more than 80% of their sample of female incest victims reported that having sex evoked the incest experience for them. As Finkelhor, Hotaling, Lewis and Smith (1989) note, "When children have been forced to be sexual, feelings of fear and disgust may become a conditioned association to sexuality in general" (p. 393). In addition, adult sexual encounters frequently occur in the dark, alcohol is sometimes involved, and sexual arousal decreases the sense of being in control. All three are factors that reduce reality testing and increase a sense of vulnerability.

The empirical fact of an association between child sexual abuse and sexual problems has been noted repeatedly (Beitchman et al., 1992) despite the fact that sexual dysfunction is defined very differently by the various studies. Lack of sexual interest, lack of sexual responsiveness, promiscuity, confusion over sexual orientation, inability to achieve orgasm, sexual dissatisfaction, fear of sex, and avoidance of sex have all been used to measure sexual dysfunction (Briere, 1984; Meiselman, 1978; Stein et al., 1988). Briere and Runtz (1988b) found that emergency mental health patients with histories of sexual abuse had three times the frequency of sexual problems (undefined) than did emergency mental health patients without such a history. Meiselman (1978) found that 87% of her sample of incest victims had sexual problems (defined as lack of desire, confusion over sexual orientation, or promiscuity) compared to 20% of controls. Saunders et al. (1992) discovered child rape victims had a 50% higher risk of sexual problems (defined as meeting *DSM-III* criteria for sexual disorders) and molestation victims a 40% higher risk than did nonvictims.

In general, other studies have supported these findings, although usually less dramatically (Finkelhor, 1979; Gold, 1986; Herman, 1981; Stein et al., 1988; Tsai et al., 1979). Only a few studies (Fromuth, 1986; Greenwald, Leitenberg, Cado, & Tarran, 1990) have found either a weak or nonexistent relationship between child sexual abuse and sexual difficulties. Moreover, Finkelhor et al. (1989) found that sexual difficulties remained related to sexual abuse when family disruption variables were controlled, as would be the case if the association were partially due to affective flashbacks of the original abuse and not to secondary factors.

In general, sexual difficulties appear to be particularly related to sexual abuse and not to trauma. Briere (1992a) found it most often associated with sexual, rather than physical or emotional, abuse.

Affective flashbacks, of course, are not the only cause of sexual problems in adult survivors. Many victims dissociate during the original assault and later find it a defense difficult to unlearn. Like it or not, they will automatically dissociate during sex, and although this prevents pain, it prevents pleasure as well. The dissociated adult survivor is rarely a fan of sex, and often her lack of interest leads to decreased sexual activity, which eventually causes problems with her partner.

In addition, many survivors enter trancelike states during the original abuse in which they numb parts of their bodies in a manner similar to the analgesia that can be obtained in hypnotic trances. This defense, once learned, also proves difficult to unlearn, and adult survivors often report feeling totally numb during any sexual activity.

Likewise, fear may reduce sexual interest. One adult survivor found that she could be sexually aroused toward her husband only when he was sleeping. When he awoke and turned toward her, she became so afraid that all sexual interest was lost.

Although sexual situations are probably the most common triggers for affective flashbacks, they are by no means the only ones. Dental phobia, for example, is frequently attributed to anxiety over pain, but it can be related to affective flashbacks of oral sex as well. For some, there may be affective flashbacks to even more general categories. Simply being in the presence of men makes some survivors uneasy.

Intimacy Allergy

Child sexual abuse is rarely physically violent, but is always emotionally violent and marked by destruction of trust and betrayal of intimacy. The intimacy is typically of a heightened and enhanced sort, built carefully by offenders for whom the child's love is both the gatehouse of access and a guardpost against disclosure. "Child molesters are very professional at what they do," bragged the offender in Chapter 2 as he revealed his modus operandi for increasing trust in children. "When you get their trust, that's when the child becomes vulnerable and you can molest the child."

It is ironic that sex offenders, who mean only harm, sometimes work harder to develop intimacy and trust with children than anyone else in the child's environment. "There's nobody better to that child than me," one offender insisted, and went on to describe how he "won all their trust."

The realization—sometimes decades later—of the manipulation behind the nurturance is more than dismaying for many survivors; it leaves them with a permanent distrust of intimacy. More than a cognitive realization that things are not always as they seem, it is a gut-level aversive reaction to intimacy, which seems almost to mimic an allergy. "Imagine," I heard a foster parent say once, "that you had an allergy to orange juice. Only imagine that you needed orange juice as much as children need love. Then imagine every time you drank it, you got profoundly ill. That's what it's like, living with these kids." She went on to say that now, when a sexually abused adolescent tried to get too close to her, she quietly set limits on it. "Because I know," she said, "That's when they run. When they get too close to you. They can't tolerate it and next thing you know they've run."

Intimacy of any sort may set up an affective flashback in the adult survivor sufficient to activate her defense mechanisms—particularly avoidance and even dissociation. "I never had a child," one adult survivor said to me, "because I know I cannot tolerate any sort of intimacy. I dissociate in the presence of intimacy." Another held her baby away from her body with stiff arms. "I can't let anybody get that close to me," she said.

Somatic Flashbacks

Although emotional flashbacks are more common, somatic flashbacks (e.g., pain or sensation in some part of the body associated with the abuse) may be evoked by triggers as well. Each time a client touches on some specific memory or topic, the clinician may notice that he rubs his arm or shrugs his shoulder or stretches his neck. When queried, he may reply that he does not know why, but his neck, shoulder, back, or other body part hurts. This frequently happens when the survivor is discussing a memory that involves some violent action in which he was grabbed or choked or otherwise manhandled.

More difficult to detect is a somatic flashback that involves the genitals, anus, or breasts, because survivors will usually not take any action that reveals their discomfort. However, once the subject of somatic flashbacks has been discussed, survivors will often volunteer that when they talk about the abuse, their vagina or anus or testicles hurt. As one multiply abused young woman said sadly, "I don't get it. I see all these movies and all these billboards and they all make sex look like this wonderful thing, and every time I think about it, my vagina hurts."

For some survivors with incomplete memories, somatic flashbacks of abuse surface before images or words do. One survivor would rub both sides of the back of her waist as she talked about a vague memory related to her mother. When the memory finally surfaced, it involved her mother grabbing her around the waist and rubbing her tiny body against the mother's clitoris. Either in sexual excitement or because pain excited her, the mother would dig her fingernails into the child's back. Hence for the child, and later for the adult, the pain of the encounter was one of its more salient features.

Summary of Affective and Somatic Flashbacks

For the adult survivor, life can be an unpredictable emotional roller coaster, where the dips occur without warning and seemingly without reason. Many survivors, even those without PTSD, respond by trying to avoid any possible reminders of the abuse and wind up with impoverished lives in which they are, even so, still not safe. A phrase used by a friend, a certain position in love-making, the odor of a pipe, Sunday morning, a 1950s car, blue suits with white shirts, any of these triggers could cause the adult survivor to have an overwhelming rush of helplessness, despair, or even terror. Worse still, the affective flashback may be to even more general stimuli: men in general, sex of any sort, intimacy of any kind. It is like walking through a mine field in the dark, usually without even the sanity-making knowledge that one is in a minefield.

Anxiety and Depression
Secondary to Cognitions

Although anxiety and depression can result from affective flashbacks, and thus be unrelated to conscious cognition, they can also result from maladaptive thought patterns, often derived from the internalization of sex offender thinking errors. Briefly put, a survivor who believes she seduced her father, who feels she betrayed her mother, who thinks she caused the breakup of the family, or who tells herself her father's abuse was proof of her own worthlessness may have anxiety and depression secondary to those beliefs and the resultant feelings of worthlessness. As seen in Chapter 3, survivors often internalize the sex offender's version of the abuse, partly because he is the only person who knows about it at the time, and therefore is in a unique position to define her reality.

Alternatively, he or she may have anxiety and depression because she has developed a "trauma-based worldview," a belief that the world is unsafe and unpredictable. Such a view may be so negative and pessimistic that it precludes all hope.

Finally, the adult survivor may be unable to make any sense of the abuse at all. Some research (Silver et al., 1983) suggests such an inability to make meaning may result in more emotional disturbance than any particular attributions assigned to the abuse. This is true even in comparison to meanings that blame the victim. These themes will be developed more fully in Chapter 6 on the cognitive sequelae of child sexual abuse.

Anxiety and Depression Secondary to Current Realities

It has become popular in the backlash literature to suggest secondary gain as a motive for accusations of child sexual abuse. This claim is ironic given the sad reality of the number and type of losses incurred by children and adult survivors who declare their abuse. No family welcomes an accusation of child sexual abuse by one family member against another. Even spouses in bitterly contested divorces are perplexed and furious, rather than satisfied, at revelations of incest. Repeatedly, one hears something like, "I knew he was a shit, but it never crossed my mind he would abuse our daughter."

A revelation of child sexual abuse, even against a despised former family member, is disruptive to the family and calls into question other bonds besides the perpetrator/victim relationship. It raises, for instance, the question of the nonabusive spouse's role. Mothers are often angry that they were not told; survivors are often angry that the mothers did not know anyway.

Time frequently does little to quiet these dynamics. The mother who could not face the abuse because of financial dependency when the children were young, often has no more financial security at age 60 and has the additional complications of impending old age. Therefore, the adult survivor who confronts her family is more likely than not to find her family denies, minimizes, rationalizes, ignores, or erases the abuse. A battle of realities ensues. The survivor is stunned to discover that, even if the family formally acknowledges the abuse, it seems to change nothing. No one talks about it, works on it, puzzles over it, or asks about it. It is as though it never happened.

Frequently, even initial acknowledgment is withdrawn. The survivor whose mother says the magic words at first, "Oh, my poor baby. That's horrible, I'm so sorry he did that to you," may find her euphoria short-lived. Within a week, she may get a furious phone call from her mother, the gist of which is, "I can't believe he would do something like that." Somewhere in the jumble of angry accusations, the survivor will hear, "I can't believe it. If I believed it, I would have to leave him."

An elderly woman, facing a limited and uncertain future, does not easily leave what passes for safety. She is not prepared to live and die alone any sooner than she has to. The survivor's protest that she does not expect her mother to leave her father after 40 years will fall on deaf ears. It is not in the mother's game plan to be married to a sex offender. It would change everything.

For many, current realities are much more severe than simply dealing with a denying or minimizing family. As noted earlier, many adult survivors are revictimized as adults by being either raped or battered (Briere & Runtz, 1988b; Herman, 1981; Russell, 1986).

Likewise, several studies have linked child sexual abuse to later prostitution (Bagley & Young, 1987; Fields, 1980; Harlan, Rogers, & Slattery, 1981; James & Meyerding, 1977; Janus, Scanlon, & Price, 1984; Rosenfeld, 1979; Silbert & Pines, 1981). Janus et al. (1984), for example, found that 24 out of 28 young male prostitutes had had a coercive sexual experience prior to entering "the life." Twenty of those 24 had gone into prostitution within a year of the sexual assault. Allen (1980) found that 66% of his sample of male prostitutes were sexually abused as children. Likewise, Silbert and Pines (1981) reported that 60% of their sample of 200 female prostitutes were sexually abused prior to age 16 by an average of two people each.

More telling than the research, however, is a pimp's description of what he looks for in selecting young women to manipulate into prostitution:

> "Beauty, yes. Sexual expertise, somewhat. That can be taught easier than you think. What is important above all is obedience. And how do you get obedience? You get obedience if you get women who have had sex with their fathers, their uncles, their brothers—you know, someone they love and fear to lose so that they do not dare to defy. Then you are nicer to the woman than they ever were, and more dangerous as well. They will do anything to keep you happy. That is how." He nods to the women and both smile. "Both those girls were had by their fathers. Now they make me rich and they are happy." (Kluft, 1990b, p. 25)

Happy indeed. Both prostitution and battering have been associated with depression, anxiety, and other psychological symptoms. Prostitution, specifically, has been associated with isolation, loneliness, ostracism, friendlessness, drug addiction, physical abuse, and depression (Janus et al., 1984). In a sample of 100 battered spouses, Gayford (1975) found that 71% had symptoms requiring antidepressants or major tranquilizers, 42% had made suicide attempts, and 21% had a primary diagnosis of depression. Hilberman and Munson (1978) found that battered wives had a host of psychological problems, including agitation and anxiety bordering on panic, intense fear when triggered by events even remotely violent, insomnia, tension, passivity, emotional paralysis, numbness, helplessness, despair, sleep disturbances, suicidal behavior, alcoholism, self-mutilation, and, not surprisingly, depression.

Therapeutically, revictimization does more than slow recovery: It stops it altogether. Healing, unfortunately, does not begin until the abuse stops. The adult survivor who spends a therapy hour processing her abuse only to return home to be battered again is striding forward on a treadmill that is moving faster than she can run. The prostitute who comes in to talk about his drug addiction only to return to life as a zombie in the streets will find that no amount of therapeutic affirmation will erase the degradation. The child who does not say enough to allow authorities to intervene will be drowning no less because she is in therapy. The most that therapy can do in such circumstances is to enable and assist the victim in finding enough strength or facing enough desperation to leave the abusive circumstances. It will be a considerable time after that before the nightmares stop.

Summary of Depression and Anxiety Sequelae

The knowledge that anxiety and depression are frequent sequelae to child sexual abuse does the clinician a limited amount of good. It is useful to know that one should look for them. Although they are frequently presenting complaints, occasionally they appear in masked form—medicated, for example, by drug and/or alcohol addiction.

But knowing that they exist is not sufficient to know what to do about them. Their relationship to child sexual abuse must be carefully examined. Are they affective flashbacks stimulated by perceptual stimuli that remind the survivor of the abuse? Are they due to maladaptive thought patterns: either the global pessimism characteristic of a trauma-based worldview, cognitive distortions adopted wholesale from a perpetrator, or the affront to meaning-making afforded by a senselessly destructive act? Is the link the adult survivor's current situation? Exile from a denying or erasing family, marital difficulties related to sexual impairment or an allergy to intimacy—all may cause anxiety and depression, not to mention the ongoing psychological damage inherent in severely abusive current realities, such as prostitution or battering.

There is no one intervention for anxiety and depression per se. All of the above etiologies would be treated differently; thus treatment efficacy is dependent not just on recognizing anxiety and depression—not a difficult task generally—but in knowing with some precision what is causing them.

Posttraumatic Stress Disorder

Definition

The essence of PTSD is a recurrent cycle of intrusive thoughts, images, and feelings followed by a period of emotional denial or numbness. The intrusive phrase may be marked by nightmares, sometimes with repetitive content. Nightmares may also shade into hypnogogic imagery or flashbacks, and survivors may waken from a nightmare only to see the perpetrator in the room.

However, flashbacks do not only occur at night. One adult survivor sometimes had flashbacks while playing softball. She would see the brother who raped her repeatedly step out from behind the pitcher and walk toward her. For whatever reasons, the flashback that occurred for her most frequently at night was of a neighbor who held her forcibly against the wall while he performed oral sex on her. When she tried to get away, he slammed her against the wall. Twenty years later she would wake in the night to find herself being slammed repetitively against a wall. Roommates and friends were sometimes in the room, but she negatively hallucinated and could not see them. Therefore, she was not comforted by their presence.

By means of intrusive thoughts, nightmares, and/or flashbacks, survivors in the intrusive phrase relive the trauma, repetitively, and seemingly without resolution. As befits their state of hyperarousal, they startle easily, and are often irritable, sometimes with episodic outbursts of aggression. They are, in fact, continually under stress, and preoccupied as they are with internal attack, back-breaking straws are seemingly everywhere.

The survivor does not feel in control of his internal world, and in some cases spends his days trying to manage, or at least survive, his painful affective states. He learns to avoid triggers that stimulate flashbacks, nightmares, and anxiety states. By doing so, he may reduce his world progressively, resulting in what Titchener (1986) terms "post-traumatic decline." The withdrawal is intensified by the fact that the person no longer trusts the world to be benign; thus even novel events unrelated to the previous trauma do not feel safe. The withdrawal may be profound.

Titchener notes, "Powerful forces drive him toward becoming a shadow person moving about but hardly participating in the social system, striving only for the space and sustenance required for a shadow's survival" (p. 8).

PTSD then involves an oscillating rhythm of intrusion and denial against a backdrop of a hyperalert nervous system. The cycle may turn over rapidly or quite slowly. Years or even decades may pass of "post-traumatic decline" in which the individual largely succeeds in avoiding thoughts, memories, or feelings about the abuse. Fearing the affective flashbacks, he may remember the events but live his life so that he has minimal contact with reminders that trigger an emotional response.

He may avoid sex altogether or dissociate during it. He may go to the dentist only under duress; the intrusiveness in the mouth may trigger affective flashbacks of oral sex. He may trust others minimally, and thus have shallow and superficial relationships. Conversely, he may feel so helpless personally that he clings inappropriately to others, thus increasing the chances that he will fall prey to abusive relationships.

History of PTSD

Evidence that trauma, in general, can cause specific psychological sequelae has been prevalent for centuries in the form of letters and diaries recording individual responses to disasters. Samuel Pepys kept a diary of his reaction to the Great Fire of London in 1666. He began it on the day he watched the fire progress toward his home while he hurriedly arranged to evacuate. It included a description of his own nightmares 6 months later and various sequelae experienced by others, including attempted suicide (Daly, 1983; Trimble, 1985).

Likewise, Charles Dickens wrote vividly of his experience in a horrific railway accident that left many dead and dying. His horror proved to be more than momentary. It was sometime later that he wrote, " 'I am not quite right within, but believe it to be an effect of the railway shaking' " (Trimble, 1985, p. 7; see also Forster, 1969). He subsequently developed a phobia of railway traveling.

Others propose that they can detect the aftereffects of trauma in those who never knew or never chose to say from whence their images came. Alice Miller (1990) suggests that the powerful emotional impact of Guernica by Picasso was derived not from the war he portrayed but was never in, but instead from the earthquake he was in but never admitted portraying. When he was 3 years old, his family fled through the streets from their house to a safer one where, 3 days later, his sister was born. Although there is apparently no information on the severity of the quake, it was sufficiently severe for King Alfonso XII to visit the area to survey the damage a few days later. It is Miller's contention that the disordered scene in the street had a permanent effect on Picasso's art. Likewise, Terr (1987) proposes that the long-term effects of trauma can be seen in the writings of Poe, Virginia Woolf, and Stephen King.

Early scientific work on this issue, however, was hampered by the issue of secondary gain. Railroad accidents increased dramatically in the late 1800s when the networks themselves expanded without an equivalent increase in safety technology. The term "compensation neurosis" was introduced in 1879 by Rigler to describe the increase in morbidity from railroad accidents following the introduction of compensation laws in Prussia in 1871. The first compensation acts for workers in the United Kingdom were passed in 1880, and certain restrictions eased in 1906. Within a few years after the 1906 changes, the number of reported accidents rose 44% despite the fact that the numbers employed had not changed (Trimble, 1985).

The changing figures led to spectacular medical battles over whether the clinical picture presented by litigants was the result of physical injuries, psychological injuries, or faking, the latter two considered equivalent in many quarters. (Somehow, psychological injuries historically have been seen as less real than physical ones.) For example, Erichsen (1882) wrote an early and influential book on "railroad spine" in which he defended spinal injuries resulting from the violent impact of railroad accidents as a legitimate physical finding, whereas Page (1883) attributed the complaints to a nervous condition. At the time, this was essentially an attack on their legitimacy as a basis for compensation.

Likewise, the impact of war on participants has been obscured by arguments over secondary gain. Initially, what we would now term PTSD was thought to have an organic basis. The term *shell shock* was first used by Mott (1919), who proposed that the condition was caused by brain lesions related to the soldier's proximity to exploding shells.

Over time, this view lost favor as evidence accumulated that the symptoms were more likely psychological in nature. C. S. Myers (1940), for example, found in his sample of more than 2,000 cases of shell shock that horror and fright were more often responsible than brain lesions. The issue of secondary gain in war revolved around safety, rather than money, as the presumed motivation for soldiers to leave the front lines.

Although war is the most readily apparent and most publicized cause of stress-related syndromes, research in the past 25 years on a variety of populations has established posttrauma symptoms as frequent sequelae to any powerful, adverse event. A wide range of traumas has been studied, including environmental disasters (e.g., floods) (Bennet, 1970; Newman, 1976); human-made disasters (e.g., atomic bombing) (Lifton, 1967); terminal illness (Nir, 1985); and exposure to violence (Pynoos & Eth, 1985; Terr, 1985a). In many of the situations studied, secondary gain, and consequently malingering, is not a realistic concern.

However, there continues to be debate over whether posttrauma sequelae are widespread in those instances in which the disasters are environmentally caused and hit entire communities (Quarantelli, 1985). Such disasters are highly visible, do not involve social isolation, and allow individuals to coordinate with others—factors that are never involved in child sexual abuse. Quarantelli makes a compelling case that, although the research is conflicting, people behave more prosocially in those circumstances and have fewer long-term sequelae than previously believed.

Although secondary gain is not a realistic concern in many of the scenarios cited above, it is by no means absent from the debate over child sexual abuse. Curiously, the charge is seldom raised that money is the motivation, although an increasing number of adult survivors sue their offenders. More often, it is charged that the adult survivor is attempting to explain and justify her own personal failures by blaming her parents. Thus even the dysfunction of many adult survivors is used as evidence, not that they were traumatized as children, but that they have something to gain by claiming they were.

PTSD and Child Sexual Abuse

The issue at controversy regarding child sexual abuse and PTSD is not whether PTSD is a sequela of child sexual abuse, but how often. There are those who contend that it is universal, or nearly universal, in victimized children and adults (Donaldson & Gardner, 1985; Frederick, 1985; Goodwin, 1990; Herman, 1992; Lindberg & Distad, 1985), whereas others believe it to be one of several possible sequelae (Finkelhor, 1988; Saunders et al., 1992; Stein et al., 1988).

Frederick (1985) diagnosed all of his sample of 300 molested children as having PTSD, as did Lindberg and Distad (1985) in their clinical sample of 17 adult survivors of incest. Donaldson and Gardner (1985) found that 25 out of 26 of their clinical sample of adult survivors met criteria for PTSD. Goodwin (1990) concluded that "the incest victim almost invariably has, at the core of her difficulties, a posttraumatic state" (p. 55). In *Trauma and Recovery* (Herman, 1992), PTSD was the only sequela to child sexual abuse that Herman discussed.

However, a review of recent research suggests that many studies conclude that it is a minority of victims who have PTSD; only a few studies find it to be universal. McLeer, Deblinger, Atkins, Foa, and Ralphe (1988) found PTSD in only 6 of their 29 hospitalized, sexually abused children. This finding was all the more surprising given that 20 of the 29 children were also physically abused. Wolfe et al. (1994) found a somewhat higher rate: Approximately half of their sample of 90 sexually abused children had symptoms of PTSD.

Kilpatrick, Amick-McMullan, Best, Burke, and Saunders (1986) found that PTSD was currently present in 10% of a sample of 126 adult survivors of child sexual abuse and was never present in more than 36%. Likewise, Resnick et al. (1993) found that

12% of their sample of women who had been raped as either a child or an adult met the criteria for PTSD currently, and 32% had met it at some point in their lives.

Norris (1992) reported that 14% of his sample of 44 victims of forcible sexual assault (as child or adult) satisfied the criteria for PTSD. Although this percentage is low overall, this was as high or higher a percentage of PTSD as that found in any other traumatized group in their study. Other traumatized groups included individuals who had experienced a tragic death, physical assault, Hurricane Hugo, a fire, a motor vehicle crash, or combat. It was seven times the number of subjects who had PTSD from combat.

Saunders et al. (1992) found that the rates of PTSD were quite varied for different types of sexual assault. Sixty-four percent of their sample of adults who had been raped prior to age 18 were classified as having PTSD at some point in their lives, compared to 33% who had been molested and 11% who had been the victim of a noncontact offense. Rates for current PTSD were 18%, 9%, and 6%, respectively. A far higher rate was found by Rowan, Foy, Rodriguez, and Ryan (1994), who found PTSD currently in 69% of 47 adult survivors.

Most intriguing, perhaps, was a study by E. Greenwald and Leitenberg (1990), which found that 20% of a sample of 54 nurses who were sexually abused as children currently had PTSD and 41% had had PTSD in the past—if symptom endorsement at the level of "a little bit" was used as criteria. If the cutoff point required subjects to endorse "moderately" for those symptoms to count, the figures dropped dramatically to 4% and 17% respectively, a rate much lower than those typically found in clinical samples. It is to be expected that clinical samples will have a higher incidence of problems because they are composed of people seeking help. However, this study begs the question of whether those studies that simply ask whether the subject has had a symptom in the past may overestimate the incidence of PTSD by including symptoms of low severity.

In summary, PTSD is definitely found in a percentage of adult survivors, but only in a percentage. Although studies vary considerably regarding the precise figure, they seldom find that it is universal. Schetky (1990), in her review of the literature, concluded that approximately half of all adult and child survivors met the criteria for PTSD.

Problems With PTSD as the
Principal Sequela of Child Sexual Abuse

The concept of PTSD as the principal sequela of child sexual abuse has proved attractive to a number of authors (e.g., Goodwin, 1985b; Herman, 1992; van der Kolk, 1987). No doubt, the reasons are both empirical and heuristic. There is a clear, documented association between PTSD and child sexual abuse, one that makes sense theoretically. Child sexual abuse is a form of trauma, and research on the impact of other traumas suggests a generic response to trauma rather than a situation-specific response. On the other hand, the notion that child sexual abuse produces the same type of trauma-based reaction as combat is also useful in counteracting the long-standing tendency of society to deny or minimize the existence and impact of sexual assault.

However, the fortuitous properties of PTSD in relation to child sexual abuse are so attractive that they can mask the fact that PTSD appears to explain only some of the reactions that some of the victims have some of the time. A number of symptoms associated with child sexual abuse cannot be subsumed under the current definition of PTSD. Suicidality, drug addiction, alcoholism, and revictimization, for example, are outside current diagnostic criteria for PTSD but are frequently found to be sequelae of child sexual abuse (Briere & Runtz, 1988b; Finkelhor, 1988). Likewise, the cognitive effects of child sexual abuse—the internalized voice of the offender, the struggle with meaning-making, cognitive distortions, and shattered assumptions—cannot be easily explained by reference to PTSD.

There are other objections as well. Finkelhor (1988) has suggested that PTSD is a frequent sequela to violent, physically dangerous situations, a suggestion backed by research on adult rape victims by Kilpatrick et al. (1989), which found that whether the victim thought she might die in the attack was a significant predictor of PTSD. Child sexual abuse is often not violent, and, in fact, many offenders carefully manipulate the children psychologically in order to minimize resistance. The negative impact in those cases comes from the depth of the betrayal rather than the severity of the violence, and there is little in the literature to suggest that PTSD is a frequent sequela to nonviolent betrayal, however profound.

Implications of PTSD for
Contact With Perpetrators

Incest offenders often push for premature apologies, supervised (or unsupervised) visitation, and movement toward reunification. Emotionally and monetarily dependent spouses may do the same, regardless of the child's degree of PTSD. Judges frequently make decisions on reunification based solely on the willingness and seeming ability of the spouse to prevent future physical attacks, without regard to whether or not the child has PTSD. The inability or professed unwillingness of the offender to attack the child physically is taken as evidence that the child is safe; whether the child feels safe is usually not considered.

Hence there may be considerable pressure for early contact between victim and offender, regardless of the child's state of psychological health. Unfortunately, in the intrusive stage of PTSD, contact with the perpetrator may increase the victim's disorganization. It will inevitably result in an upsurge of anxiety, intrusive thoughts and images, nightmares, dissociative defense mechanisms, and cognitive impairment.

Adult survivors also may be in the intrusive phase of PTSD, sometimes following decades of denial. Families confronted by their adult children, even when such families admit the offense occurred, often pressure the victim to forgive the perpetrator instantly. "It was a long time ago. You've got to go on with your life." "What can he do? He's said he's sorry." "You can't blame everything on what happened to you as a child." "Forgiveness is the Christian way."

One woman confronted her family one afternoon after driving up to their summer home. Her father admitted he did molest her (although he denied having molested cousins who also accused him of it), but by dinner several hours later—it was simply expected that the victim would, of course, stay for dinner—the conversation at the dinner table centered on the leg of lamb. It was generally concluded that it was difficult to get good lamb.

Likewise, one woman summoned her courage to reveal to her family that her uncle raped her when she was 5 years old, strangling her in the process. She struggled not to pass out, convinced that if she did so, she would die. He threatened her with a gun if she told. That summer she received an invitation to a family reunion. The uncle was also invited.

Families and the courts consistently underestimate the impact of contact with the perpetrator on survivors in the intrusive phrase of PTSD. Witness the legal requirement—modified in some instances only for young children—that witnesses testify in the presence of the alleged perpetrator. The notion that face-to-face confrontation between the alleged perpetrator and the alleged victim will assist the court in making a determination of truth is based presumably on the notion that liars will be unable to face the accused and testify convincingly, whereas genuine victims will have no difficulty. Apparently, victims are thought to have no reason to feel shamed, be evasive, or have difficulty looking the perpetrator in the eye. Liars supposedly would be overcome by the perfidy of their ways when faced with the honest countenance of the accused. Clearly, this assumption was set historically long before any serious understanding of the impact of trauma on victims or of the sophistication and psychopathy of lying.

What actually happens in many cases is that the requirement of face-to-face confrontation prevents the victim from telling her story as accurately and coherently as she is able, given that she may be fighting considerable internal disorganization, anxiety, shame, and fear while on the stand. Does this really assist the court and the jury in making a determination of fact, given that the presence of the alleged perpetrator may prevent the victim from providing the very evidence they would need to weigh?

Victims in the intrusive phrase often are at least aware that they are unable to have contact with the perpetrator, given the violent emotional response it occasions. However, in the denial phase of PTSD, the victim may "make nice" and attempt to maintain the same family ties she would have maintained had the incest not occurred. Obviously, this will occur when the victim is in cognitive denial and does not remember the abuse. However, it also occurs when the victim does remember but is in emotional denial.

There is a recent trend for "interactional assessments" of alleged victims and perpetrators. Such assessments bring alleged victim and alleged perpetrator together in the same room. A trained observer supposedly can tell whether or not the child has been abused by noting the interaction between the two. Presumably, fear, anxiety, and distress would all suggest abuse, whereas an absence of negative affect and/or the presence of positive affect toward the offender would argue otherwise. The theory does not take into account the skill of sex offenders in grooming their victims, the capacity for children to attach even to harmful parent-figures, or the tendency of children with PTSD to "make nice" in the avoidant phase.

In the avoidant phase, the victim numbs herself to the point where she is able to tolerate contact with emotionally triggering phenomena. Unfortunately, the contact may feed the emotional numbness because it is unlikely she can let down a defense that is still needed. One might not recommend that most survivors of the Holocaust try to live in the literal shadow of Auschwitz. Simply put, it would seem to be a bad idea. However, such is the invisibility and denial of incest, that survivors with PTSD are routinely asked to visit, stay with, forgive, take care of, and even have dinner with their perpetrators, while all the time appreciating the difficulty in getting good lamb.

Summary

The association of long-term anxiety and depression with child sexual abuse is not a controversial one, although much more has been written documenting the association than addressing the etiology. Although revictimization as an adult no doubt explains some of the sequelae, it appears that child sexual abuse makes an independent contribution in addition to, or in the absence of, adult revictimization.

The depression and anxiety that adult survivors often experience may be (a) derived directly from affective flashbacks, (b) secondary to cognitive distortions, or (c) secondary to current realities. Affective flashbacks may be triggered by either highly specific stimuli, such as an odor similar to the offender's aftershave lotion, or by general phenomena, such as sexual activity, dental work, intimacy, or even men per se. Some survivors experience somatic flashbacks as well. These consist of pain or sensation in specific parts of their bodies when discussing the abuse.

In addition to specific affective symptoms, adult survivors show high rates of PTSD, a disorder characterized by an alternating rhythm of intrusive thoughts, feelings, and/or nightmares interspersed with periods of withdrawal in which triggers to affective flashbacks are successfully avoided or otherwise distanced. Both intrusion and withdrawal are set against a backdrop of a heightened physiological arousal that results in an exaggerated startle reaction and possibly in an increased likelihood of anxiety reactions.

PTSD can be found as a sequela to any powerful, traumatic event, whether natural (floods, fires, earthquakes) or human-made (atomic bombing, experiencing or witnessing violence). But although it is certainly associated with child sexual abuse, there are difficulties in describing it as the only, or even principal, sequela of child sexual abuse. Only some victims have PTSD. Those who do not are sometimes seriously affected by the abuse in other ways. PTSD does not explain the cognitive sequelae to abuse, nor does it currently include suicidality, revictimization, or drug and alcohol addiction.

Survivors with PTSD often find their symptoms exacerbated by contact with the perpetrator. For those in the intrusive phase, the offender is the ultimate trigger for affective flashbacks. Avoidant symptoms are likewise worsened because the survivor must numb herself or dissociate in order to distance emotionally what cannot be distanced physically.

Affective symptoms are at the heart of the aftereffects of child sexual abuse. They constitute the core dysphoria, which changes the way survivors think about the world and that forever after must be managed either by avoidance (through distraction, dissociation, or denial) or medication (through drugs and alcohol, self-mutilation, or even suicidality). To change these affective symptoms, client and therapist must first get to the root of them, whether those roots be affective flashbacks, belief systems, or current realities. Without such differentiation, the therapist is equivalent to the physician who knows the patient has stomach pain, but who does not know whether it is coming from the appendix, the gall bladder, or an ulcer.

6

Sex Offenders in the Head
Effects of Child Sexual Abuse on Victim Thinking

A Trauma-Based Worldview:
Meaning, Malevolence, and Mastery

At 4 years of age, Jonathan and several other children were sexually abused at a day care center by the day care provider's son and by her brother. The first to tell, Jonathan was further victimized when the other parents initially refused to believe him. Instead, they raised $1,500 for the legal expenses of the day care provider—an effort that ended only when their own children disclosed that they had been abused as well. A further trauma for Jonathan was that his younger sister was at the same day care center and he was forced both to watch her be abused and to take part himself.

Jonathan's initial response was to dissociate periodically. Even 3 years later, he was often found at school wandering around in the bathroom dazed. His teachers found it hard to attract and hold his attention. He had difficulty concentrating.

By age 10, the remnants of Jonathan's dissociation were found in his addiction to reading. He read voraciously, even at recess, instead of playing with other children. Furthermore, he read fantasy, a childhood analogue to the adult survivor who dissociates through an addiction to romance novels. Still, he was better off in every way. His previous accidents—climbing on a roof and falling off, accidentally shooting himself with his father's bee sting kit, fooling around with a spray-paint can until it exploded—had stopped. He was less hostile to the sister from whom he had distanced himself after the abuse. He no longer curled up in a fetal position at home when he became angry and upset, and he was no longer as afraid, or so it seemed.

When Jonathan was 10, his family went on an outing to Boston with some friends to see a play. At the end of the play, the theatergoers poured out onto the street, momentarily flooding it. Jonathan and his sister were less than 5 feet away from their parents and the other five adults. By chance, his father noticed a man walking toward them who kept his eyes steadily on Jonathan— something that struck his father as odd. As the man came abreast of Jonathan, he put his hand on the child's shoulder and partially bent down as if to say something. Suddenly, he grabbed Jonathan's arm and began to disappear with him into the crowd. Jonathan's father had started moving when he saw the man's hand on his son's shoulder. Even so, he barely caught Jonathan around the waist before he was pulled away. The man let go.

Sitting in my office, the father had a gray face, and he looked physically ill. "It was so fast," he said repeatedly. "You wouldn't believe how fast it was. The whole thing was just a few seconds. No one saw it. None of the other adults saw it. It was just so fast." And then he added, "I don't know why I'm so upset. After all, nothing happened."

Nothing happened. In the Chowchilla kidnapping case (Terr, 1985a, 1985b, 1990), an entire busload of schoolchildren were kidnapped and held in a buried truck underground. Within 27 hours, the older children had dug a way out and all of the children had returned home physically safe. The town rejoiced and put up a plaque to express their gratitude to God that their children were returned unharmed and that nothing happened.

How, then, does one explain Jonathan, who reported to me that he was not surprised by the kidnapping attempt? He knew bad things would happen to him; there was no such thing as good luck. However, there was such a thing as bad luck. He drew a boy walking under a cloud to show me how he saw himself.

How, then, does one explain the Chowchilla children, who, 5 years later, still believed they would die young, still believed there was a fourth kidnapper out there who was stalking them (there was never any evidence of one), and still believed they were likely to be kidnapped again?

How does one explain my adult client who was physically abused as a child and whose brother committed suicide? A psychic told her after age 52 that things would be golden. She assumed it meant she would die. It did not seem possible to her that the psychic could be saying that things would be "golden" while she was still alive.

The assumption that nothing happened to Jonathan or the Chowchilla children is predicated on a notion that psychological trauma does not occur unless the victim is physically injured. It did not occur to Jonathan's father, a bright and well-educated man, that the meaning of the attempted kidnapping and of the sexual abuse at age 4 would change Jonathan's sense of safety in the world, and therefore his view of it. Perhaps the Chowchilla parents assumed that getting their children back physically safe meant they also got them back psychologically safe.

However, when a child or adult is terrorized, regardless of whether they are harmed physically, something does indeed happen. Psychological trauma can and does occur in the absence of physical injury and brings with it changed notions about the safety, reliability, trustworthiness, and predictability of the world as well as a diminished sense of the efficacy of the self (Briere & Conte, 1993; Famularo, Kinscherff, & Fenton, 1990; Janoff-Bulman, 1992; Johnson & Kenkel, 1991; Mullen, 1993; Roth & Newman, 1993; Spiegel, 1990). Simply put, trauma appears not only to change the way people feel; it changes the way they think as well.

Trauma does not do this by making the person cognitively aware that dire events happen in the world. The average person is all too familiar with the endless wars, diseases, accidents, and losses of all kinds that are a routine part of biological life. On the contrary, the sense of safety that nontraumatized individuals have was never derived from a rational appraisal of the universe in the first place, but was developed inductively instead, through generalizing from early experience with a nurturant caregiver. Nontraumatized individuals feel safe because they were safe, are safe, and thus expect to remain safe. As Milton Erickson points out, the unconscious appears to learn on the basis of experience or allusions to experience, such as metaphor or stories, but not on the basis of a logical or abstract process (Haley, 1985).

Were logic involved, no one would be likely to feel safe: The chances in this culture of being exposed to trauma appear considerable. Norris (1992) found that over the course of a lifetime, the probabilities were high of being victimized by fire (11%), by robbery (25%), by a car wreck sufficient to injure someone (23%), and by having a loved one die from suicide, homicide, or accident (30%). Overall, the chances of suffering some sort of trauma were 69%, a figure that has been corroborated by other studies of lifetime trauma (Kilpatrick, Saunders, Best, Von, & Veronen, 1987; Resnick et al., 1993). Resnick et al. (1993) found the lifetime probability of trauma to be 69%, whereas Kilpatrick et al. (1987) found exposure to crime-related trauma to be 75%.

Despite the fact that, in actuality, the world is dangerous and dicey, nonvictimized individuals appear to have an unrealistically optimistic view of the world (Taylor, 1989; Tiger, 1979). Those who have not been traumatized describe far more positive than negative life experiences (Matlin & Stang, 1978), believe they are above average (Greenwald, 1980; Taylor, 1989; Taylor & Brown, 1988), think things will work out well (Janoff-Bulman, 1992), overestimate the amount of control they have over events (Langer, 1975; Wortman, 1975), and, finally, underestimate the prevalence of negative events and overestimate the probability of positive events (Janoff-Bulman & Frieze, 1983; Janoff-Bulman, Madden, & Timki, 1983; Perloff, 1983; Taylor, 1989).

New Age culture (e.g., Redfield, 1993), with its emphasis on the meaningfulness of coincidences, on individual choice in regard to seemingly random events, and on everything happening for a reason, appears to be old age after all. The need to feel safe in the world remains constant from generation to generation; only the packaging differs.

However, for trauma victims, even years after the trauma, the "Pollyanna Principle" (Matlin & Stang, 1978) has been shattered. Famularo et al. (1990) found that subjects with chronic (as opposed to acute) posttraumatic stress disorder (PTSD) believed that life would be difficult, hard, and short. In a series of studies, Janoff-Bulman and colleagues have repeatedly demonstrated that victimized and nonvictimized groups differ in fundamental assumptions about the nature of the world—particularly about whether the world is benevolent and meaningful, and whether the self has efficacy (Janoff-Bulman, 1992). Other authors (e.g., Horowitz, 1976; McCann & Pearlman, 1990) have catalogued the disparities slightly differently, but have agreed that cognitive schemas can be changed by traumatic victimization.

This chapter will describe cognitive sequelae of child sexual abuse, including the development of a trauma-based worldview and its component beliefs about meaning, mastery, and malevolence. In addition, I will explore process and content thinking errors characteristic of survivors and compare them with thinking errors of offenders.

Meaning

Joan Didion (1979) caught the bewilderment of the trauma survivor when she wrote:

> We tell ourselves stories in order to live. . . . Or at least we do for a while. I am talking here about a time when I began to doubt the premises of all the stories I had ever told myself, a common condition but one I found troubling. . . . I was supposed to have a script, and had mislaid it. I was supposed to hear cues, and no longer did. I was meant to know the plot, but all I knew was what I saw: flash pictures in variable sequence, images with no "meaning" beyond their temporary arrangement, not a movie but a cutting-room experience. (pp. 11-13)

The notion that life is orderly and meaningful appears fundamental to most people's sense of the world. Stories have points; fables have morals. No less a thinker than Einstein foundered on his refusal to accept random theory in physics. "God does not play dice with the universe," he said, and, driven by the need to find order and meaning in his later years, drove full speed down a scientific blind alley.

Lerner (1980) termed this need to find order the "just world theory," that is, the widespread belief that people get what they deserve. His research has demonstrated repeatedly that what happens to people dictates how other people feel about them. People who have negative outcomes are devalued, even if the outcomes are randomly assigned and subjects know that they are. The devaluing appears to be automatic and unconscious rather than rational and planned.

Of course, I assumed I was immune to such blaming of the victim. After all, I had a name for it, could recognize it, and understood its purpose. But a few months ago, I read in the local newspaper of the resolution of an unsolved murder that had occurred in the area several years ago. A businessman in a local town had answered the door one night only to be killed by a shotgun blast. Only recently did a neighbor of the man confess that he committed the murder after brooding for years over some minor disagreement. It was a totally irrational murder of a completely innocent victim. With a jolt, I realized that I had read the original report of the murder years back and had simply assumed that the businessman, with no history of wrongdoing, had been secretly involved with drug trafficking.

That tendency to blame the victim may be irrational, and is hardly laudatory, but it seems fundamental to a sense of safety. Without it, all individual effort is called into question. As Lerner and Miller (1978) note, "Without such a belief it would be difficult for the individual to commit himself to the pursuit of long-range goals or even to the socially regulated behavior of day-to-day life" (p. 1030).

Major trauma of any sort can shatter this matrix of meaning, order, and predictability. Although meaning in particular seems to be a casualty of natural disasters, the sense of meaning can be destroyed by human-generated trauma as well. Lifton (1963), for example, described the disbelief of the survivors of Hiroshima that such a disaster could occur. For them, there was a "vast break-

down of faith in the larger human matrix supporting each individual's
life, and therefore a loss of faith or trust in the structure of existence"
(p. 487).

The search for meaning can be lifelong. Silver, Boon, and
Stones (1983), in a sample of 77 women who were incest victims
an average of 20 years ago, found that 80% were still searching for
some way to make sense of the experience. More than 50% felt
that they could make no sense of it at all, and said things such as,
"I always ask myself why, over and over, but there is no answer"
(p. 89).

Those who could not make sense of it fared worse than those
who could; however, the type of meaning (e.g., blaming the self
vs. blaming the perpetrator) did not correlate with outcome. The
inability to make meaning was associated with the severity of intrusive, recurrent, and disruptive ruminations, with level of distress, with worse social adjustment, lower levels of self-esteem,
and less resolution.

However, contrary evidence does exist. Morrow (1991) found
the opposite, that an inability to make sense of incest did not correlate with outcome, whereas who got blamed did. Intriguingly,
the major difference in the samples was age. The Morrow study
was of adolescents, whereas respondents in the Silver et al. (1983)
study ranged from 18 to 72. In the latter study, the incest had occurred an average of 20 years previously. It may be that the need
for meaning-making only increases with age.

Malevolence Versus
Randomness Versus Benevolence

In Colorado, at the entrance of the Rocky Mountain National
Park, there is a sign that says, "The mountains don't care." Apparently, the National Park Service has noted the tendency of hikers
to believe in the benevolence of nature, and found that such a
belief was not conducive to hiker longevity.

It is quite striking that part of the Pollyanna tendency of the
nontraumatized seems to be to romanticize nature, given that it
is, in fact, the most ruthless of arenas and one in which might
inevitably makes right:

> There is not a people in the world who behaves as badly as prey-
> ing mantises. But wait, you say, there is no right and wrong in
> nature; right and wrong is a human concept. . . . The universe
> that suckled us is a monster that does not care if we live or die—
> does not care if it itself grinds to a halt. It is fixed and blind, a
> robot programmed to kill. (Dillard, 1974, p. 180)

Dillard (1974) surmises, "Cock Robin may die the most grue-
some of slow deaths, and nature is no less pleased; the sun comes
up, the creek rolls on, the survivors still sing" (pp. 179-180).

For the trauma victim, the natural, if irrational, tendency to
see benevolence in the world may be lost, and survivors may go
beyond appreciating randomness and accepting indifference to
expecting malevolence. For sexual abuse survivors, the sense of
malevolence is often focused on people rather than nature. "What's
he doing to that little girl?" Sarah found herself asking every time
she saw an adult male with a 5-year-old girl. At the time, she had
no memories of sexual abuse and came into treatment partly because it seemed like such a strange thing to be thinking.

However, the distrust is not always related to people. Survivors frequently have a vague feeling that the universe has singled
them out and that they are doomed. Athena was physically
abused, burned, humiliated, ridiculed, and sexually abused as a
child. All her adult life, she carried with her a sense of doom. She
did not expect people to be kind; she did not fantasize about the
lottery; she did not think that the safe would fall on someone else.
She did not truly believe that the world was random. She thought
she was somehow selected for ill treatment and that all of her en-
deavors would inevitably end poorly.

Likewise, after a series of traumatic accidents and illnesses as
a child, Tim decided that it was going to be "one thing after another." He spent his time trying to imagine the age at which his
luck would run out completely and he would die; he thought it
would surely be in adolescence. As an adult, a single negative
event could cause a powerful affective flashback to that sense of
doom that could last for weeks.

The loss of the sense of benevolence in the world means that
the trauma victim no longer feels as though someone is protecting

her from harm. What happens to her does not seem to really matter very much at all in the larger scheme of things. The sense that one is looked after, watched over, and cared for by some larger force—the legacy of good, early nurturing—is lost. "Why angels turn their backs on some," Bonnie Raitt sings, "is a mystery to me."[1] At one level of trauma, the victim rails against the negligent angels; at another, she decides there are no angels to rail against. The internalized "good parent" often projected into the sky as God or onto nature as a benevolent spirit shatters, and in its place is only a sense of being very small and very lost.

This sense of the world's indifference, even malevolence, that sexually traumatized individuals have is often not a functional and discriminating sense of wariness or caution that protects them from exploitation. On the contrary, it may make them feel needy and desperate, and thus implicate them in inappropriate relationship choices. Abandonment by the fates and by God makes it all the more difficult to tolerate being alone. The consequent clinging and dependency may mean that survivors end up in relationships with partners who seek enmeshment rather than intimacy. Ironically, universal distrust often seems incompatible with the type of discriminating distrust that is truly protective. If one is caught out on the ice and thinks all ice is thin, one is likely to step out blindly.

Mastery

In the face of meaninglessness and malevolence, mastery does not exist. As Spiegel (1990) notes:

> Trauma can be understood as the experience of being made into an object: the victim of someone else's rage, of nature's indifference, or of one's own physical or psychological limitations. Along with the pain and fear associated with rape, combat trauma, or natural disaster comes a marginally bearable sense of helplessness, a realization that one's own will and wishes become irrelevant to the course of events, leaving either a view of the self that is damaged; contaminated by the humiliation, pain, and fear that the event imposed; or a fragmented sense of self. (p. 251)

The ability to protect oneself is fundamental to a sense of efficacy, and efficacy seems fundamental to a sense of self. The failure of the outside world, of God or the fates, to protect the individual puts a much higher onus on her to protect herself. Those who feel that the universe is benign, that things work out in the end, and that they have a guardian angel puzzle at the hypervigilance of the adult survivor.

By contrast, the adult survivor is engaged in an endless search for safety; and safety, like the desert mirage, seems to lie in all kinds of places that it does not. Fearful of helplessness and scornful of chance, the survivor believes in neither the goodwill of the fates nor the kindness of strangers. As a result, she controls far too much, far too often. Spouses grow angry; children pull away. Letting go—the Zen antidote for anxiety and practically an AA mantra—is not a state she knows anything about. She feels like a zebra being asked to lie down in the sun and nap when there are lions in the neighborhood.

There are schools of thought that claim that "all victims are offenders and all offenders are victims," and point to the controlling and sometimes angry behavior of the adult survivor as examples of predation. But the surface equation fails because the core dynamics behind the adult survivor's angry outbursts are not predatory or addictive at all: They are simply a hunger for safety and a desperate search for ways to medicate pain. "Probably the greatest lesson I have learned from abused children and adults," Gil (1991) wrote, "is that everything they do after they have been abused is designed to keep themselves feeling safe" (p. 59).

Where there should be an internalized benevolent parent—the model for human projections of God—there is, instead, the internalized offender, with his harsh, blaming, judgmental, and occasionally sadistic attacks. Incapable of self-soothing, the victim turns to distraction instead, and works, drinks, drugs, sexualizes, clings, rails, or simply makes endless lists in her too busy life. "What's the worst thing about dealing with your daughter?" I asked a survivor whose acting-out daughter was wreaking havoc in the family. "You're going to think I'm awful," she said. "She messes up my schedule," and then she burst into tears.

The helplessness and lack of a sense of efficacy that lies at the heart of controlling behavior comes not only from the onslaught of the outside world, but also from the survivor's experience of being overwhelmed by her own affect as well. Images, memories, dreams, intrusive thoughts, affective flashbacks, somatic flashbacks, full flashbacks—she is in as much danger internally as externally, and equally at sea. The truth is, she cannot control her own feelings any more than she can control the world around her.

In her attempts to restore a sense of control to her life, she is likely to blame herself for her troubles, an easy solution given that she has in all likelihood internalized the offender's pattern of blaming her. Self-blame, however, is doubly determined. It functions both as an internalization of the offender, and as a hat to hang her hopes of future control. If she caused the abuse last time, perhaps she can keep it from happening next time.

For years, I was puzzled as to why some rape victims clung so tenaciously to the notion that the rape was their fault for walking down the wrong street, for wearing a skirt above their knees, for being out at night. But what would any of us want to believe? That we could wear longer skirts, pick different streets, and stay in at night, thereby guaranteeing that we would never be attacked again, or that it could happen any time, day or night, no matter what we wore or where we walked?

It is not surprising, then, to learn that those who, despite following careful rules for staying safe, were raped anyway, were the most likely to experience chronic fear afterwards (Scheppele & Bart, 1983). After all, what could keep one safe after that?

Blaming the self for certain behaviors (behavioral self-blame) has been found in several research studies to be effective in restoring a sense of control (e.g., Janoff-Bulman, 1979; Wortman, 1976). Because suspect behaviors, such as wearing a short skirt, can be changed, the victim believes that she can prevent attack in the future. Taking action to make specific changes—for example, changing one's residence or phone number following a rape (Burgess & Holmstrom, 1979) or taking self-defense courses (Kidder, Boell, & Moyer, 1983)—have been associated with better recovery from trauma.

By contrast, blaming the abuse on who one is (characterlogical self-blame) is not associated with effective coping. The victim who believes that "I'm a bad person, that's why my father did those things to me" simply gets more depressed (Janoff-Bulman, 1979; Peterson, Schwartz, & Seligman, 1981).

The survivor's experience of being unable to protect herself from trauma is analogous to her experience of the meaninglessness of the world at large. Her own behaviors were meaningless —ineffectual and irrelevant—in the face of the attack. It is easier to believe that she did it wrong than that what she did did not matter at all. There is a world of difference between having a negative effect and having none, whereas psychologically, positive and negative impacts both at least make the self feel that one's efforts counted. Both of the latter involve some degree of power, and both suggest mattering. To have no impact at all on events is to feel more than helpless; it is to feel less than human. Small wonder that the adult survivor often blames herself for the abuse; she is assigning herself a position of power.

Conclusions Regarding a
Trauma-Based Worldview

Which view—the "Pollyanna Principle" of those never victimized or the trauma-based worldview of the survivor—one takes as reality and which as distortion depends, no doubt, on the role of trauma in one's own personal life. However, both sides would agree that it is better to have hope than not, and what the traumatized person loses most of all is a sense of hopefulness. The greatest of the defenses, its loss—a bitter one—leaves the survivor living in a universe that feels malevolent at worst, random at best, and over which she has no control in either case.

In Toni Morrison's *Beloved*, Sethe, traumatized by slavery, wakes up in the morning and thinks of her daughter's use of the word, "plans." She herself had only made one set of plans in her life—to run away from slavery—and they "went awry so completely she never dared life by making more. . . . Would it be all right?" she wonders. "Would it be all right to go ahead and feel? Go ahead and *count on something?*" (Morrison, 1987, p. 38).

The trauma victim's view of the world as a "monstrous world running on chance and death, careening blindly from nowhere to nowhere" (Dillard, 1974, p. 180) is not a world in which she is likely to feel safe enough to count on something, certainly not a world in which she can feel "precious." And feeling precious is the antidote to despair.

Cognitive Distortions

There are two types of cognitive distortions: process and content. Adult survivors, most likely through the mechanism of internalizing the sex offender's distortions, make both types of errors. Whereas the content distortions appear to be similar to those made by the offender, process distortions tend to be the opposite, fitting together with the offender's distortions, black against white, much like an Escher print.

Content Thinking Errors

In terms of content errors, both perpetrator and victim may agree on a series of propositions to which an objective observer might vehemently disagree. However, both predator and prey are likely to believe the following:

- The abuse was the child's fault because of her behavior (an analogue to behavioral self-blame), because of who she was (characterological self-blame), or even because of her category (i.e., girls and women "drive men wild").
- If the child's body responded physically to the offender's manipulations, it means the child wanted to have sex with him and thus was responsible for the abuse happening in the first place.
- It was the child's responsibility to stop the offender from abusing him.
- If the child responded to the abuse by "freezing" rather than actively fighting off the offender, it means he wanted the offender to molest him.
- The offender could not control his behavior.

- The abuse was the fault of the perpetrator's wife for not having more or better sex with her husband.
- The abuse was not the offender's fault because he was under stress, sick, or had a problem.
- The offender never meant to hurt his victim.
- In the case of incest, it was the daughter's responsibility to take care of her father sexually and emotionally.
- The victim is overreacting to the abuse.
- The victim needs to just forget about the abuse and get on with his life.
- The victim should forgive the offender, and it is his failure if he cannot.

Such thinking errors, although deeply entrenched, may not lie close to the surface and thus may be difficult to expose. Logically, many adult survivors would not agree with any of these propositions, especially for other children. But the "head vote" and the "heart vote" may differ on these issues, and clues to the client's deeper belief system may appear in her affect. A client's inability to get angry at the perpetrator, for example, may relate to other issues: difficulties with anger in general or fear of retaliation. On the other hand, it may also relate to a perpetrator's thinking error that the abuse really was not his responsibility. He was ill. His wife denied him sexually. The victim was much too seductive as a child.

Likewise, the survivor's difficulty in talking about the abuse could relate, for example, to affective flashbacks. Then again, it could be due to a cognitive distortion associated with guilt over not having stopped the abuse. His impatience with his own process often relates to his belief that he should be totally over this by now. After all, it was decades ago.

Process Thinking Errors

Process or automatic thinking errors (Yochelson & Samenow, 1976) are likewise usually out of the client's awareness. Their most striking feature is not how similar they are to the offender's process thinking errors but rather how diametrically opposite.

Grandiosity Versus Self-Effacement

Sex offenders, like criminals in general, are often privately grandiose and narcissistic. They consider themselves unique, above both the law and conventional morality. Rules were made for others; for them, their own needs or desires have the force of moral law. They suffer narcissistic injury when thwarted or held responsible for their behavior.

There is not a term for the complementary process in victims, but every clinician would recognize it. It is a diminishing of self, a withdrawal of one's needs or wishes from consideration. Self-effacement perhaps comes the closest, but fails to capture the implosive quality. Although offenders appear to see no needs but their own, victims fail to see their own at all. Offenders minimize their acts; victims minimize themselves. When the same abuse inflicted on them is described as happening to someone else, they are outraged for those others, but never for themselves.

I Can't Versus I Should Have

Sex offenders automatically say "I can't" to anything that is uncomfortable. They "can't" control their behavior, get to group on time, do their homework, stop frequenting arcades, withdraw from the church youth group, tell their spouses about their molestations, or articulate why not. "I can't" is "I won't" in costume.

The adult survivor, by contrast, is obsessed with "I should have." They "should have" known the nice teacher was a child molester, stopped the abuse from happening, stopped their parents from drinking, prevented the siblings from getting abused, forgiven everybody, and gotten over all of it by now. Whereas the offender takes no responsibility for things for which he is responsible, the adult survivor takes responsibility for things for which she is not responsible and could not control in any case.

Victim Stancing Versus Victim Blaming

Offenders are prone to "pity parties" in which they attempt to manipulate other people into feeling sorry for them. Incest offenders, particularly, seem to use this in their grooming of children, and children are often persuaded that they need to "take care" of Dad, who is suffering so much. Such carefully groomed children are often angry at their mothers for supposedly not meeting the fathers' sexual or emotional needs. "Pity parties" also protect offenders from disclosure. How could a child tell on someone for whom he feels so sorry? He would surely not want the offender to go to jail. Likewise, victim stancing often prevents others who may find out about the abuse from going to the police, and it helps the offender persuade people that he does not really have a problem. He was just under so much stress at the time.

Adult survivors, by contrast, often "victim blame" rather than "victim stance." They seem to have little empathy for themselves but much sympathy for the perpetrator. They have internalized the offenders' view of themselves, which is frequently a critical, judgmental view. The negative self-images may be encapsulated to their alleged sexual "provocativeness," or may extend to their sense of self in general.

The difference between a "pity party" and genuinely dysphoric affect is that plays for sympathy in the former are often a way of passing negative affect along rather than feeling it. The clinician listening to an offender victim stance often will be puzzled by the fact that the offender does not seem to actually feel all that bad, but is attempting to make someone else feel bad about him and for him instead. By contrast, victims often respond to their genuinely dysphoric affect by obsessing about whether they are just trying to get people to feel sorry for them. Ironically, offenders who victim stance never seem to question themselves.

Superoptimism Versus Trauma-Based Worldview

Like criminals in general, sex offenders appear to underestimate the chances of getting caught. One criminal told me how he carefully obtained a second license plate prior to committing a burglary so that he could switch plates a block away. Although the plate was in the car, at the designated block he said "to hell with it," told himself it was ridiculous to change plates because there was no way he could get caught, and drove off. Someone saw his car at the scene and his failure to change the plates was in fact the mistake that caught him.

Likewise, sex offenders are often quite bold about their activities, so bold that victims are frequently not believed when they disclose. It is not unusual for a sex offender to molest a child with others in the next room. It is not that unusual for them to molest a child with the door between the two rooms open. One offender met another couple at a motel for weekly card-playing sessions while the children from both families slept in another room with the door open. He frequently got up to "check on" the children, and, with the door open, molested them while their parents sat in the next room. Another offender reported that it increased his sense of excitement to know that his wife was just in the next room and could walk in any moment while he was molesting his daughter.

It is not unheard of for offenders to molest a child while the unknowing spouse is in the same bed. Victims have reported the offender quietly playing with their genitals while their mother lay on the other side of him. Offenders routinely get up in the night on the pretense of going to the bathroom and go instead into a child's bedroom. One minister was watching a football game with his best friend, another minister. He left to go to the bathroom, walked instead into the friend's 15-year-old daughter's room, and fondled her genitals while masturbating to ejaculation. The sleepy and confused teenager's report was later corroborated by the offender's confession.

Unfortunately, the optimism of offenders is often well-justified. The spouse or friends are usually the first on the stand to testify that the incidents in question could not have happened because the spouse or friends were in the next or same room or bed.

Adult survivors, on the other hand, often have a trauma-based worldview in which they expect bad things, not good things, to happen to them. Nothing ever seems like a sure thing. Instead of gaining confidence when things are going well, many are superstitiously afraid to enjoy anything for fear of offending the gods. They grow nervous waiting for the inevitable catastrophe. They have a profound pessimism about getting caught for things they did not do.

Failing to Consider Others
Versus Failing to Consider Self

Sex offenders rarely take the point of view of others, particularly of their victims. The following conversation was with a man who molested his daughter for 5 years:

Interviewer: *You tell me how much you love your daughter and yet you did something deliberately that injured her severely. How do you think she felt about being molested?*

Offender: *I don't know. I really don't know.*

Interviewer: *What do you mean you don't know?*

Offender: *It never crossed my mind. It never crossed my mind. I never thought about it once in all those years.*

As described previously, many offenders simply project their own desires onto the victim and fail to appreciate his point of view entirely.

The victim, however, appreciates the offender's point of view but assigns little importance to his own. He sees his energy, his time, and his effort as expendable and does not factor them in when counting cost. He will absorb considerable injury to the self to save minor injury to others. "I can't refuse to go to the family picnic," he will say, even though the uncle who raped him while strangling him as a 5-year-old will be there. "It would upset everyone." Instead, he will believe he can tolerate the affective flashbacks, intrusive memories, and nightmares that will likely follow. A victim who is seriously suicidal may refuse to cancel a dinner party for fear of inconveniencing her guests.

Externalizing Versus Internalizing

In short, the adult survivor internalizes blame. He often takes responsibility for what he did, what he did not do, what he did not know to do, and what he could not do. Offenders, by contrast, often simply evade, deny, and ignore responsibility, rationalizing their own behavior while implicitly or explicitly blaming others for any problems.

Conclusions

Sexual assault affects victim thinking as well as feeling and may alter the most basic notions about the nature of the world. Assumptions about the meaningfulness and benevolence of the world as well as the survivor's degree of personal efficacy in it may be changed.

In addition, the duet of predator and prey is marked by interlocking thinking errors. In the private reality that offenders project onto victims, there is agreement on the two sides on certain propositions about the responsibility for the abuse. However, the resonance between perpetrator and victim goes beyond specific beliefs and extends to patterns of belief or "process" thinking errors. Although still fitting together like puzzle pieces, process errors are complementary rather than identical. Offenders victim stance; victims victim blame. Offenders are grandiose; victims have a diminished sense of self. Offenders center their thoughts and behaviors around their own needs exclusively; victims center their thoughts and feelings around those of others. Sex offenders deny and evade responsibility; victims assume far too much. Sadly, offenders are often optimistic about the future, whereas victims are all too often full of dread.

Note

1. "All At Once," by Bonnie Raitt. © 1991 Kokomo Music. INTERNATIONAL COPYRIGHT SECURED. ALL RIGHTS RESERVED.

7

Managing Chronic Pain

Every form of refuge has its price.
"Lyin' Eyes," by Don Henley and Glenn Frey[1]

W hether the episodic attack of the affective flashback or the seamless dysphoria of prolonged anxiety and depression, chronic pain—and ways to avoid it, manage it, minimize it, or medicate it—is often central for the adult survivor. For some, dealing with pain has become so habitual that they no longer know, if they ever did, what they are avoiding or even that they are. Survivors may interweave denial, distraction, dissociation, relationship addiction, drugs, alcohol, self-mutilation, and suicidality so artfully and automatically that they could not name any of these coping strategies, only the intolerable affective state that surfaces if the interweaving stops. Often misidentified as "the problem," such strategies are, in fact, homegrown solutions to the real problem: intractable chronic pain, often set against a backdrop of a trauma-based worldview that precludes hope. Usually discussed as sequelae to abuse, rather than homegrown solutions, methods of avoiding and managing pain are, by whatever name, well-documented in the research literature.

Figure 7.1. Continuum of Denial in Victims

Avoidant Techniques

Denial

Every trauma victim wishes she could erase the disfiguring event; some can, though ironically, not the ones who wish they could. The very wish that it could be otherwise demonstrates these victims' inability to avoid awareness. Those who do erase do so when caught in a situation that cannot be tolerated or escaped. For some, the mind dissociates at the time; for others, it distances afterwards. Decades later, the memories may burst through consciousness; they have been time bombs ticking through the intervening years.

Denial exists on a continuum. If the event is known, it can still be redefined—rationalized or minimized in some important way. If the event is known and accepted as abuse, the mind can still minimize its impact, deciding that it was, after all, a small and unimportant event, one of little consequence. "Denial ain't just a river in Egypt," a greeting card declares, and indeed, this strategy has more subtlety, presents more variety, and deserves more respect than is commonly accorded. Figure 7.1 lists the spectrum of denial to which sexual abuse survivors subscribe.

Amnesia: Denial That Abuse Happened

Hotly debated in the legal arena and the media, the issue of the loss and subsequent recovery of traumatic memories has polarized the field. However, it is difficult to see how extreme positions on either side can be defended. The work of Loftus, Ceci, and others does demonstrate that misinformation can distort memory, although these findings are consistently strongest when unimportant details are changed (Ceci & Bruck, 1993; Ceci, Toglia, & Ross, 1987; Loftus, 1993; Loftus & Davies, 1984). Suggestion can not only distort real memories, but it can quite possibly create wholly false memories. Loftus, for example, has found that she was able to implant in adults a new and totally false memory of being lost as young children in a shopping mall (Loftus, 1993). However, she was able to do so by using the subject's family members, who claimed to be actual participants in the event. The typical "suggested abuse" scenario is quite different. Family members typically can apply far more pressure than can the most trusted therapist, and, in abuse cases, the pressure of family members is against the revelation of abuse, not for it.

However, even assuming that false memories can be suggested by others, it is nevertheless an illogical leap to say that because some recovered memories are false, that all are false. Some ordinary memories are false. It does not mean they are all false. It is equivalent to saying that because cancer is sometimes misdiagnosed, it does not exist. In fact, there is considerable evidence that some adults, either through repression or dissociation, do not remember early traumas for years, sometimes even for decades, only to have them surface eventually. Briere and Conte (1993), for example, found that 59% of their sample of 450 sexual abuse victims had amnesia for the abuse at some time in their history, whereas Herman and Schatzow (1987) found 64%. Twenty-eight percent of Herman and Schatzow's sample were described as having severe deficits of memory. The Briere and Conte study is open to the criticism that there is no independent validation of the abuse. Some might argue, then, that the alleged victims did not recover memories; they invented them. Herman and Schatzow (1987), however, found that the majority of victims in their sample of 53 who looked for verification of memories found it in some manner. Likewise, Feldman-Summers and Pope (1994) found that 41% of their sample of psychologists who remembered sexual or nonsexual abuse as a child had had a period of no recall. Of those who had such a period, 47% were able to find some sort of corroboration of the abuse.

However, the strongest evidence of the validity of some recovered memories was found in a study by Linda Williams (Williams, 1992, 1993, in press-a, in press-b) in which she researched hospital emergency room records of 129 children examined because they or their families had reported sexual abuse. Thirty-eight of the subjects interviewed 17 years later did not report the abuse when queried. Specifics of the interviews suggested that the majority of women did not remember the abuse. One told the tale of her abuse—a striking tale involving the murder of the alleged perpetrator by another victim's mother—but reported it as happening to someone else in her family before she was born (Williams, in press-a). Sixteen percent of the subjects who remembered the abuse did report the abuse but mentioned that they had recovered their memories. In total, 47% of the total sample had some period in which they did not remember the sexual abuse (Berliner & Williams, 1994).

Likewise, Lenore Terr (1994) writes in *Unchained Memories* of a number of abuse victims whose recovered memories in adulthood were corroborated by others. Marilyn Van Derbur, Miss America of 1958, may have only recovered her memories of abuse by her father when she was 24, but her sister Gwen had never lost hers. A scientist Terr calls Gary Barker recovered memories as an adult of his mother strangling and sexually attacking him, and torturing him with electricity. His brother had never lost the memory of the electricity torture.

Eileen Franklin Lipsker recovered memories not only of her father molesting her, but of his raping and then killing her 8-year-old friend. Although no physical evidence was ever unearthed that linked George Franklin, Sr. to the murder, he himself provided corroboration of a sort when he was first interrogated by the police. His first question was, "Have you talked to my daughter?" And although the jury was never allowed to know it, his apartment was "filled to the brim" (Terr, 1994, p. 24) with child pornography, books on incest, and, of most concern, child-size dildos.

For some, then, the abuse is set aside and cognitively negated. If the abuse did not occur, the child, and later the adult, can at least escape some of the very difficult affect that may accompany memory. When Gary Barker's memories of his mother's sadistic sexual assaults returned, they were so devastating that he passed out.

Remembers but Does Not Admit Abuse

Of course it is possible to know that abuse occurred but refuse to admit it, thus withholding it from a shared consensual reality and denying oneself the confirmation of that joint reality. The survivor simply does not allow the abuse to be part of her "day child" (Terr, 1994), the part of her that operates in the real world. Although she may feel that this protects her from shame, in reality, it blocks her from finding solace and isolates her with memories that she cannot integrate into her social reality. Reality is indeed a consensual experience, and the failure to share a private reality with anyone affords it only a half-reality in the mind of the survivor.

The half-reality of the unspoken and the unheard can be seen most dramatically in sex offenders. Many will deny culpability in circumstances in which there is enough evidence to convict beyond a reasonable doubt. In such situations, denial is sometimes diametrically opposed to their best interests. Denial (postconviction), for example, may prevent them from gaining entrance to outpatient treatment programs and probation, and they may be sentenced to prison instead.

The naive observer often assumes that such intransigence could only be a sign of innocence, but experience with offenders who later admit suggests convincingly that it is not. "It isn't so," the offender appears to think, "unless I say it's so." "They can't really know I did it." It is not real, somehow, unless he makes it part of his shared social reality. Reality is not what happened, from the offender's perspective, but what people think happened, and he will play to the audience for his version to become the generally accepted truth.

Observers often underestimate what offenders gain and what victims lose when the offender refuses to admit. The fact that many offenders will choose incarceration over admission is a clue to the importance of what they gain. Reality may not be the product of the most august imagination, as Wallace Stevens thought

(Stevens, 1969), or even of the most accurate; in some sense, it is the product of consensus instead.

The combination of amnesia and denial of abuse in victims has implications for the accuracy of report rates of sexual abuse. Lawson and Chaffin (1992), for instance, found that only 43% of prepubertal children with sexually transmitted diseases admitted any sexual contact. It is not clear in the study whether this is due to a refusal to admit the abuse or to forgetting it. No doubt for a combination of reasons, rates of disclosure overall tend to be low (Salter, 1988; Sauzier, 1989; Sorensen & Snow, 1991).

Denies It Was Abuse

Remembering the event and admitting so does not mean that the victim is out of denial. It is possible to relabel the event as an accident, as an understandable reaction to stress, or as someone else's fault other than the perpetrator's. The survivor may believe that the event was inappropriate, but not necessarily abusive. In short, victims frequently reframe, rationalize, or minimize sexual abuse. This tendency is so pronounced that it affects how sexual assault questionnaires must be worded to obtain an accurate picture. Koss, Gidycz, and Wisniewski (1987) note that only 27% of those college women who had had an experience that met the legal definition of rape were willing to call it "rape."

Nor is this phenomenon restricted to sexual assault. DiTomasso and Routh (1993) determined that 21% of their sample had been physically abused according to specific questionnaire items they endorsed, whereas only 1.5% would label their experiences as physical abuse.

The issue is a bigger one than that of underreporting. A key question for a victim is whether or not she sees the perpetrator as a sex offender. If she considers the abuse sufficiently "understandable," based on her own "seductiveness," on her mother's lack of availability, or on her father's stress level, she will not see him that way. It is a numbingly familiar scenario for clinicians to be confronted with a distraught mother who is devastated by the fact that the father/brother/mother/uncle who abused her has now abused the grandchild entrusted to him or her.

Although some will see malice in the mother allowing an offender to have access to her child, more often, in my experience, it is the product of this type of denial. The mother may have remembered her own abuse, but she never accepted it as abuse and never accepted the fact that her perpetrator was actually a sex offender. She saw the behavior as idiosyncratic and atypical—no doubt the product of something that she did to provoke it—and denied its meaning and implications.

Denial of Impact

Survivors sometimes deny that the abuse was affectively charged or had any particular impact on them. Goodwin (1985b) notes that the use of dissociation, repression, and other defenses makes this a frequent finding in posttraumatic stress disorders. Survivors either attribute this lack of importance to the inherent insignificance of the abuse itself, to their indifference to pain, or simply to the passage of time. At times, their own sense of helplessness will lead to denial of impact. "There's nothing you can do about it. You just have to forget about it."

Denial of impact is akin to the psychoanalytic defense of isolation of affect, a division between cognition and affect that allows individuals to discuss extremely painful events without emotion. It is associated with intellectualization, a cognitive discussion of issues without accompanying emotional processing. Trepper and Barrett (1989) discuss the same phenomenon in offenders. In all likelihood, it was internalization of the offender's thinking errors that caused the survivor to minimize the seriousness of the abuse in the first place.

It is striking to see survivors minimize the impact of sexual abuse on their lives even while having symptoms such as sexual dysfunction, intimacy allergy, drug and alcohol addiction, posttraumatic cycles of avoidance and intrusion, and lifestyle constriction. All of these symptoms seem significant to the observer, and all of them can be traced to the original abuse. Denial of impact turns out not to affect impact at all, merely the awareness of impact.

What purpose, one may ask, does denial of impact serve if it neither protects the individual from awareness of abuse or, in reality, mitigates its impact? For some, denial of impact is denial of vulnerability and of helplessness, both of which may produce exorbitant anxiety in the survivor. Knowledge of impact, of the seriousness of abuse, of the rippling circles of sequelae—all speak to an inability to protect the self and to helplessness in the hands of the offender. "Sticks and stones may break my bones," the survivor seems to be saying, "but abuse will never hurt me." It is, perhaps, the same impulse that causes a physically abused child to say, "You might as well stop hitting me, Dad. It doesn't hurt anymore." The victim is locked in a power struggle with the offender, stretched thin through the decades but never broken; by denying the importance of the offender, she is cutting him down to size.

As such, it may be useful at the time, as all such coping mechanisms are, but as a long-term strategy it wants for much. For what begins as disempowering the offender ends by disempowering the self. The survivor who does not take the impact of abuse seriously does not take her own pain and suffering seriously. To maintain the offender's lack of efficacy, she must turn on the self, branding her own fears and anxieties as "stupid" and "unjustified." The paradox is that by opposing the offender, she ends up agreeing with him. He would argue, too, that her fears, anxieties, depression, sexual problems, difficulties with intimacy, addictions —all are "stupid" and "unjustified," and most certainly not his fault.

I was once asked to do a training session for a group with a strong feminist orientation. As a fellow feminist, I was delighted and not at all upset at being "vetted." No, I did not recommend labeling adult survivors as "borderline." No, I did not think only MDs and PhDs should treat survivors. Yes, I believed in multidisciplinary teams. All went well until the question about multiple personality disorder. What was wrong, I asked, with the concept of multiple personality disorder? "We don't like to think of it as a disorder," I was told. "We like to think of it as multiplicity."

I thought about that stance a good deal. It came too close, for me, to minimizing the impact of trauma, to saying trauma is not bad for people. Yet the survivors of childhoods that produce multiple personalities are survivors of torture, sensory deprivation, and sadistic attacks. It may be more fair to call it a coping strategy than a disorder, but it is a lot more than an alternative lifestyle.

Impact of Denial

Avoidant defenses such as denial reduce the cognitive field. The victim simply does not know what is too painful to be known. Or knowing it, he refuses to acknowledge it, and thus keeps it from being validated as part of a shared reality. Or knowing and acknowledging it, he turns the telescope around and deludes himself into thinking it is much further away from him than it is. Although active attempts to avoid pain are understandable and inevitable—there is pain so searing that even the memory of it scars—it is still true that "every form of refuge has its price."[1] The price of negating memory and/or impact is that, in Lynn Sanford's terms, the survivor's "cognitive life raft" disappears (L. Sanford, personal communication, September 17, 1994).

Without memory, without an understanding or felt experience that abuse is at the heart of his difficulties, the survivor is lost. He may be globally symptomatic and functioning poorly in every area of his life, or he may have encapsulated symptoms that affect only a few areas. In either case, he will have difficulty with meaning-making. Why is sex so aversive? Why is intimacy so frightening? Why, without drugs and alcohol, is he so profoundly sad? Why is he afraid so much of the time, at peace so little? Why does life seem so meaningless? Why does the future seem so bleak?

He does not know where he is because he does not know where he has been. Instead, he is likely to turn on the self as somehow inherently flawed, defective, and worthless. Decades ago, the offender treated him as though he mattered little. Without knowing that, understanding it, and feeling it, the survivor is likely to end up agreeing with him.

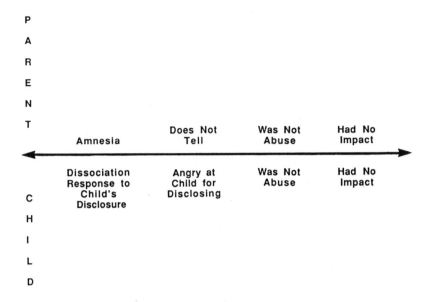

Figure 7.2. Parents' Defenses to Their Own Abuse and to Their Child's

Reactions of Adult Survivors When Their Own Children Are Molested

The adult survivor in denial is at particular risk if her own child is molested. Although this issue has not been addressed in the research literature, it is my clinical experience that she will often use the same defenses in responding to her child's molestation that she used for her own. Figure 7.2 lists the correspondence between adult survivors' defenses in response to their own molestation and their response to their child's.

Amnesia

Although I had never had a case in which it seemed clear, I had wondered for some time if the loss of memory in regard to the survivor's abuse was somehow duplicated when faced with her child's abuse. For the most part, mothers who ignored their child's disclosures appeared to remember them, even if they did not believe them. In some cases, they insisted that the child's original disclosure was so vague that they were not aware he was referring to sexual abuse. The following case, however, suggested that dissociation may explain at least some mothers' failure to act.

Three sisters and one brother lived with their families in four separate apartments in one house. One of the sister's children disclosed at school that her father (the current husband of one of the sisters) had sexually molested her. Knowing the proximity of the apartments, the school interviewed the other children in the house as well. Quite a few of them also reported sexual abuse, and the abuse was reported that day to the appropriate child protection agency. Despite the school's objections, the child protection worker refused to interview the children until the following day. The school was concerned, appropriately as it turned out, that the proximity of the apartments would result in a premature confrontation between the offender and the other families.

As the school personnel expected, some of the children told their parents of the school interviews, and a fight ensued in which the offender wandered from apartment to apartment all night arguing with the families of the children he had molested. In the early morning, he grabbed his gun and strode off into the woods trailing threats of suicide. A single shot was fired within hearing range of the apartments.

By the time the shot was fired, the children were all waiting for the school bus, and as it was leaving, the school bus bearing the confused and frightened children passed the ambulance coming to the house. The offender had, in fact, killed himself.

One of the sisters came to me for a consultation. She reported that the offender had raped her several times, but she never told her sister (his wife) because she did not want to upset her. "There's just one other thing," she told me, "that sticks in my head. My son tried one time to tell me something about Uncle Bob, but it was the strangest thing. He opened his mouth, and I could see his mouth moving, but I couldn't hear anything."

"What happened after that?" I asked.

"I don't really know," she said. "I don't remember much after that. I remember being in my neighbor's house, and I remember going to the state hospital."

My client, who had an extensive mental health history with repeated hospitalizations, had dissociated, wandered around the neighborhood, and was hospitalized that day.

"It's a funny thing," she said. "He (my son) denies this ever happened, but I know it happened. I remember seeing his mouth move."

With such a catastrophic response to his disclosure, it is little wonder that her son never again reported sexual abuse by Uncle Bob.

Does Not Want Child to Disclose

The parent who never revealed her own abuse is often horrified when her child discloses hers. The mother equates disclosure with exposure, and reveals, by her fear of others knowing, the extent to which her own abuse is shame-based. By consigning abuse to the autistic world of a private reality, she attempts to diminish it. In this, she treats her child's abuse exactly as she does her own and for the same reasons. She rarely knows or admits that this diminishment is an attempt to avoid her own affective flashback, which it is, but describes it as a way to protect the family instead.

Protecting the family is experienced as a higher value than holding the offender accountable or protecting the child from further abuse. The child is viewed as having betrayed the family by telling "strangers," and such children are frequently pressured to recant, a dynamic elegantly explored by Roland Summit (1983) in his classic paper on the child sexual abuse accommodation syndrome.

Was Not Abuse

Parents who were abused as children often make as many excuses for their own child's perpetrator as they did for their own. Perpetrators are thought to have molested because of alcohol, stress, or by accident. "I think something happened," more than one mother has said, "but not what she said." An inquiry into what the mother thinks happened will often elicit a vague response to the effect that the child's father would never do anything to hurt her and/or a tale of accidental touching. "Perhaps he fell against her in the hall," one mother said. "The halls are really narrow, and he could have slipped." Her 10-year-old daughter had described digital penetration.

The mother may blame the child for being "provocative," or herself for an aversion to sex. She will often blame anyone other than the offender. Quite clearly, she believes that, whatever happened, the child's perpetrator is not actually a sex offender any more than hers was.

Denial of Impact

"What's the big deal?" mothers sometimes say. "I was molested as a child and it never bothered me. She needs to quit whining about this and get on with her life."

"You can't let it bother you forever. She needs to just forget about it."

"He does fine until she comes in here. I don't think it's good for him to come in here and dwell on it. He needs to get on with his life."

"You can't blame everything on what happened as a child. He has to quit blaming everything on that and take responsibility for his life himself."

"Stop whining and act like a man."

When a parent denies the impact that abuse has on the child, it is sometimes because she has yet to face the impact that her own abuse had on her own life.

Summary of Survivors' Reactions to Their Child's Molestation

The impact of denial will often affect not only the survivor's life, but her attitude toward any molested child with whom she comes into contact. Her own children are particularly at risk, given that she is likely to identify with them and thus project her defenses onto their situation. If she dissociated during her own abuse, she may dissociate upon evidence of her child's. If she did not report her own, she may equate reporting with public shame and be furious at her child for reporting. If she insisted that her own abuse was not abuse and that her perpetrator was not really a sex offender, she may mislabel and rationalize her child's abuse. If she denied the impact of her own abuse, she may follow suit one generation later. All of these reactions are counterproductive to her child's well-being. The literature suggests that maternal support is an extremely important predictor of recovery in the child (Johnson & Kenkel, 1991; Mannarino, Cohen, & Berman, 1994). Her denial may have minimized her own pain as a child, but it runs the risk of increasing her child's.

The answer to the often-asked question of how to break denial in mothers who refuse to believe their abused child is, alas, not an easy one. If the mother's denial is based on her defenses to her own abuse, she is unlikely to change unless she deals with her own past. Only when she separates her inner child from her real child is she likely to recognize and accept the differences between the two; only then can she distinguish between the path that made sense for her and the one that makes sense for her child. The other primary reason for maternal denial—relationship addiction related to an inability to tolerate being alone—is likewise frequently a sequel to her own abuse. She must heal herself before she will stop making it difficult for her child to heal.

The Inconstancy of Denial

The victim in any type of denial will often end that denial with an oscillating cycle of admission and denial. A client of mine told me in one session that her father forced her brother to molest her while he watched, a fact that she had forgotten for years. In the next session, I made some passing reference to her comments regarding her brother, and she became enraged with me, shouting at me that this was not so, that I had made it up. Her brother never, never molested her. I was taken aback, and wondered if I had confused cases. In fact, when I went back to my notes, she indeed had reported abuse by her brother, and in the next session, she again confirmed it. Yes, she said sheepishly, she now remembered saying that.

Denial is not a door that victims exit; it is a line that victims walk back and forth many times before moving forward. If some survivors who recover memories do not write them down or tell someone, the memory will slip below the waterline again, perhaps to surface later, perhaps not.

Distraction

Some adult survivors of child sexual abuse live their lives in a flurry of activity. They work, volunteer, garden, exercise—all in a driven and compulsive way that exhausts and uses up the self rather than nurtures it. They do not stop when they are tired; they may not even know when they are tired. They become addicted to the pace, and in all likelihood, the internal chemicals that accompany it (van der Kolk, 1987, pp. 72-73). It is possible to not think of a white elephant—not by not thinking of it, but by thinking of other things so intently that one leaves no room for it. Given the inability of the brain to attend to more than one thing at a time, a killing pace of activity rivets the attention and produces accompanying emotion that successfully competes with memories of abuse and the affect attached to them. "Down times," when the mind wanders and is not sufficiently engaged to prevent the old memories and their affective sidecars from returning, are simply not permitted.

This need to avoid "down time" is at the heart of some survivors' inability to be alone. The issue is not always dependency on others, nor is it necessarily a loss of the sense of self when not attended to. In some cases, it is the inability of the survivor to manage his affective states and control his thoughts unless distracted by company. More than a few survivors turn on television immediately when faced with an empty house. "At least it's company," they say. In reality, it is distraction.

Likewise, revictimization experiences are sometimes not reenactments of trauma at all, but rather methods of distraction. Relationship addiction, in which a survivor goes through a series of intense, unstable, and volatile relationships, may function as distraction. A current crisis may occupy the mind and heart so completely that it anchors the survivor in the present, and thus prevents drifting in the past. Dancing as fast as you can may keep the bogeyman at bay, but only as long as the music never stops.

Dissociation

Dissociation has been linked frequently to childhood sexual abuse (Briere & Runtz, 1988b, 1988c, 1990; Chu & Dill, 1990; Elliott & Briere, 1991b; Lindberg & Distad, 1985). Lindberg and Distad (1985), for example, found dissociative reactions in one third of their sample of incest victims, although without a control group, the figure is difficult to interpret. Briere and Runtz (1988b) compared emergency walk-in patients with a history of child sexual abuse with those without this history and found that twice as many of the former "spaced out" (42% vs. 22%), three times as many had derealization experiences (33% vs. 11%), and almost three times as many had out-of-body experiences (21% vs. 8%). Anderson et al. (1993) found that 88% of their sample of outpatients had a dissociative disorder. Dissociation has been found to be elevated in nonclinical samples of sexual abuse survivors as well (Briere & Runtz, 1988c).

Other traumas have been linked to dissociation, and in fact, at least one study (Swett & Halpert, 1993) found that the combination of physical and sexual abuse was related to dissociation, whereas sexual abuse alone was not (although physical abuse alone was). Similarly Chu and Dill (1990) found that both forms of abuse combined produced particularly high dissociation scores.

The defense of last resort, dissociation occurs when trauma cannot be prevented, endured, or escaped. If the body cannot go away, the mind does. The essence of dissociation is, as the name implies, separation. It is the process of separation that defines the response rather than the content, for the content varies. The process of separation may occur between the sense of self ("I") and the body (out-of-body experiences, analgesia), between the sense of self and former identities (fugue states, multiple personality disorder), between the sense of self and the present circumstances (disengagement, flashbacks, shutdown), between the sense of self and the past (amnesia), or between the sense of self and the emotions (detachment/numbing). A complete description of each of these can be found elsewhere (Briere, 1989, 1992a; Putnam, 1989; Ross, 1989). Only out-of-body experiences, observation, analgesia, and disengagement will be discussed here.

During traumatic episodes, the sense of self may "leave" the body and hover somewhere in the room, often watching the abuse from the ceiling. Of course, the mind does not actually leave the body; it just switches perspectives and—much like the computer it is—translates the sensory data into a different configuration. Later, this process may become observation (Briere, 1989, 1992a), a process in which trauma survivors habitually watch themselves and their interactions from the internal viewpoint of a third person. They do not see or remember events from their own personal perspective. This defense is quite closely allied with emotional numbing because by adding cognitive distance, it reduces emotional involvement.

Analgesia is akin to the physical numbness and lack of feeling that can be induced by hypnotic trance (Rossi, 1980). Milton Erickson used self-hypnosis to manage the chronic physical pain that his polio and related physical problems produced. "It usually takes me an hour after I awaken to get all the pain out. It used to be easier when I was younger. I have more muscle and joint difficulties now" (Rossi, 1980, p. 112). However, for the adult survivor, the analgesia is not produced as a conscious strategy to avoid pain. Rather, it is an unconscious strategy developed in some cases to block physical pain, and in other cases to block physical pleasure. The latter occurs because pleasure during sexual abuse produces a cognitive dissonance that is intolerable to the victim.

For some, the analgesia becomes habitual and surfaces whenever the survivor engages in sexual activity. Despite the analgesia, the body may function normally. A woman, for example, may lubricate in response to sexual stimulation, but will feel numb and derive no pleasure from the experience.

For others, particularly those who were violently attacked and/or physically beaten, the analgesia occurs primarily in the presence of pain. Thus some adult survivors report unusually high pain thresholds. One survivor nearly died twice, once when an ovarian cyst ruptured and once when she had an acute attack of appendicitis. When the ovarian cyst ruptured, she called the doctor who, because of her calm demeanor, said on the phone, "One thing's for sure. It isn't an ovarian cyst rupturing because you'd be in much worse pain."

When her appendix ruptured, she was standing in the emergency room filling in insurance forms. She continued to finish the forms and waited her turn. When she went into shock, the staff realized the seriousness of her problem. She said later, "I thought my husband understood how sick I was because he was going to park the car, and I said, no, drop me off at the door. I never do anything like that."

On a follow-up visit after completing therapy, she said to me proudly that her recent visit to the dentist had hurt so much that tears had run down her cheeks. "Through the novocaine?" I asked, puzzled. "I've never used novocaine," she said. "I've never needed it."

Disengagement is a separation of the sense of self and the present environment. Thus it is a frequent defense during therapy sessions, where discussion of trauma may threaten amnesia or trigger affective flashbacks. Although some other forms of dissociation—analgesia and observation, for example—may occur in the presence of a clear sensorium, disengagement does not: Survivors report feeling "spacey." In therapy, some clients simply appear to drift off, as though thinking of something else for a moment or daydreaming. However, when queried, they respond that they were not thinking of anything and seem to be unaware of having lost focus. One woman did this habitually several times in each session. An indication that she was dissociating was that she made small smoothing motions on her skirt each time, which did not occur at times when she was simply thinking of something else.

Other survivors disengage by becoming confused. They may forget what they were saying, what the therapist was saying, or have such difficulty in understanding that their reactions resemble aphasia. They may totally forget what was said during the last session. One survivor, a scholar of considerable repute, lost the ability to read when dissociative.

Therapeutically, dissociation can be used as a marker for the importance and threat-value of clinical material. When the client dissociates, it is appropriate to wonder what is being discussed that is so distressing: It may be important to slow down so that the material can be integrated, given that dissociation blocks understanding, retention, and affect, as it was intended to do.

Summary

Dissociation presents in a variety of ways: out-of-body experiences, analgesia, fugue states, multiple personality disorder, disengagement, flashbacks, shutdown, amnesia, and detachment/numbing. In any form, it is a more powerful method of avoiding pain than denial or distraction, because denial only blocks awareness and affect after the fact, and distraction merely keeps both from surfacing. By contrast, dissociation blocks awareness and retention of events at the time of occurrence, and later can block awareness of triggers to the abuse—witness the dissociating survivor's difficulty in understanding what is being said to her during therapy. Memories laid down while dissociative may be stored, but if so, most likely they will be state-dependent, that is, only accessible while in a similar state (Putnam, 1990).

Unfortunately, dissociation is not encapsulated to the extent that denial and distraction are. Denial may be restricted to the sexual abuse, and thus affect the adult survivor little in other areas. Distraction may frequently affect the adult survivor by contributing to certain specific problems—primarily workaholism and relationship addiction. Dissociation, however, has the capacity to interfere with the survivor's ability to function in the world in any area. The dissociative survivor may be unable to work, read, or concentrate on anything, and may even be dangerously unaware of his surroundings. The power of dissociation is its ability to separate the victim from trauma; the weakness is that it can separate him from present reality as well as past.

Medicating Pain

When chronic pain cannot be successfully avoided, the adult survivor will often self-medicate by means of drugs and alcohol, self-mutilation, or suicidality. Unlike avoidant techniques, the use of medicating behaviors or substances inevitably reduces the survivor's ability to function successfully.

Drugs/Alcohol

Drug and alcohol addictions have been found repeatedly to be higher in sexual abuse victims than controls, sometimes strikingly so. Briere and Runtz (1988b) found alcoholism to be 2.5 times as common and drug addiction 9 times as frequent in 67 survivors of child sexual abuse. This was true even though both clinical and control samples were taken from walk-in emergency patients where the incidence of alcohol and drug addiction could be expected to be high in any case.

Likewise, Peters (1988) found elevated rates of both alcohol and drug addiction—albeit a slightly different pattern. In a community sample of 50 African American women and 69 white women, the 54 women (46%) of the sample that reported contact abuse were 2.5 times as likely to have drug abuse histories, and 3.5 times more likely to have alcohol abuse histories than nonabused controls. Noncontact abuse did not appear to contribute to risk.

However, most startling were the results of the Los Angeles Catchment Area Study (Stein et al., 1988), a large-scale, community, random-sample study. Of those males who were sexually abused as children, 45% were diagnosed as drug abuse/dependent, compared to 8% of controls. The figures for women were lower—14% versus 3%—but nevertheless represented more than a fourfold increase in risk. Alcohol abuse rates for women were also elevated: 21% in abused women versus 4% of controls. Alcohol rates for men were high in both groups (36% vs. 23%) but not significantly different from each other. Yet even higher rates have been found. Anderson et al. (1993) determined that 65% of their sample of outpatients were substance abusers.

Although most of these studies have been done with outpatients or community subjects, inpatients who were molested as children also have been shown to have higher rates of alcohol and drug addiction. Singer, Petchers, and Hussey (1989), for example, have found that adolescent psychiatric inpatients had more regular use of cocaine and stimulants, more alcohol and drug use in general, and more reported episodes of being drunk or drugged than nonabused adolescent psychiatric inpatients.

In addition, Benward and Densen-Gerber (1975) found that 44% of their sample of drug abusers in a residential treatment program were incest survivors. However, there is research with very dissimilar patterns. Cavaiola and Schiff (1989) found an extremely low incidence of sexual abuse in their sample of chemically dependent adolescents in a residential program.

Internal Drug Addiction

In addition to external chemicals, internal chemicals may be used to self-medicate. Van der Kolk (1987) wrote of an "addiction to trauma" (p. 72) that he felt was likely based on elevated levels of endogenous opioids in response to trauma or traumatic reenactments. Reenactments of trauma—for example, prostitution in survivors of child sexual abuse—might actually be methods of increasing production of such endorphins if trauma has become an established trigger for them. Likewise, it may be that the tendency of some survivors to experience flashbacks and abreactions repeatedly, without any apparent movement toward resolution, could be due to the increased levels of internal opioids that traumatic material produces. The body may produce whatever experiences are needed in order to trigger the endorphins on which the body has become dependent. Some support for this hypothesis can be found in animal research. Van der Kolk (1987) notes that animals who are continually traumatized produce so many endogenous opioids that they suffer withdrawal symptoms upon termination of the stress (p. 71).

Summary of Drug and Alcohol Addiction

Many people find drugs morally reprehensible and are judgmental about survivors who use them. Although there is nothing good that can be said about drug addiction, perhaps the angry and sometimes hostile tone of onlooker outrage can be mitigated slightly if one remembers that few surgery patients turn down a morphine pump for pain relief following surgery. Forced to choose between the several days of physical pain following surgery and the sometimes decades of psychological pain following sexual abuse, few would consider surgery more traumatic. In a fumbling, confused, and often desperate way, the adult survivor is doing nothing all that different from the surgery patient asking for narcotic relief. He is seeking relief from pain wherever he can find it.

Self-Mutilation

Although it is easy for the nontraumatized to grasp how drugs and even thoughts of suicide can provide solace to those in need, self-mutilation remains an almost opaque form of pain relief. Self-mutilation is self-torture—whether it takes the form of cutting the body, burning it, or banging it against objects—and there is truly something grotesque about such a profound turning against the self. Few behaviors on the part of a client have such a capacity to produce such angry countertransference reactions in a therapist, and the end result is often rejection and abandonment of the client. This does little to decrease the dysphoria that the client was medicating in the first place (Briere, 1992a).

Self-mutilation has been frequently associated with child sexual abuse (van der Kolk, Perry, & Herman, 1991; Walsh & Rosen, 1988). For example, de Young (1982) found that more than 50% of her sample of 60 incest victims had self-mutilated; these mutilations included attempts to break bones and self-poison.

The functions and purposes of such behaviors appear to be multiple. Most important, self-mutilation may well produce compensatory endorphins that result in withdrawal as they dissipate (Schetky, 1990; van der Kolk, 1987). Van der Kolk (1987) has noted, for example, that "in our experience, a variety of chronic self-destructive behaviors such as wrist cutting and anorexia nervosa have responded to clonidine, which also blocks the autonomic manifestations of opiate withdrawal" (p. 72). Thus self-mutilation may produce endorphins that successfully medicate pain, but that upon dissipation, increase the dysphoria, thus resulting in the need for more pain relief, and so the cycle continues.

However, self-mutilation also may be a trump card played by a desperate survivor for whom solace lies not in drugs or alcohol but in attention and nurturance from significant others. Initially, self-mutilation is almost certain to produce increased concern and renewed efforts to help. Shortly, however, onlookers discover that they are helpless to stop the self-mutilation that merely becomes more habitual as it produces the hoped-for care and attention. The onlookers become vicariously traumatized from being close to someone who is torturing herself, and withdraw in frustration, helplessness, and often anger. Inevitably, whether dealing with significant others or therapists, the survivor's chances of being rejected and abandoned are increased by self-mutilation.

Many survivors have an unconscious belief that others could reduce their dysphoria if they chose. Herman (1992) notes that "The greater the patient's emotional conviction of helplessness and abandonment, the more desperately she feels the need for an omnipotent rescuer" (p. 137). Thus survivors sometimes escalate the behavioral messages they send in the hope of eliciting the help they believe is available, but withheld.

Other survivors, however, self-mutilate—not to produce endorphins or elicit attention or compel rescue, but to deliberately punish the self. The internalized perpetrator in some survivors is extremely hostile, and the internal anger toward the self that the survivor feels may be relieved by a catharsis of anger toward the self.

Pain production may be the target of the self-mutilation, not just in those who wish to punish the self but also in those who are experiencing derealization or depersonalization. Pain will sometimes ground the dissociative survivor, that is, break through the dissociative haze and tell her she is "real." Ironically, it is also used by other survivors to induce dissociation and separate from the present reality. Survivors talk about the ritual of self-mutilation, about how cutting in a methodical, slow, and ritualistic way will induce a trancelike state.

Thus self-mutilation is a surprisingly flexible method of pain control. It can produce endorphins, elicit nurturance, compel rescue, self-punish, and either ground dissociation or produce it. However, its considerable short-term power to alleviate pain is matched only by its long-term propensity to increase it. The side effects—messages about the worth and value of the self, for example—are entirely negative.

The proponents of proper etiquette were probably right. We are not nice to people because we like them; we like people because we are nice to them. In the same manner, treating the self as "precious" is not just an effect of good self-esteem, it is a cause as well. The adult survivor does not just self-mutilate because she hates herself, she hates herself because she self-mutilates. It appears the "just world theory" (Lerner, 1980; Lerner & Miller, 1978) functions intrapersonally as well as interpersonally. The individual will assume that punishment, even self-punishment, is meted out to her for a reason. If she self-mutilates, it must be because she deserves it, and to deserve torture, she must be very bad indeed.

Suicidality

The ultimate method of pain control is suicide, and many survivors, caught in a chronically dysphoric affective state, fantasize about suicide with an almost religious fervor. "Suicides have a special language," Anne Sexton wrote. "Like carpenters they want to know *which tools*; they never ask *why build*" (1966, p. 58).[2] Thoughts of suicide become thoughts of solace, and some survivors will fantasize as ardently as prisoners of war do about methods of escape.

That survivors do more than fantasize has been well-established. In a series of studies of crisis walk-in and psychiatric emergency room patients, Briere and colleagues (Briere, Evans, Runtz, & Wall, 1988; Briere & Runtz, 1986, 1987; Briere & Zaidi, 1989) found that the percentage of sexual abuse victims who had attempted suicide ranged from 51% to 79%, whereas control groups averaged 30%. Other researchers have also found differences in those with a sexual abuse history. Herman (1981), for example, found that 38% of her sample of sexually abused outpatients versus 5% of controls had attempted suicide, and de Young (1982) reported that 68% of her sample of 60 incest victims had made attempts, 66% of those more than once. Likewise, Bryer et al. (1987), in a study of 66 inpatients, found that women with a history of suicidal ideation, gestures, and/or attempts were three times more likely to have been sexually or physically abused as children than were inpatients without these symptoms. Unfortunately, the study did not distinguish between the two types of abuse.

Although some community samples have found differences (Bagley & Ramsay, 1986; Sedney & Brooks, 1984), others have not (Peters, 1988). Therefore, the jury is still out on whether suicidality is more pronounced in nonclinical populations. Even those community studies that find differences often find that a small percentage of survivors have made attempts: 5% in Bagley and Ramsay's study had made a suicide attempt or deliberately inflicted self-harm.

Unfortunately, suicidality does not turn out to be a long-term effect that emerges only in adulthood; sexually abused children have elevated rates of suicide attempts as well. Lanktree et al. (1991) reported that more than one third (36%) of their sample of sexually abused outpatient children had made suicide attempts versus 8% of other child outpatients. Wozencraft, Wagner, and Pellegrin (1991) found that suicidality in their sample of sexually abused children was more common in older incest victims who had not been removed from the home and whose mothers were less supportive of treatment. Even in a drug treatment program (Cavaiola & Schiff, 1988), adolescents who were chemically dependent and abused were twice as likely to have made a suicide attempt (46% vs. 23%) than adolescents who were chemically dependent but not sexually abused. They were 27 times more likely to have made an attempt than nonabused, nonchemically dependent adolescents (46% vs. 1.7%).

However, more survivors will fantasize about suicide than will attempt it. For some, the thoughts alone are sufficient to provide solace even as they do for some terminally ill patients. These thoughts remind the overwhelmed survivor that she has choices and that she is not trapped in a world she can neither endure nor change. Suicidal fantasies become as comforting and soothing as a transitional object. "Dazzled," Anne Sexton (1966) writes, "they can't forget a drug so sweet" (p. 58).[2] Clients are often surprised by their therapist's lack of enthusiasm for this form of solace.

Where there should be an internalized soothing introject—an image of parental warmth and loving—there is none, either because poor parenting early in the survivor's life failed to provide a model that could be internalized, or because trauma disrupted the sense of basic trust that had developed. Ironically, instead of going back to scenes of early nurturance for images of soothing and pain cessation, the client without any such images goes forward to the end of her life, and can imagine no greater soothing than being without pain. For her, suicide is simply a way to stop hurting.

There are those, of course, for whom suicidality is in the service of an interpersonal agenda, a way to compel attention, secure nurturance, or temporarily prevent abandonment. I once saw a woman on emergency who had made her tenth suicide attempt when a man she tried to pick up at a party refused to take her home.

Without question, the client's motives for a suicide attempt are critical for treatment. The client who sees death as the ultimate analgesic needs reconnection to the world and sufficient external soothing to begin to develop a benign and loving introject. You have to be around kind people a long time, Vaillant notes, in order to internalize them (G. Vaillant, personal communication, October 26, 1994).

However, the client who uses suicidality as a way to manage interpersonal relationships is likely to be made worse by too much "holding." Dramatically increasing attention and concern in response to an attempt can be dangerous for such a client.

Conclusions

Sexual abuse survivors often respond to intractable chronic pain—whether the episodic pain of the affective flashback or the chronic pain of a major affective disorder—by either avoiding or medicating it. Such avoidant and self-medicating behaviors are not, properly speaking, sequelae, but responses to sequelae. The survivor will avoid by denial, distraction, or dissociation—each of which blocks information at a different point in time.

Dissociation is the most powerful of the three because it will block awareness and memory at the time of the abuse, but it also has the most harmful side effects. Later in life, the same classes of stimuli that trigger affective flashbacks for some may trigger dissociation instead of, or in addition to, such flashbacks for others. Dissociation, however, does not take the abuse away; it takes the person away. Its lack of specificity and precision combined with its power make it function less like a laser and more like a tank. While blocking awareness of abuse and/or abuse related stimuli, it can separate the survivor from her environment or from her body almost entirely, rarely a helpful response postabuse, and sometimes a risky one.

Distraction keeps the survivor moving so fast that old memories and affective flashbacks simply do not surface. Although distraction does not impair the survivor as globally as dissociation does, it can produce a frenzied, anhedonic lifestyle, and its crisis orientation is often implicated in relationship addiction.

Denial can block awareness through amnesia, but more often it inhibits awareness of meaning, awareness of impact, and disclosure. It puts a different spin on abuse and thus blunts the survivor's awareness of its import. Although denial is more specifically encapsulated to the abuse than either distraction and dissociation, it too can affect the survivor's life in other areas, most notably by reducing her capacity to understand and support her child should he, in turn, be abused.

For the adult survivor to give up avoiding and medicating the pain, she must understand and be committed to facing it. Pain that was unendurable as a child without options is, in fact, endurable decades later by an adult with many options. Although few survivors believe it at the onset, it is nonetheless true that the shortest way through psychic pain is a beeline.

Notes

1. "Lyin' Eyes," written by Don Henley and Glenn Frey. © 1975 Cass County Music/Red Cloud Music. INTERNATIONAL COPYRIGHT SECURED. ALL RIGHTS RESERVED.

2. Excerpts from "Wanting to Die," *Live or Die* by Anne Sexton. Copyright © 1966 by Anne Sexton. Reprinted by permission of Houghton Mifflin Co. All rights reserved.

8

Links Between Offenders and Victims
Summing Up

W hat, then, do we know about the links between offenders and victims? How does the information on offenders in the first three chapters inform our knowledge of victims? How do the sequelae of abuse as discussed in Chapters 5, 6, and 7 relate to offenders? What, then, are the tasks of therapy and how can they be accomplished?

The compulsivity and repetitiveness of sex offenders as demonstrated in Chapters 1 and 2 suggest that sexual offending is not an accident that happens to offenders. It is not an illness that descends on them and then mysteriously passes. It is not a problem that they eventually solve. If not actually an addiction, it is a compulsive behavior that does not necessarily get better with time or with promises to do better. Religion is used more often to evade treatment than to support it. Remorse may interrupt the pattern, but rarely controls it. Nothing cures it.

Adult survivors are rarely aware of this. The nature of grooming, as demonstrated in Chapter 2, is such that survivors will internalize the offender's thinking errors. Among these is inevitably some attribution of responsibility for the offense to the child. The adult survivor who believes the abuse was his fault is at risk of leaving his child with the offender if that offender is a relative —his own abuse notwithstanding. After all, his son is an innocent little child. There is nothing about him that would cause the grandfather to abuse him. No, indeed, there is not. But then again, there was nothing about the adult survivor as a child that caused the offender to molest him, either. The survivor who does not understand that sexual offending is a compulsive disorder, owned and operated by the offender, will not treat the offender as a child molester. At worst, he will feel guilty for causing his father to abuse him.

Such adult survivors—still partly groomed by relatives/ offenders—do not object to the offender baby-sitting, taking in foster children, becoming active in youth groups, or becoming involved with women whose children are of the same age as the survivor when molested. After all, it was a long time ago and he was not really a sex offender.

The adult survivor's problems in understanding the nature of the disorder are complicated by many offenders' high standing in the community (as noted in Chapter 1). Much of what happens between offender and victim is a battle of realities. The respect that many offenders are accorded by others increases the adult survivor's doubt of her own reality. It is easier for her to hold her reality that the offender was dishonest and dishonorable if others agree with her, even if for other reasons.

The offender's high standing in the community will affect the survivor in other ways as well. People judge accusations by whether or not they are consistent with their experience, by whether the person is considered to be the kind of man who would do that kind of thing. It makes an enormous difference in a small community whether a man accused of being a barn-burner is someone with a history of petty thievery and vandalism who has never held a steady job, or whether he is the local, deified doctor. In child sexual abuse cases, it is all too often the local doctor, and he does not seem like the kind of man who would do that kind of thing.

This battle of realities began long ago in childhood, when the abuse itself began. A world that believed or pretended the abuse was not occurring (implicit denial) placed the child in the position of owning a private, unacknowledged reality. Such realities, un-validated and unacknowledged, are more like half-realities, eas-ily subject to forgetting and denying. Terr writes that children who suffered trauma in a group setting (e.g., the Chowchilla kid-napping) suffered no memory loss (Terr, 1985a). Is this surprising, when others went through the trauma with them and were there every step of the way to acknowledge it? Even so, what if the Chowchilla children had returned from their kidnapping ordeal and everyone in town acted as though nothing had happened? Would their memories of it have been the same?

Because of the silence surrounding the abuse, the offender's voice will ring loudly. His comments, his manner, his attitude about the abuse—all are subject to internalization by the child vic-tim and are often carried decades later by the adult survivor. It is imperative for the therapist to understand how the offender thinks. His thinking will interweave with the adult survivor's more authentic voice as a spreading weed interweaves among garden plants. The first rule of gardening is to know which plants are weeds and which are not. Just so, the therapist must learn to recognize the sound of the offender's voice—whether outside the survivor's head or inside it.

There are other reasons to study offender thinking as well. The points of contact between offender and victim—supervised visitation, unsupervised visitation, apology sessions, reunification —all offer opportunities for the offender to make comments or take actions that reflect thinking errors. The therapist who studies offenders knows what to expect in such interactions and can pre-pare his client better than the therapist who knows nothing of offenders. The price of not understanding offender thinking er-rors was graphically demonstrated in Chapter 4 by apology let-ters that reoffend. Some of the letters would have gotten by some therapists—after all, the offender was saying he was sorry and that the abuse was not the victim's fault.

In studying offenders, the therapist will discover that sadistic and nonsadistic offenders act differently, think differently, and have different motivations. They leave different footprints on the hearts and minds of survivors as well. The nonsadistic offender who projects his sexual arousal onto the child wants to believe that the child desires him sexually. He reduces physical discomfort rather than increases it, and he pretends emotional suffering does not exist. He believes what he needs to believe (i.e., that the child desires him) to be sexually aroused. He is living a sexual fantasy. Because he ignores the reactions and feelings of the child, he leaves behind victims who are more frightened of not being known emotionally than of being known, more fearful of emotional invisibility than visibility. Such victims tend to thrive in therapy, where a premium is placed on listening carefully to the survivor and understanding her or him as precisely as possible.

If the nonsadistic offender is oblivious to the child's true reactions to the abuse, the sadistic offender, by contrast, listens very carefully. He attends to the child's pain and suffering because he finds it sexually arousing, and he uses the child's reactions as a guide for increasing the suffering and therefore his own pleasure. He leaves behind victims who do not want their thoughts and feelings known for fear that others will use those thoughts and feelings against them. Emotional invisibility feels safe; emotional visibility produces a reaction close to terror. Therapy must go slower for such clients because decompensation in response to such affective flashbacks is common.

Affective flashbacks can occur in response to other stimuli as well. Hearing the offender's name, smelling an odor reminiscent of his aftershave lotion, having sex, going to the dentist—all may trigger affective memories of the abuse. Obviously, having direct contact with the offender is a particularly powerful trigger. Those survivors with PTSD, especially, may find that the intrusive phase is exacerbated or the avoidant phase aborted by contact with the offender. Facing the offender in court, in an apology session, or at a family reunion may destabilize the adult survivor and take her back emotionally to the abuse. One sibling offender, in a confrontational therapy session with his sister, said, "Part of me wants to talk about this, and part of me just wants to say, 'To heck with this, let's just go make love.' " His sister had a full panic attack at his words. Pale and shaking, she nearly bolted from the room and was able to remain only by sitting extremely close to her therapist instead—and as far as possible from the offender.

In addition to affective flashbacks, the survivor's psychological symptoms may result from cognitive changes secondary to the abuse. She may have developed a "trauma-based worldview," a profoundly hopeless sense of personal vulnerability and lack of efficacy in the face of what seems to be a random or even malevolent universe. If the survivor has escaped a trauma-based worldview (and even if she has not), she may still have cognitive changes secondary to internalizing the offender's thinking errors. Certain beliefs—for example, that the child was responsible for the abuse, that the child sought or enjoyed the abuse—are internalized exactly as they are believed by the offender. Process thinking errors, however—such as victim stancing or superoptimism about not getting caught—are internalized as opposite to the offender's. Instead of victim stancing, survivors may victim blame. Instead of being superoptimistic, they may have a trauma-based worldview.

The dysphoria produced by affective flashbacks, by a trauma-based worldview, or by internalized thinking errors may cling to the survivor for decades. Many survivors know little of self-soothing pain and turn instead to denial, distraction, or dissociation—all ways of avoiding pain—or, failing that, to ways of medicating it. Drugs and alcohol, suicidality, self-mutilation, or living in a constant state of crisis may all function as psychological narcotics whose function is to numb pain that has eluded avoidance.

However, understanding the links between offender and victim is only the first step. What, then, are the goals of therapy? How does a therapist help a client get an internalized sex offender out of her head? How can someone who knows only how to avoid or medicate pain learn to self-soothe? What can be done about affective flashbacks? Knowing all of the above, how does one use that information in therapy? What is therapy, anyway? How does it differ from a simple, intellectual discussion of the issues? The final chapter of this book will turn from the science of sequelae to the art of healing, from negotiating the forest of research studies to crossing open ground.

9

Crossing Open Ground
Trauma and Transformation

> *But we need to understand healing for what it really is; it is not a*
> *vanishing act, but rather learning to live with, in, and through*
> *pain, to adjust to our wounding, which cannot ultimately be de-*
> *nied, and to be willing to risk opening to change that will lead to*
> *transfiguration.*
>
> —Ross (1988, p. xviii)

What Is Therapy and What Is Not?

Not everything that happens in a therapist's office is therapy.
A surprising number of therapists commit grotesque errors;
among the most egregious is having sex with clients. This phenomenon seems particularly correlated with child sexual abuse.
Twenty-seven percent of Gil's sample of 99 survivors were revictimized by therapists (Gil, 1988), as were 30% of de Young's sample of 10 incest victims (de Young, 1983). In a sample of 12 incest
survivors, all of whom had been sexually abused by their therapists, Kluft (1990a) found that 28% of the total number of therapists they had seen had been sexually abusive. The average number of therapists/perpetrators per client was 1.9. One woman had
been victimized by six.

By contrast, the figures overall for therapists who have sex
with clients range from .6% to 10%, and tend to hover between 5%
and 10% for male therapists and 2% to 3% for female therapists (Bouhoutsos, Holroyd, & Lerman, 1983; Derosis, Hamilton,

Morrison, & Strauss, 1987; Gartrell, Herman, Olarte, Feldstein, & Localio, 1986; Holroyd & Brodsky, 1977; Kardener, Fuller, & Mensh, 1973; Pope & Bouhoutsos, 1986; Pope, Levenson, & Schover, 1979).

The factors most associated with therapist/client sexual contact seem to be, first, the client's sexual abuse as a child, and second, the severity of her symptoms (Kluft, 1990a). In de Young's (1983) study, the sexual abuse often began shortly after the incest was revealed. It is particularly disturbing to discover that perpetrator/therapists are abusing the most highly symptomatic clients, and thus the most impaired, at their most vulnerable moments. A client of mine was raped by a previous therapist during a flashback. The therapist, against whom several other women also brought suit for similar behavior, was eventually jailed for insurance fraud.

Less grotesque, and surely more common, is the practice of self-disclosure on the part of therapists. It is not unusual for a client to mention in therapy that a previous therapist spent much of the hour discussing her own issues; the therapy eventually felt more like a social exchange than a therapeutic endeavor. Clients sometimes come with astonishing detail of a previous therapist's private life, including the specifics, for example, of a troubled marriage.

In such cases, it seems that over time, the therapists talk more than the clients. This is not surprising, given that the adult survivor was often groomed to be a "parentified" child and thus can quickly fall into the role of caretaking the therapist. Although self-disclosure is often described by such therapists as "being real" with the client—which it may well be for the therapist—it is frequently simply a reenactment of caretaking a parental figure for the client.

Equally problematic, "therapy" can easily turn into an intellectual discussion of the issues with little affective involvement. One client, a therapist himself, asked his own therapist why, when he had become teary over his mother's death, the therapist had changed the subject. "Well," the therapist replied, "I have trouble with affect."

Therapy is, of course, none of the above. It is a different concept of therapy entirely that George Vaillant celebrated when he wrote:

> Sacred places, too, allow us to imagine, to sustain paradox, and to wonder. In the painted caves of Altamira and Lascaux, or upon the artifact-surrounded, Oriental rug-draped couch of Sigmund Freud, or in an Aboriginal dance at a sacred site in Australia's Northern Territories—in such sacred places art, religion, ego, metaphor, play, and dreams intersect. The caveman's shrine, the analyst's office, the child's playhouse are places separated from and yet bound to reality. . . . In sacred places, wonder reigns supreme. Transitional objects (symbols of early relationships) are everywhere. Sacraments and tragedy, rage and ecstasy can all be tolerated. Land can belong to two moral peoples at the same time; wine can become a savior's blood, and straw can be spun into gold. Perhaps a better term than sacred places would be playrooms or spiritual kindergartens for adults. (Vaillant, 1993, p. 339)

What, then, happens in a therapist's office that permits wonder to "reign supreme"? What are the conditions that turn an ordinary room into a "spiritual kindergarten"?

Enter the client, with at least some, and perhaps many, of the symptoms discussed in Chapters 5, 6, and 7. His usual ways of avoiding or medicating pain have broken down to some degree—or else he would not be there.

Enter the therapist, who picks up her notes just so, turns just so, and sits in the same seat in the same place. She cocks her head a certain way, and says the same phrase each time—whatever it may be. "Where would you like to start?" She is speaking to the unconscious—both hers and the client's—as surely as a writer who sits in the same seat wearing the same baseball cap and using the same coffee mug each time she writes. She is using ritual to close the door on outside reality, to define this time and space.

It is a discipline, this honoring the boundaries. Except for the brief discussions of the weather or other such in the transitions, the therapist asks no questions that are not for the benefit of the client. If the client mentions a workshop, a play, a book in which she might personally be interested, she does not inquire. I once had a client who was molested by her famous and talented father. I knew in which field he was but did not know his name. I am sure the client thought I knew. Had I asked, it was clear she would have been happy to tell me. I never asked. His name had nothing to do with her therapy, and the asking would have been only to satisfy my own curiosity, which was, I admit, considerable. Three years later, she mentioned it in passing.

Because the therapist is so firm about keeping his own issues absent, he makes space for an entirely different dynamic to be present. Kierkegaard (1959) wrote that the poet suffers the torments of the damned and, by a trick of fate, his suffering comes out of his mouth as beautiful music that others applaud. Even so, the therapist resonates affectively to the client like a reed instrument. He does not swap stories. He does not raise his own history or his own experience, lest his own affective response blind him to the client's. It is not a Ping-Pong ball going back and forth across a table; both players are on the same side of the net. The client's pain, played through the therapist as instrument, comes back perhaps a little more formed, with more sense and shape. The client often hears the echo better than her original shout.

> A man burdened with a secret should especially avoid the intimacy of his physician. If the latter possess native sagacity, and a nameless something more,—let us call it intuition; if he show no intrusive egotism, nor disagreeably prominent characteristics of his own; if he have the power which must be born with him, to bring his mind into such affinity with his patient's, that this last shall unawares have spoken what he imagines himself only to have thought; if such revelations be received without tumult, and acknowledged not so often by an uttered sympathy as by silence, an inarticulate breath, and here and there a word, to indicate that all is understood; if to these qualifications of a confidant be the advantages afforded by his recognized character as a physician,—then, at some inevitable moment, will the soul of

the sufferer be dissolved, and flow forth in a dark, but transparent stream, bringing all its mysteries into the daylight. (Hawthorne, 1850/1986, p. 114)

To do what Hawthorne described so well (it is ironic indeed that such an elegant description of the therapeutic process should have been written 6 years before the birth of Freud), the therapist must do more than think about the issues. He must be affectively present. He cannot be making grocery lists or planning dinner. It is a peculiar skill to be able to detach, even dissociate, from one's own affective response and be resonant instead with another's, with an affective intensity unmatched in normal social exchange. The therapist must vibrate like a tuning fork, not to his own history, but to the client's.

When he does this well, images and metaphors come forth that capture the client's experience more fully than a rational listening process could elicit. The client is not just angry. It is a cold, hard, seething anger that never breaks the surface, or perhaps it is a dull, aching, repetitive anger like the throbbing of a headache. It could be an electric anger that charges certain moments with a dangerous intensity, where far too much could happen far too fast. When he listens in this focused way, shapes and nuances of emotions seem clear, sometimes even obvious; by contrast, the logical process of recognizing and labeling "anger" seems impoverished.

If you tell a client he is angry, he may agree with you with little affective involvement. However, if you catch the coloration of the anger, even if your words are imprecise and halting, his "yes, yes, that's it" will come back bearing an emotional charge never elicited by a logical assessment of the issues.

To do this, the therapist must shut off outside reality as completely as possible. Her field of vision narrows; she may literally get tunnel vision. The world in which she is sitting is, for the moment, the only world there is. If she has Ericksonian inclinations, she may use microanalysis to focus her concentration more intensely. When does the client blink? On what words? When does he sigh? When does he look away? When does his breathing change? She may match the client's respiration, breath for breath, to try on the client's experience more readily.

This can sometimes yield surprising data. I once matched respiration with a large woman with a poised and articulate exterior. To my surprise, her breathing was shallow and rapid, far too shallow for her size. For a long time, it was the only clue I had to the massive and debilitating anxiety that lay beneath the polished surface.

Live Affect

Vice President Al Gore relates a tale of Gandhi in which a woman asked him to tell her son to stop eating sugar. He ate too much, she thought, and it was bad for his health. Gandhi agreed to confront the son but asked for a 2-week delay first. When the eventual meeting was successful, the overjoyed mother thanked him profusely, but asked, puzzled, why he had requested the delay. " 'Because,' he replied, 'I needed the two weeks to stop eating sugar myself' " (Gore, 1992, p. 14).

Because the therapist is affectively present, she is able to request the client to do the same. The coin of therapy is live affect on both sides. When the client is not affectively present but sends his intellect to the table instead, education may be taking place, but therapy is not. The essence of therapy is affective change, and affective change does not occur in the absence of affect.

Some therapists are better than others at detecting live affect in the client. The client may mention two or three different issues in the same sentence. Where does his voice catch? Where does he look away? Where does he shift position? Where does he raise his hand to cover his mouth? Where does his tone change ever so slightly? One of the issues may well be more important than the others, but that cannot be determined by assessing their relative importance in the literature or in the lives of other clients, but only by seeing or hearing the nonverbal clues of this particular client.

However, at times, the issue that the client is discussing obviously may be important—incest, for example, is unlikely to loom small in any client's personal landscape. But the client may recite the facts with no discernible affect. Ironically, without affective involvement, even cognitive schemas will not change because they are driven by affect and not by logic. The client who believes she deserves what the perpetrator did to her will have her mind changed not by a logical analysis of the worth of human beings or the fallacies in sex offender thinking, but by learning to nurture her own inner child instead.

Discussion without affect must be confronted, however gently. "What are you feeling right now? I notice when you say that, you smile, and yet you're talking about horrible things. What is the smile all about?" The client who is dissociating from her own affect must be brought back, not to the affect she felt at the time the events were happening—for that may only be a memory unless she is having an affective flashback—but to her current affect. Her current affect is the most accessible and the most potentially live. Her life, most likely, is being controlled by her need to evade, minimize, and medicate her current affect; yet it is learning to recognize and live with her current affect that is key.

Vaillant has commented on the importance of early nurturing by saying, "We learn to anticipate future pain effectively only if someone first sits beside us while we learn to bear our current anxiety" (Vaillant, 1993, p. 331). The process is the same for learning to bear past pain. Someone must still sit beside us in our current anxiety.

In addition, intimacy is not possible without live affect, and whatever else therapy is, it is also about learning to tolerate intimacy without loss of boundaries, emotional visibility without shame, trust without fear of exploitation. The client who is not affectively present is not vulnerable, and thus cannot learn that vulnerability is not necessarily weakness in the presence of malevolence. It is paramount, then, that the therapist know when the client is affectively present, and when the affect presented is, instead, a stale and distanced version of what the client is really feeling. Being good at detecting live affect is as important as knowing which way the wind is blowing when at sea.

Safety and the Therapeutic Relationship

"I'm scared of life," the 4-year-old said to the astonished therapist. A sense of safety does not come easily to the traumatized. Nor can a therapist even attempt to provide a totally safe place. To enable a victim to become a survivor, the therapist's office must not only be a place where the client is held emotionally, but a place where she confronts the dragons. "Beyond this point," the old maps read, "there be dragons," and crossing the threshold to the therapist's office is always moving into dragon country.

"What do you think about seeing a counselor?" I asked a 9-year-old who had told me almost immediately he was "good at forgetting things." He had much to forget. He had repeatedly watched his father batter his mother, and he had been battered and emotionally abused himself. "Scary," he said, and went on to say that he did not want to remember the things he was good at forgetting and he did not want to remember what they felt like, either.

To some extent, what makes the therapist's office safe is that it embodies all the things that are lost in a trauma-based world-view: meaning, efficacy, and benevolence. Therapy involves, first of all, an active and continual search for meaning. The implicit assumption is made that although the universe may be random, the client's motivations, feelings, and behaviors are not. Together the client and therapist must find the narrative line. Typically, clients have already developed meanings, but such meanings are often irrationally hostile and attacking of the self. The new meanings developed in therapy will be at once more logical and more kind.

Likewise, to feel efficacious is to feel that one matters. By focusing intently on the client's beliefs, feelings, and behavior, the therapist communicates clearly and continually that the client does indeed matter. Human beings can have no more value to themselves than the highest value ever assigned them by another, and for that valuing to count, it must be assigned by someone the person either loves or respects. The client/therapist dyad is often a strong, if transferential, bond—entirely sufficient to allow the therapist to help redo the not-mattering messages that poor parenting, sexual trauma, and/or the randomness of the universe have communicated.

Therapy is predictable, and predictably benign. Many adult survivors have difficulty regulating interpersonal distance. Either they were rejected and abandoned as children or intruded on by assault or enmeshment—sometimes both. The therapist, by contrast, never changes his interpersonal distance with the client. He is close enough to be intimate, but the peculiar boundaries of therapy are such that he never demands anything emotionally in exchange, and he never leaves his office to become a real-world figure in the client's private life.

No doubt many parents believe it is their differential response to good and bad behavior that socializes the child. So it may be, but it is the invariant constancy of parental love regardless of behavior that gives the child a self to be socialized. Many clients—either because they never internalized a good enough parent or because they have internalized a hostile perpetrator—are full of self-loathing. In therapy, however, the client does not have to be "good" to keep the therapist close; no one either goes away or attacks if he is "bad." Therapy provides a place where intimacy leads to neither abandonment nor enmeshment. When learning a trapeze act, it is always better to start out with a safety net.

Therefore, the predictability that the therapist embodies is not restricted to regularity of time and place—although with the severely traumatized, this type of predictability is also helpful. Of more import for most clients is the predictability of the interpersonal distance. "You were so close," Jean Valentine wrote, "I could have touched the dead childhood in your face" (Valentine, 1965, p. 14).[1] That degree of closeness can be tolerated by clients only if the therapist makes it clear that the closeness is still a respectful, and absolutely invariant, distance away.

Telling the Tale

Much has been written about the necessity of the client "telling the tale" in order to heal (Herman, 1992). It is likely all true. The client may heal in the absence of specific memories of trauma, but cannot heal in the absence of emotional visibility. Reality is indeed a consensual experience, and the client's view of herself must be validated by another for it to take hold. Those negative parts of the self that remain totally hidden will remain totally shame-based. Darkness produces good mushrooms, but poor flowers.

The client will not always agree. Telling the tale is a reliving of the experience and automatically produces affective flash-backs. Persuading an adult survivor to go back fully into such old and uncomfortable territory is as difficult as persuading someone with a snake phobia to hold a live snake. Instead, she may strip the tale of all those aspects that make it live. She may describe and summarize her experience rather than relive it. She may tell the tale hurriedly with little emotion, then say quickly, "Well, what do I do about it?" She is fending the snake off with a long stick made of words. She may not remember—an even longer stick. "What color was the rug?" one therapist asks. She finds that victims always know the color of the rug, and somehow the perceptual details take them back.

And back they must go for change to occur. The client must tell her tale as fully as did Nisa, the !Kung woman who told the story of her life to her anthropologist friend:

> She ended her story in a fairly usual way, saying, "That's all, and life went on." An unusually long silence followed. Then she added, thoughtfully and slowly, "No. There's still something in my heart about this that isn't finished. My heart is still shaking. The story hasn't come completely out. I'm going to talk more about it until it does. Then, I'll go on to another. Then my heart will be fine." (Shostak, 1981, p. 40)

Hearing the Tale

The client's ability and willingness to tolerate the process of dragging things out of her anxiety closet is only half the issue. How that tale is received will determine whether the client is re-victimized or empowered.

I once asked a high-level chess player what it was like to play at his level. Having nothing but burned out neurons in the chess center of my own brain, I was curious what it would be like to think in that way. He paused a long time—chess moves were easier for him than words. "Imagine going to a strange city," he said finally. "Imagine that you've never been there at all before. Then imagine starting to walk in that city. You turn left, then right. You go down this block and that and you keep walking for a long time. To play well, you have to know what that city is going to look like at the end of all that, and it has to be as real to you as this wall," and he thumped the cafe wall next to us.

I think he was trying to tell me that playing chess well was more than a rational process of planning moves and anticipating countermoves, computing probabilities, remembering textbook maneuvers, and recalling classic games. You had to have a sense of where you would be at the end of all that, a sense as clear and present as a wall.

What was it like, after all, to lie in bed, hearing the sound of your mother's voice drift up the stairs as she tells your father how bad you have been that day? What was it like waiting for the inevitable footsteps to sound on the stairs, waiting for the beating and the rape? At what point, at which step exactly, would you start to drift and where would you go? Could he hurt you badly enough this time that you would come back? Did you wonder if you would think this time you were dying? Did you wonder if you would?

Although the therapist must grasp this emotionally as clearly as though he were there, he must resonate, not identify, with it. It is not his pain. Taking it on as his own will lead to sleepless nights, antidepressants, and a need to control the client in order to control his own affective response.

Neither must he project onto the client his own experience and his own affective response that, however similar, will simply make the client feel more invisible. Perhaps it is the emotional equivalent of Piagetian concrete operations, this ability to hold the client's affective world and the therapist's at the same time without merging the two of them—living one and resonating emotionally to the other.

I have never had much patience with the dilemma of whether the tree falling in the empty forest produces a sound. The issue seems to me to rest simply on the definition of sound. But the client who tells her tale to an empty room, however emotionally charged her rendition, is not having a cathartic experience nor an abreaction; nor will anything be eased or changed or transformed inside her. She must tell her tale fully, from the heart—and someone must bear witness.

Meaning-Making

The tale, once told, must be made sense of. A quilt with a discernible pattern must be stitched together from the cast-off squares of cloth: the images, beliefs, and fears, the pictures in her head, the snippets she remembers, the holes where she does not. Some of this work may be soothing. The client may have never heard of affective flashbacks, and may be relieved to find that her sex life (or lack of it), for example, makes sense. She may have never considered that her problems with intimacy might be an understandable, almost inevitable, response to betrayal. She just thought she was a "cold fish." She may have resisted the pressure to forgive the offender—she simply could not make herself—but blamed herself for her intransigence. A good cognitive life raft will help her build a coherent reality strong enough to compete with the family myths.

However, some of the work is not soothing. It is jarring and disruptive and can potentially increase the need for self-medication. In particular, coming to terms with what I call "load-bearing walls," the "benign transformation," and "malignant competition" can lead to a temporary increase in symptomatology and even disruption of a sense of identity.

Load-Bearing Walls

In the sense-making part of therapy, inevitably, some close attachment figures look different from the perspective of the adult than they did from that of the child. Dora, for example, adored the grandmother who told her she loved her, who introduced her to books, who took her for the entire summer and got her away from her abusive parents. Life without the grandmother was dire indeed. Beatings, emotional abuse, and sexual abuse by both parents were almost daily occurrences. Dora was stupid; Dora had ruined her mother's life by being born; Dora was too selfish and egocentric ever to be a parent; it would be better for everyone if Dora just went away and died. Both parents drilled these statements into Dora's mind. From the standpoint of the child, the grandmother was her rescuer. Once, the grandmother even stopped Dora's father from beating Dora!

But from the standpoint of the doctoral-level academic that Dora became—no doubt in part because of the love and the books her grandmother provided—her grandmother was a mixed blessing. It turned out that Dora's grandmother told her her parents were right. She was just as bad as they said she was. She was, in fact, "scum-of-the-earth." However, she, the grandmother, was such a wonderful person that she could love Dora anyway. Her love was nothing that Dora deserved. It was the gift of a magnanimous spirit for which Dora should be forever grateful and was (not coincidentally) one of the major weapons in the chronic war that the grandmother waged with Dora's mother.

Even the beating that her grandmother interrupted was used against Dora. Her father exiled her grandmother from the house for several years because of her "interference." She blamed Dora for this. If Dora were not such a despicable child, it never would have happened. For the rest of her life, she talked about what supporting Dora cost her.

There were surprises for Dora as she discussed her mother and father. Memories surfaced that distressed and depressed her. But Dora was always aware to some extent of her parents' malevolence, and had built her identity knowing that fact. She did not identify with either parent, and if she internalized their negative messages, it was never to the extent that she did her grandmother's. However, when rethinking her grandmother's role, Dora's depression deepened and grew dangerous. Her sense of her own identity became shaky. She became disoriented.

Likewise, Lucy's aunt played a double role. Although she too provided nurturance and warmth to the battered child, she also told her that Lucy's father's beatings were Lucy's fault. She needed to shut up, stop provoking him, and everything would be fine. In addition, she did not stop her own husband (Lucy's uncle) from sexually abusing Lucy, nor did she admit awareness of it. That she knew or should have known is indicated by a memory Lucy has of her aunt coming home unexpectedly one day to find that her husband had invited several neighborhood children over and was entertaining them on the deck. The aunt was furious, and Lucy remembers her saying, "You know you're not supposed to do that. You're not allowed to be around children." Nevertheless, she allowed him to take Lucy down in the basement every week, and she never asked any questions.

When renovating houses, one can knock down walls with impunity until one comes to a load-bearing wall. Slamming into one will likely cause the roof to cave in, and so it feels to the clinician who inadvertently comes across unknown betrayal in a major attachment figure of the client. Such figures are introjects, part of the internal landscape for the client. They are part of who she thinks she is. She has internalized what she believes to be their goodness; their approval of her—however tainted to the outside eye—looked like sweet water at the time. To say that nothing was as it seemed is to raise the question of whether the same is not true of her as well. As one client said, "If she's not who I thought she was, I'm not who I think I am." These figures are people onto whom the child held to grow, and in some sense, onto whom the adult holds still. When they are suddenly jerked away, the child, and the adult, lose their balance.

When a therapist stumbles onto a load-bearing wall—and it is nothing one ever expects, given the initial glowing reports of the attachment figure—she must then slow down, backtrack, and to some extent, soft-pedal. This figure is an integral part of this client's identity. Because she identifies with the figure, she will take malevolence in her as though it were malevolence in herself. Her sense of self-worth will instantly plummet.

Remind the client of the good, as well as the negative, parts of the figure. Give full due to what such attachment figures gave to and did for the survivor. Settle in for the grief. This is no grave to dance on. What you will hear is a wild keening instead.

Benign Transformation

Harry Stack Sullivan wrote of the "malevolent transformation" —a change in the child occasioned by the realization that he is living among people who mean to do him harm (Sullivan, 1953). Few children, however, can tolerate the knowledge that they are living among enemies. Instead of becoming malevolent themselves, they turn malevolence in the parents into benignity to make the world less frightening.

This is not the only way in which load-bearing walls get built. The child genuinely may not see malevolence. Lucy did not know what to make of the phrase, "You're not allowed to be around children." She remembered it because of the affect with which it was said, but it took an adult understanding of pedophilia to decode it.

By contrast, Cynthia did make the benign transformation. As a child who needed to see her mother as benign and simply overwhelmed—a stance she maintained until her 40s—she actively distorted data. Her mother had embezzled money from her employer and was caught. Although charges were never filed, she lost her job and could not get another. Her father was a minister and also became unemployed. The family was too proud to ask for or accept aid. The poverty that followed simply defeated her parents, or so Cynthia thought. The lack of food, the lack of heat, the bills piling up in the mailbox—all were put down to well-meaning but ineffectual attempts to deal with the world.

But in her 40s, Cynthia found herself in therapy talking about the fact that her brother was accepted at a college but never went because he was denied financial aid. It was only years later that she found he was denied financial aid because her parents had "forgotten" to return the financial aid form. They never revealed that to the brother.

Oddly enough, something worse happened with her other brother, who received a full scholarship to a college but was never told that he had.

Cynthia also applied for a scholarship, but was turned down without explanation. Two months later, for whatever reasons—either because her mother had a change of heart or because she thought it was too late—her mother told her that she had found the letter requesting that her SAT scores be forwarded to the scholarship committee in her father's coat pocket. He had "forgotten" to mail it. Cynthia went to her guidance counselor, lying to him, of course, and claiming it was her mistake. Despite her claim, he was furious with the parents. Through his advocacy, the college was persuaded to accept her anyway.

Apparently, the counselor understood. Cynthia does not know what he told the college, but they never asked her parents for anything again. They accepted her and provided a full scholarship that included room and board. They even paid her dental bills.

Other memories tumbled out once Cynthia admitted the possibility of malevolence. One year, her mother "forgot" to buy her a present for Christmas. There were presents for everyone but her, and she, of course, had bought or made presents for everyone.

She remembered a game. "What would you do if . . . ?" the mother would say, and then would describe some bizarre situation in which the child was accosted or kidnapped or otherwise in some sort of terrible danger. The family lived in such dangerous neighborhoods that the "game" was all too realistic. Cynthia would answer gamely. She was a creative child. But her mother would demolish all her arguments: "What if no one could hear you yell? What if the windows were locked?" The child would finally break down and cry. This would seem to satisfy the mother. Once the child admitted total helplessness and defeat, the mother would stop, ending the game on that note. The game was billed as a way of learning to cope with adverse situations, but the agenda seems to the adult eye to be somewhat different.

All this the child transformed into benignity, into accidents, into well-meaning attempts to be helpful that backfired. It was much later that she allowed herself to see a different pattern.

One may ask whether the therapist should confront the benign transformation at all if it is going to be so stressful to the client. Why risk an increase in symptomatology and distress? If someone thinks that he or she grew up with love and used that belief to form his or her identity, why challenge it in any way?

First, it is rarely the therapist's choice. The client will raise the disturbing data because there is a tension between her belief and certain anomalous memories. Once raised, the therapist may provide the label—malevolence; people of the lie; in some cases, even sadism—but she provides neither the data nor the tension that impels the client to explore the issue.

Second, malevolent attachment figures tend to be a major source of cognitive distortions for the adult survivor. While sending positive messages about themselves to the child, they inevitably send negative messages about the child. Love is a catalyst for internalization, and cognitive distortions that ride on the back of love slip past the victim's defenses. The general message is usually that the attachment figure is good, but the child is not. She is stupid, or evil, or ineffectual, or worthless—someone for whom it is not worth remembering a Christmas present or sending in a financial aid form.

Third, these major attachment figures are often a part of the client's present life, and they may continue to reabuse the client emotionally. The client who did not appreciate the figure's double role as a child will not appreciate it as an adult. Thus she will not protect herself, not stay alert for put-downs and victim blaming, and will not understand why she emerges from interactions with such people with an increase in anxiety and depression. It is impossible to heal while being reabused.

Malignant Competition

There are probably many forms of malevolence. One that surfaces frequently in abusive families is malignant competition. In nonabusive families, parents identify with the achievements of their children. They may even make up for past failures by living vicariously through their children's successes. This may be so pronounced as to be unhealthy—witness the number of Little League fathers who were not successful in sports as children, but who push their own children far beyond the children's desire or skill level. Even so, the core of the phenomenon is identification, not malevolence.

In families where malignant competition rules, parents feel diminished, rather than augmented, by their children's successes. They cannot tolerate the child doing well in any area they have staked out as theirs, and they communicate this so powerfully that the child knows achievement comes at the price of attachment and fears that it might even come at the price of annihilation.

Such children, grown large, have certain areas where either they never allow themselves to be successful or they may underachieve generally. One woman was accepted into the Junior League and called her mother, thinking she would be proud of her. She knew that her mother had always wanted to belong but had been turned down. The mother, instead, was furious.

This same client then began to make sense of why she became so anxious when she tried to learn a musical instrument. Music was her mother's turf, and the message, never owned or acknowledged, was that the daughter was not to succeed there.

Generally, individuals with this family dynamic frequently achieve at a level far below what would be predicted based on their socioeconomic background. One survivor, raised in an upper-middle-class and well-educated family, fell so far below the poverty line that she did not always have heat in the New Hampshire winter. She drifted from job to job, never holding any one job for very long. Despite the expensive preparatory schools she attended, she was never able to complete college. Such behavior is often thought to be the result of poor mental health in general, but sometimes it is the product of this very specific dynamic. The client has the capacity to achieve more and function better, but does not dare to do so.

There is no antidote to malignant competition except to detach from the attachment figure who is the source of it. As long as the client fears the loss of love, she will accept the terms of the relationship as given. As long as loss of love is equated with total annihilation, she is hopelessly entrapped. Even when she detaches, she will have to permit herself achievement slowly and gingerly, one tiny accomplishment at a time. Perhaps she can learn one song on the violin—not become a violinist, just learn that one song. She can then discover that nothing horrible happens as a result, and perhaps learn another song.

She may detach, of course, while still having contact with the person, or she may sever all contact as she chooses. However, if she does have contact, she would be well-advised to keep her successes to herself. Rage, sabotage, passive aggression, and undermining are likely to be responses to her news. She will not be thanked for sharing.

Methods of Countering Thinking Errors

Internalization

Therapists derive their authority from the transferential aspects of the relationship, that is, the extent to which they call up the most ancient of bonds, that of the early parent-child. To a good-enough mother, babies can do no wrong, and to a good-enough therapist, the client is valued regardless of his difficulties. With such territory come issues of identification and internalization. Even as the client internalized the perpetrator's views of him, so he may internalize the therapist's views of him, and for similar reasons. Not only was the perpetrator often a major attachment figure, but his views, beliefs, and attitudes spoke particularly loudly in the silence of the secrecy surrounding sexual aggression. Being the only game in town always ensures a good audience.

To some extent, too, the therapist occupies a similarly privileged position. Few others will ever know the extent of the trauma as the therapist comes to know it. Few will have access to those particular aspects of the victim's experience or of his reactions that he considers shame-based. How many other people is the client likely to tell, for example, that she reaches orgasm by fantasizing about cutting her father's throat, as one client did? How many people are likely to have a real sense of what it was like to wait for those footsteps?

The secrecy of the perpetrator/victim bond is replaced by the privacy of the therapeutic relationship. This is all to the good. One heals through disclosure, not exposure. The difference in whether the revelation of sexual abuse leads to healing or retraumatization lies in whom you tell under what circumstances.

But although the therapist is in a unique position to be internalized by the client, that does not mean that the client will easily replace the perpetrator's beliefs with those of the therapist, however logical and "right" the latter's beliefs may be. The therapist may believe fervently that sexual abuse is not a 3-year-old's fault, but find that only his client's head agrees with her. The "heart vote" remains tenaciously committed to the notion that the 3-year-old indeed should have known better, trusted less, and, short of violence, not consented.

The primary route to changing those beliefs is indirect. What the client internalizes from the therapist is not her specific beliefs, but her attitude toward and opinion of the client. The client is more susceptible to changing his sense of whether he matters, whether he is worthwhile, whether his agendas are important, whether or not he is expendable in the service of others' needs than he is his specific beliefs. It is the therapist's treatment of the client, her predictability and her affective presence, not her belief system, that will change the client's opinion of himself.

Partially, this inability to absorb another's belief system happens because the client has a natural resistance to being told what to think or feel. Therefore, he will react defensively to the therapist's specific beliefs. However, the therapist's attitudes about and opinions of the client are communicated indirectly and thus are not subject to conscious screening. For similar reasons, Erickson routinely tried to design interventions that would bypass the conscious mind, believing that its natural defensiveness would interfere with interventions it knew about (Rossi, 1980).

Of course, this is not to say that insincere praise and lectures on the worth of human beings in general, and the client in particular, will have any impact on the client except to alienate him. The therapist only rarely says anything to the client that might be considered to be praise. Praise, as much as blame, rests on outside judgment, and the goal of therapy is for the client to take over the function of soothing himself. Developing a reliance on outside judgment will only make the client vulnerable to the next perpetrator who uses a carrot instead of a stick to gain access.

Instead, the therapist supports the client while he learns to make sense of his own life as well as to provide his own sense of solace. She demonstrates support rather than talks about it by the most finely tuned listening, the most compelling affective presence, and the most focused attention of which she is capable. For the adult survivor, a sense of "mattering," rather than a borrowed belief system, is the sine qua non for confronting the internal critic who taunts him.

Differentiation and Internal Confrontation

In addition to internalization, there are a number of specific techniques that more directly confront thinking errors in the adult survivor. The tradition of dividing the client's internal landscape into differentiated parts or "voices" has a long history in both traditional psychoanalytic therapy (Kernberg, Selzer, Koenigsberg, & Carr, 1989) as well as more recent and less orthodox approaches (Harris, 1969). In their treatment of so-called "borderline personalities," Kernberg et al. not only divide the self into parts, but specifically label some parts of the psyche as the "punitive, sadistic parent" or the "sadistic attacker." Although they believe these creations to be fantasized and distorted recreations of real experiences, more likely, as Herman (1992) has noted, they "accurately reflect the early relational environment of the traumatized child" (p. 147). In short, the "punitive, sadistic parent" and the "sadistic attacker" probably existed in the real world and were simply internalized by the client.

This approach of differentiating the self into parts is particularly well-suited to confronting perpetrator-based cognitive distortions for several reasons. First, one cannot challenge a cognitive distortion unless one recognizes it; therefore, dividing the self into different "voices" is a necessary prerequisite for confrontation.

Second, recognition and differentiation allow the confrontation to be internal between parts of the self rather than external between the therapist and the self. Confrontations between the therapist and the client simply allow the client to unify behind the opposing view. The most effective confrontations (and those that evoke the least resistance) occur internally.

This notion, that confrontation (as well as solace) must be internal rather than external, is a cornerstone of therapy that frees rather than infantilizes. The reason for this lies in the universal propensity for power struggles. It is a truism that if Hank is ambivalent about an issue, and Mary, in conversation (or therapy), takes responsibility for one side of that ambivalence, Hank is then freed up to support the other side wholeheartedly. In short, if someone pulls on one end of a rope, the natural tendency is to pull back.

It is for this reason that therapists do not try to "cheer up" depressed clients. Telling someone to "count his blessings" inevitably makes him feel worse. Instead, the therapist says, in effect, "My God, that's terrible! Given all that, it's a wonder you don't feel worse," to which the client, in effect, replies,"Well, it's not *that* bad."

Imagine that a client comes into therapy for a weight problem. Imagine, too, that she announces in therapy that she got up at 2 a.m. the previous night and ate an entire German chocolate cake. What would happen if the therapist then lectured her on the inadvisability of eating German chocolate cake? Is there any doubt that responsibility for controlling the client's eating would thereby be transferred to the therapist? Before long, the client would most likely be eating German chocolate cake for breakfast while telling the therapist, "I don't know, doc. It just doesn't seem that therapy is helping me that much. I can't seem to control my eating." Soon, the therapist would begin to feel depressed, helpless, and ineffectual, whereas the client would likely feel lighter, freer, and strangely efficacious—if fatter.

It is for this reason that working with seriously suicidal clients is so difficult. Although the therapist cannot but take a clear and consistent stand against the proposed suicide, he runs the risk of thereby allowing the client to avoid her own ambivalence, transfer responsibility for controlling her behavior to the therapist, and unify behind her suicidal intent.

With suicidal clients, the therapist must walk a tightrope between taking no more responsibility than he has to for keeping the client safe, while still communicating that the client matters and that her death would be a terrible thing. The therapist takes no more responsibility than he must because the client's own internal ambivalence about dying is too important an ally to waste. The therapist's voice against suicide must not speak so loudly that it drowns out the client's ability to hear her own.

It is connection, not control, that motivates clients to continue their relations with the world of the living. The issue is simply how much the client has to lose by dying. Antisuicide pacts and contracts to call before attempts often work despite the risks cited above. They work not because they have any ability to control the client's behavior, and not because truly suicidal people are "Boy Scouts" who feel compelled to keep their word even in the most extreme of moments—they work because they embody an ongoing connection to the therapist that makes the therapist's presence felt at the worst and most impulsive of times. They imply connection; they demonstrate connection; they continue the "holding environment" (Winnicott, 1965) beyond the hour of therapy. They remind the client of a soothing presence in the midst of abject despair. To want to live in the world, dying must be loss, not an end to loss.

Using Different Voices in Internal Confrontation

When listening for the different parts of the self, the therapist should be aware that certain voices are likely to be present. Survivors frequently have an internal, perpetrator-based critic. This voice may or may not be sadistic, depending on the dynamics of the abuse, but is frequently hostile and blaming of the victim in any case. In addition, a voice one might term "the guardian" is often present. This is the internal voice that has discounted all evidence of the abuse for the years, sometimes decades, since it occurred. The client himself tries to make sense of whatever specific memories he has while dealing with these two interlopers. The client, for example, may make the following series of statements:

Client: *I have this odd memory, well, part of a memory, really, just this picture I see. It's this penis coming towards me in the shower. I'm maybe five and it's coming right at me, and it's standing up and I'm scared. It's funny. The whole thing is so clear I can see each pubic hair distinctly.*

Guardian: *But that's ridiculous. If I had been sexually abused as a child, I would have known it. It's not the kind of thing you forget.*

Perpetrator: *Besides, I'm probably just trying to get attention.*

In this example, the client reports a perceptual memory. The guardian then uses logic to try to protect him from the meaning of the memory, and the perpetrator makes an ad hominem attack on him.

For the therapist, therapy is often akin to listening to an orchestra and trying to pick out the different instruments. She then labels the instruments:

> Wait a minute. I hear different things here. First, I hear this straightforward memory that you have. You may not know what it means or what to make of it, but you have this funny memory. Then I hear a voice that's almost like a guardian or a protector that's trying to talk you out of it, that's arguing with you, and then I hear this voice belittling you and saying you're just looking for attention. Attention, of all things! Where did you hear that? Who said that to you?

The therapist in this case is not trying to persuade the client in any direction regarding the meaning or significance of the memory. She is simply noting the client's own process and reaction to the memory. She is, and should be, more confrontational with the hostile critic who is attacking the client than with any other part of her psyche, even as she will be more supportive and less confrontational with the child's voice when it emerges.

In this case, the perpetrator voice may derive from an actual sexually abusive offender or may be a spouse enabling a perpetrator. The phrase, "just trying to get attention" is likely a verbatim recounting of something said to the client as a child. It is a phrase that is frequently addressed to children but almost never to adults.

The guardian must be treated carefully as a self-protective part of the client and not as an example of internalized malevolence. Clients who are frustrated by holes in their memories will often turn on themselves and attack the guardian, but the therapist must not support these attacks. The way home is characterized by increased compassion, not increased self-loathing.

More chances may be taken with the perpetrator-based, hostile critic, but even there the therapist must keep in mind that the perpetrator introject is now part of the client and must be treated as such. Direct confrontation is appropriate; shaming or humiliation never are. Even with confrontation, the therapist must be careful to confront only part of the client, which she then specifically labels as a derivative internalization of the perpetrator. If she generalizes it to the client herself, she simply continues the cognitive distortions of the perpetrator.

For example, I once had a disastrous encounter with an inpatient unit over this issue. I referred Dora, a survivor of beatings, burning, and sexual abuse (who was previously described under "load-bearing walls") to an inpatient unit because she had made a very serious suicide plan to be carried out in a few months if she did not get better. This particular client had never made an attempt before, had never threatened one, had never acted out in any form, but had struggled for many years with a debilitating and severe posttraumatic depression. She was not manipulative; she was worn out.

Part of her depression related to self-loathing that was based on the internalization of the offenders' projections. Both parents told her with many words in many ways that it was she, not they, who was evil and sadistic.

In the initial interview with the unit, Dora's husband told the interviewer how sad it would be for him if Dora died. He was upset and his eyes filled with tears. Dora looked out the window at the rain. She later said that she was finding solace in the pattern of the raindrops on the window—that is, dissociating to avoid her husband's pain. When I spoke with the interviewer, she told me that she interpreted this behavior as Dora "dismissingly" ignoring her husband and not caring that he was in pain.

In any case, she turned to Dora and said, "Did you know you were sadistic?" Dora startled, she was so surprised. "What do you mean?" she asked. "The suicide plan," she was told. "It is sadistic." "Do you have any other evidence?" Dora asked. "I don't need any," she was told. "The plan is strong evidence." Dora was distressed at this and said almost pleadingly, "What you are doing is very harmful. I have worked for a long time in therapy to understand it was my father who was sadistic and not I."

"Well," she was told, "I'm not saying your intentions are sadistic or your character is sadistic, but your behavior is sadistic" —a distinction that held little comfort for Dora, who subsequently refused to enter that unit or any other.

All questions aside as to whether this client's suicidality was in any way related to sadism, and laying aside, too, the issue of whether an initial interview is an appropriate time to confront a client with whom one has no therapeutic alliance, one is still left wondering if telling a client she is sadistic is not destroying the city in order to save it. Certainly, clients sometimes turn on others, including their families and their therapists, even as they frequently turn on themselves. Herman (1992) has noted that "a destructive force appears to intrude repeatedly into the relationship between therapist and patient. This force, which was traditionally attributed to the patient's innate aggression, can now be recognized as the violence of the perpetrator" (p. 136).

How one labels the "violence of the perpetrator" has much to do with whether the violence becomes internalized even further —driven deeper by adding the therapist's authority to that of the offender—or whether the client begins to shed it like an onion shedding its skin. In survivors, the internal critic must not be treated as though it were the person, the whole person, and nothing but the person, but as though it were a borrowed and ill-fitting suit that needs to be returned.

It may seem a minor distinction, a question of hair-splitting words, to argue whether a sadistic, perpetrator-based voice is present within the client or whether it is the client. For the client, however, the question is no less than who and what she is— hardly a minor issue.

Effect of Labeling Different Voices. A survivor cannot detach from or discount a voice he cannot recognize. Labeling such thoughts as perpetrator based automatically drives a wedge between the client and the critic. Prior to labeling, the client believed that the continual belittling and hostile comments were simply true, and never considered them as a point of view, much less a biased point of view, much less a perpetrator-based, biased point of view. Raising that possibility tends to help the client separate his own, more authentic voice from the perpetrator internalizations.

Eventually, clients will begin to recognize the different parts themselves and weigh their counsel accordingly. One client realized that each statement about abuse was followed immediately with an "undoing" statement by the guardian or the perpetrator. She would make a statement and then, jokingly, clap her hand over her mouth to stop the equal and opposite reaction from occurring.

Internal Instead of External Confrontation. In addition, mental imagery can be used to facilitate an internal confrontation between differentiated parts of the self. A survivor who recognizes a part of himself as an "inner child" is often hostile to that child; the internalized perpetrator frequently (sometimes continually) attacks him. Attacking the child occurs far more often than its opposite—despite the popular image of adult survivors carrying teddy bears and care-taking their symbolic inner children. For the therapist to object directly to the client attacking himself has limited utility, given that confrontation from the outside is frequently seen by the client simply as more criticism. However, the therapist can ask the client to use mental imagery to imagine a confrontation among the different voices. The therapist weights the confrontation indirectly by how she sets up the exercise. For example, she may describe the exercise as follows:

> Imagine yourself at any age. What age do you see? What are you wearing? What does your hair look like? How are you feeling?
>
> You know you frequently tell me that as a child you were to blame for your father's behavior. Why tell *me?* Tell *her.* Let's see what this is like from her point of view. She is being raped in the

night, something she doesn't understand or have a clue how to deal with. She is frightened and confused and deeply wounded. You are a lot of what she has to hold onto. She will want to know from you how you feel about the abuse. Tell her how you feel about it.

If the therapist sets the stage carefully by portraying the child as the confused and frightened little girl she surely was, he makes it very difficult for the client to attack her further. However, if it looks as though she could, then the therapist needs to intervene, and ask for the name of a child the client loves—a relative's or friend's child, usually. Then she can be asked how she would feel if that child had been sexually abused. "Go ahead and tell her it's her fault."

It is almost always impossible for the client to do so. For most survivors, the cognitive distortions of the offender are specific to the victim, and she does not generalize them to other children. Would she tell another sexually abused 3-year-old it was her fault? Certainly not! She will be offended at the thought. Thus, instead of the usual pattern of learning empathy for others by imagining how one would feel in the same situation, adult survivors often must learn empathy for the self by imagining how they would feel if it were somebody other than themselves who was suffering. Empathy for the self can be felt only if reflected off a third person. This technique—of going outward in order to go inward—is applicable to any situation in which the survivor's perspective on herself is distorted by offender-based cognitive distortions.

In facilitating internal confrontation, the therapist is attempting to remove the buffer zone between two very different parts of the self. His goal is for the two sides to literally rub together; through that friction, a new vision will emerge. Admittedly, he intervenes in the confrontation by weighting the odds in favor of the inner child. It is not his intention to have a fair fight; the point is, it never was a fair fight. The power of the offender, his degree of certainty, his level of sophistication—all of them overmatched a small child. It is the therapist's job to change the odds.

Summary

Meaning-making should be called "remaking meaning" because few survivors come to therapy without previously assigned meanings attached to the abuse, their role, and the offender's role. The nature of offender psychology is such that he will almost inevitably have found ways to victim stance (himself) and victim blame (her). To the extent that the victim internalized the offender's thinking errors, she will present with both her point of view and with his.

On some level, she will retain the experience of the victim in terms of fearfulness, powerlessness, and confusion while at the same time judging and criticizing herself. She will vacillate between feeling like prey—with all the frightening vulnerability that entails—and predator—with all the self-blame that engenders. Her anxiety and depression will be exacerbated by the self-loathing that results from living with a hostile critic in her head. Consequently, the therapist is forced from the start to consider ways of confronting meanings that denigrate the victim while excusing the offender.

That task is made more difficult by the fact that some accurate meanings that do not denigrate the victim will nevertheless not initially soothe. The therapist may run into "load-bearing walls," "the benign transformation," and/or "malignant competition," all of which will prove internally disruptive in the short run.

In addressing these issues, the therapist may use specific techniques, such as differentiating parts of the psyche as different "voices" and facilitating internal confrontation between those parts. However, the client's internalization of the therapist's stance toward him is probably more important than any specific technique.

The therapist's stance—that it is the survivor's needs and not the therapist's that are important, that the client is valuable and worthwhile and that his pain must be taken seriously—is in direct contradiction to the internal offender's position. Thus there are usually three people in the therapist's office: the client, the therapist, and the perpetrator, and underneath the gentle tones of therapy, there is always a fight going on.

Reducing and
Managing Chronic Pain

Self-Soothing

The running child tangles her legs and lands in a heap. Her lip is cut, her knees are scraped, she is crying. A good-enough parent does not say, "How many times have I told you not to run on asphalt?" She does not say, "You're not hurt. Stop crying! You're always crying about something. I don't think you're happy unless you're crying." She does not say, "Stop crying or I'll give you something to cry about." She does not continue to watch TV. She rushes over and says, "Are you OK? My poor baby. Let me clean that up for you." And she kisses the hurt places and makes them better. Bandages are in order—for their decorative value if nothing else—Barney bandages or Ninja turtles, perhaps.

Even as she puts on the bandages, she also establishes a template, a model, a method for handling pain. Throughout the brief exchange, she communicates to that child numerous "mattering" messages, all of which contribute to the sense that the child is precious. The mother's soothing presence in due course will be internalized by the child. She will find, in times of distress, that she has a compassionate presence inside her head that encourages her, nurtures her, soothes her, and forgives her transgressions, real or imaginary.

For some children, of course, it is not a scraped knee in the driveway, it is a violent father who is beating and raping their mother in front of them and/or doing the same to them. Even if the mother were able to soothe the child at such a time, she would find that the degree of trauma makes it far more difficult.

More often the trauma is invisible: child molestation by a trusted relative or friend. A parent cannot soothe what she does not know exists.

Some such children grow up never having developed the ability to self-soothe, and others may have once had it, but became overwhelmed by an internalized, perpetrator-based critic. The problem such children face is daunting: They must manage misery with a poverty of tools.

Without the ability to self-soothe, the victim will almost inevitably turn to some of the avoidant and/or self-medicating techniques discussed in Chapter 7, all of which have negative side effects. Initially, therapy is likely to make matters worse. Telling his tale fully will trigger affective flashbacks, whereas making meaning may relieve much of the self-blame but will do nothing but increase the sense of betrayal and loss. In short, the victim will feel worse before he gets better. It will not be possible simply to ban the ways—dysfunctional though they may be—that he avoids or medicates his pain unless he learns to self-soothe instead.

Survivors are frequently told by well-meaning friends, even therapists, and by self-help books to take care of the self. Hot baths, long walks, meditation, yoga, retreats—all are suggested as ways of internal caretaking. However, none of these are effective if, for example, the client at the same time is berating himself for wasting time and not being productive. Clients frequently say truthfully that they are too tense to meditate, and if they take a hot bath they are drumming their fingers on the side of the tub waiting impatiently until they can "go do something."

Although one may argue which comes first—the chicken or the egg—ultimately it seems that self-soothing internally must precede self-soothing externally. There may be exceptions. The rare client who sticks with yoga, despite the impatient internal messages, may find that it eventually diminishes the sound of the perpetrator-based critic. Ordinarily, however, it is futile to suggest external self-soothing to a client who knows nothing of internal self-soothing.

Some texts (Herman, 1992) suggest focusing on issues of safety and stability before the therapist begins uncovering work. Although this is highly desirable, it is not always possible. Clients with severe intrusive symptomatology and chronic anxiety and depression are often unable to reduce them without uncovering therapy. Intrusive memories, flashbacks, and nightmares do not respond often to external self-soothing in the absence of internal change. To reduce such symptomatology, the client must learn to identify and challenge the internal, perpetrator-based critic who constantly attacks him, and he must learn to self-soothe instead of self-medicate.

Of course, this is not to recommend aggressive uncovering therapy with unstable clients with a propensity for cutting and/or suicidal ideation. It is to say that therapy cannot always wait until the client gets better to begin, and to say, too, that therapy must from the very beginning include the development of internal self-soothing as a primary goal. In this process, there are a number of specific techniques that may be useful.

A Safe Place

Affective flashbacks are often so searing that the client needs a method for diminishing her anxiety on the spot. Asking her to imagine a safe place will result in a mental image incompatible with anxiety and fear. Mental imagery, by its nature, is perceptually specific; asking the client to elaborate details will only add to the power of the image. This exercise also allows the client not just to feel better but to feel safe, a feeling she may not know and that she must learn to recognize if she is to make choices that avoid revictimization.

By calling attention to the issue of safety, the therapist implicitly asks where the client feels safe in the real world and suggests a new filter through which to view people, places, and situations: safe/unsafe. It is a small exercise that can open up a large dialogue and it has considerable power to soothe.

Note, too, whether the client uses invisibility as her metaphor for safety. A client whose safe place is a small boat in the middle of a gigantic ocean, for example—so big that no one could ever find her—is using invisibility. This occurs when the abuse involved a sense of exposure and shame, when the offender was sufficiently violent that the child despaired of ever winning a direct confrontation, or when the offender was sadistic and used the victim's reactions as a guide to increase her suffering. Therapy must proceed slowly with such clients because therapy involves emotional visibility, and emotional visibility will produce affective flashbacks.

Affirmations

As popular psychology insists, affirmations are useful, although not the panacea some suggest. There are now books of affirmations on every topic for every category of person. In all probability, there is a book of affirmations somewhere specifically for workaholic women over 6'5" with short alcoholic mates. The client would be well-advised to save her money; the most effective affirmations are developed by the individual for exactly her issues with precisely her language.

Affirmations are simply statements that the client makes over and over to himself until they become implicit and unspoken "tapes" that replace his usual negative thinking. Eventually, they are overlearned to the point that they become largely unconscious, part of his assumptive world; they will play frequently without triggering conscious awareness. Basically, affirmations are conscious attempts to self-soothe by self-talk.

For example, a client may have such severe affective flashbacks that she loses reality testing. When reminded of the offender, she may become so frightened that she begins to worry that he is stalking her, that he is going to kidnap her and make her go home again, even though the abuse occurred when she was a child and she is now an adult. One woman, whose mother was raped and murdered when the woman was a teenager, always had the fear that the murderer knew where she was and would eventually come after her.

If this belief is part of a paranoid process, affirmations will be of little use. However, survivors are often sufficiently anxious about contact with the offender that they appear paranoid when they are not. Their distress is often based on trauma-generated fear rather than groundless suspicion and mistrust.

Such a client would be asked, What was the single most reassuring thing she could say to herself? What would help her feel better if she could believe it? The therapist monitors to make sure the affirmation is not hostile to the self—for example, "That's stupid, an example of what a crazy I am," and that the affirmation does not empower the offender, "He wouldn't do anything like that" (which suggests he could if he chose). Better messages are "He wouldn't do it; he knows he couldn't get away with it" or "I can stop that from happening." However, the actual wording must be the client's own because foreign wording and rhythms are more difficult to internalize.

The client then says her chosen phrase to herself numerous times a day, whenever she is feeling anxious about kidnapping. She is learning not only the specific counter to this specific fear; she is learning the process of comforting the self. It is part of the process of developing a compassionate presence inside her head where one never existed before. Although awkward and contrived initially, although slow and laborious, this process nevertheless will cumulatively sculpt such a presence—one affirmation at a time, one mental image at a time.

Mental Imagery and Self-Soothing

Redoing. Intrusive memories bring with them affective flashbacks and physiological fear responses. For this reason, mental imagery can be well used to change the intrusive image in such a way that the emotions and the physiological responses change, even though the imagery has no impact on the memory itself. For example, John's sexually, physically, and emotionally abusive father demanded total obedience at the dinner table. Children were not to speak unless spoken to and then only certain topics, certain comments, and certain affects were permitted. He would ask each child about his day; they were to report amicably a variety of interesting things that happened. Disappointments, failures, and negative feelings were not permitted. John hated those dinners and the sense of being controlled that accompanied them.

In a redoing exercise, John had his father begin dinner as usual, but when he started to speak, a lion rose from behind John's chair and bellowed at his father so forcefully that it caused his hair to stream out behind him in the breeze. The physiological and emotional response to this image was quite different from that to the original—laughter and relaxation versus anger and fear. John then began to develop a new association and a new emotional response to memories of the dinners. Eventually, memories of the dinners would produce more mixed and more modulated responses.

The images must be the client's own, and some clients will suggest graphically violent images, particularly in response to memories of the sexual abuse itself. Such images appear to be therapeutic for some clients, although the therapist may find them difficult. Obviously, they should not be encouraged in any client who has a history of or tendency toward violence, for in such clients the line between fantasy and reality may be too thin.

Violent images are problematic for the least "macho" clients as well as the most. Phobic clients who were violently traumatized are often afraid such images will provoke the offender. Even in fantasy, they fear retaliation.

Finally, it is generally better if the redoing images are fantastic, and even humorous. Reality-based scenarios of fighting back are likely to make the client feel worse about not having done so. However, no client can expect himself to have a lion behind his seat waiting to roar at his father. Fighting back would be part of a realistic safety plan, but there is no point to a realistic safety plan for one's childhood sexual abuse. The childhood is gone; the child is gone. Only the offender in the head remains. Finding the perfect squelch decades later may sound fruitless, but it produces a surprising degree of satisfaction.

Dialogue With the Inner Child. The inner child is the client's concept of herself as a child extended into the present. It organizes and names the most vulnerable aspects of the client's personality; these are, by definition, aspects behind her adult defensive structure. Inner children do not drink and take drugs (unless they are adolescents) and are not relationship or work addicted. The concept is useful because it suggests how the client may access parts of her self behind her own defenses in a way she could not otherwise do.

The adult's relationship to the inner child is diagnostic. When asked to imagine an inner child whom they would then hold and rock, many clients rebel. They are not even able to imagine themselves getting near an inner child. Some say bluntly they cannot stand her. Others show a lack of empathy unmatched in their interactions with others.

One client, for example, who was severely physically abused by her mother, stayed out of her mother's way by spending all day in the attic. Without insulation and heat, the attic was bitterly cold and dark in the New England winter. I asked this client (who was magical with other children, including her own) to imagine climbing the stairs as the adult she was now to comfort the child. She climbed the stairs in fantasy only to bellow at the little girl, "What's wrong with you? What are you doing up here?" She could say nothing else. She could not imagine putting her arms around the small child in the cold and the dark, although the mere mention of *another* child in that situation would have elicited tears.

Those clients who cannot directly nurture the inner child are asked to take one small step at a time. Perhaps they can say one comforting thing to the child, move closer, or let the child sit near them.

The most severely traumatized clients, those whose capacity to avoid revictimization is minimal, can sometimes make use of the inner child where other techniques fail. Unable to empathize with the self, they may retain a capacity for empathy with others. Externalizing the self through the mechanism of the inner child can bring it under the client's protective wing—a wing that disappears when the client speaks as "I."

Rhonda's childhood was characterized by severe neglect and emotional and physical abuse. As one small example, her grandmother had once found the three small children after they had been left alone for 3 days. The baby's diaper was filled with maggots. Grandmother was disapproving and judgmental of the mother, but did nothing to protect the children. When they ran away to her house, she returned them home. Rhonda's father was alternately warm and sadistic. He would put Rhonda's preschool arms around his neck, hold them tight, and swim underwater until she could hold her breath no longer and started drowning. Only then would he emerge. He told her he was training her to be an Olympic swimmer.

Teachers tried to intervene and have the children removed, but the mother fought tenaciously when threatened. Judges—unaware of the difference between fusion and love—concluded that the mother loved her children because she was so upset at the prospect of losing them. The children were only removed once, briefly, and Rhonda remembers it as the happiest time of her life.

As an adult, Rhonda was raped by a psychopathic employer who then convinced her that "the only safe place was by his side." He "wore me down," she said, until she agreed to marry him, and for a decade he controlled every aspect of her life. He was sexually sadistic and extremely emotionally abusive. Rhonda finally freed herself from the relationship and took the bold step of suing him for battery.

Before the case was ever heard, however, Rhonda was already in another relationship with a sexually abusive male and had also allowed her abusive mother to move in with her. Her mother had been living in a shelter, and the other siblings were furious that Rhonda had rescued her from the consequences of her irresponsible lifestyle. Once ensconced in Rhonda's home, her mother refused to let Rhonda be alone for a moment, and followed her room to room talking nonstop. She was as controlling and emotionally abusive as ever, although no longer physically assaultive. Rhonda felt responsible for her mother, as she did for her violent boyfriend. She had no concept of responsibility to herself.

Through the decade of her marriage, Rhonda had been in and out of therapy with several therapists. It was difficult to treat her, partially because of the countertransferential rage her situation evoked. It was easy to tell Rhonda what to do, and hard not to. As a result, she had been ordered, coaxed, lectured, and warned—all of which simply externalized that part of her ambivalence that wished to leave the abusive relationships and consequently freed Rhonda to stay. Early on in my relationship with her, I referred in passing to her boyfriend as a "rapist"—which I thought merely a factual description—and received a lecture on "seeing the good in everybody" in return.

Clearly, she had no concept of herself as someone worth nurturing or protecting, although she had well-developed, almost obsessive drives to take care of others. Her mother had ensured the latter when Rhonda came back to pick up some belongings after having finally moved out for good. When she opened the garage door, the prize show dog Rhonda had been forced to sleep with as a child—sleep with so that she could pick up any feces he dropped in the night—was tied to a 4-foot chain without food or water. He lay dying.

Rhonda was asked in therapy to imagine an inner child. "It's not happy," she said. "I don't like doing it." The child she described was a baby standing in a crib on a bare mattress with feces smeared all over her. She had been there a long time. This was, in fact, a memory of an incident and was confirmed by her mother, who for years had told a "funny" story of Rhonda smearing the feces. She was asked to comfort the child. She could easily, she said, until she realized that the child was not supposed to be "a baby," it was to be her. She stopped short at the door, unable to enter. Odd, she said, she could do it easily, would want to do it, would have to if it were any other child. She was at a loss. She found she could not imagine herself going in. She began to cry—something not seen in her bland and affectless descriptions of previous trauma.

That session she worked on trying to enter the room, approach the child, and say something. "This is hard," she kept saying. Finally, her therapist said, "As long as your mother is living in your house, that child is going to be in that crib. You have some choices here. You can't evade them anymore. You can keep your mother in your house, but the price is selling that kid down the river. That's the reality. Up to you." Using Rhonda's compulsive need to take care of others, particularly children, the therapist facilitated an internal confrontation rather than lecturing her from an outside point of view. It was only a beginning, but previous therapy had failed to find even a starting point.

Self-Soothing Versus External Soothing

The most important aspect of any self-soothing exercise lies in the term "self." When the client leaves the office, the means of soothing need to leave with him.

It is impossible for the therapist to avoid providing solace in any form: The type of attention paid by the therapist, the ability to hear the client more fully than others have heard him previously, the ability to empathize with shame-based parts that others know nothing about—all will surely comfort. Because of this, it is particularly important that the therapist be mindful of the dangers of too much external solace in order to minimize those risks.

Soothing that stems only from the therapist will increase the client's distress. He must then stay in the therapist's presence and/or stay connected to him in order to feel safe. The client must either please the therapist or control him. Either option will produce rage in the client. The extreme alternation of rage and dependency characteristic of so-called borderline personalities is often, in fact, a failure of the client to develop self-soothing skills and a failure of the therapist to encourage them.

High-functioning clients with encapsulated sequelae may have already developed the ability to self-soothe and thus may find internalizing the therapist's compassionate presence to be automatic. These are not, by definition, the clients frequently diagnosed as "borderlines."

However, the more severely disturbed clients, those who do become diagnosed as "borderline," may replace internalization of the therapist with a chronic dependence on him as observing ego, meaning-maker, and external soother. Such clients can never leave therapy, nor can they tolerate the therapist's absences, illnesses, or vacations with equanimity. One therapist consulted me on a case in which he had not taken a day of vacation in 5 years without giving a particular client the phone number where he would be. The client would call each day and rage at him literally for hours about the therapist's alleged cruelty in leaving him. In such extreme cases, such clients may call day and night, eventually generating such anger in the therapist that the therapeutic relationship becomes distorted and counterproductive.

Likewise, much of what is considered relationship addiction is often simply the client's ability to soothe through others and not the self. She must take care of her alcoholic boyfriend so that he will soothe her. When she is alone, she experiences no soothing in any form. This is often seen in adolescent sexual abuse survivors who appear to rebel against their parents by becoming seriously involved with a boyfriend. A closer look, however, suggests that the teen has become fused with the boyfriend rather than attached. They do everything together. She forfeits all other friends, all other interests, all other activities. She sees him in school, after school, and on the weekends. In a surprising number of cases, she ends up living at his parents' house or he at hers.

Eventually, when he leaves for whatever reasons, she may then make her first suicide attempt. She feels safe and soothed in his presence, even as a small child does with a parent, and the emptiness that follows his departure is intolerable. What looked like a search for independence and adolescent acting out was, in fact, simply a transfer of parental dependency. If the therapist is not careful, he can end up in the same position as the boyfriend.

Conclusions

Therapists must directly teach methods of self-soothing and not assume that the client will sooner or later simply internalize the therapist and thus let go. A nonabused 5-year-old, whose parents had divorced, once drew for me a picture of her in her dad's house and one of her in her mom's house. In each one, she drew inside her head a picture of the missing parent. She held each one in her head, she said, when she was in the other's house so that she would not miss them. It was a simple trick for a nontraumatized 5-year-old with object constancy, a trick no one had to teach her. It is an achingly difficult one for a traumatized adult, one someone needs to teach her.

Management Strategies for Chronic Pain

The two options for constructively managing chronic pain are to reduce it as much as possible and to self-soothe what is left. Much of what has been described above will diminish it. To the extent that dysphoria is secondary to cognitions, developing a cognitive life raft, remaking meaning, and challenging the internal, perpetrator-based critic will all be helpful. Even affective flashbacks—which are not secondary to cognitions—are less upsetting when the survivor understands what they are and how they function.

However, it frequently occurs that the chronic pain of child sexual abuse cannot all be made to disappear, and survivors must make choices regarding management. The goals of therapy differ depending on the areas of impairment and the degree of trauma. For the most severely traumatized, just developing a sense of self again may be a dramatic gain. In general, however, the goals for pain management include a conscious (rather than unconscious) choice of strategies and a reduction in the amount of pain such that it diminishes to a "background level." The residual pain should not interfere with functioning or with the ability to enjoy life. Within that framework, choices may be made. For example, affective flashbacks may respond to habituation, avoidance, or self-soothing, all of which can be under the survivor's conscious control.

As outlined in Chapter 6, unconscious strategies for managing conscious pain tend to take on a life of their own. Many are addictive (e.g., drug or alcohol addiction); some have egregious side effects (e.g., suicidality, self-mutilation); most generalize beyond the situations for which they were developed and intrude on general functioning (e.g., dissociation). By being unconscious, these management strategies do not give the survivor the option of reducing the pain itself, for example, by habituating to the stimuli. She cannot choose how far to tolerate affective flashbacks before she intervenes because the strategies are triggered automatically outside of conscious awareness.

Assume Roberta has affective flashbacks whenever she passes a 1950s beige car, particularly if it is a certain model. Understandably, she has no knowledge of what affective flashbacks are. Although she has always remembered being abused by her father on Sunday drives, she is not aware of having any reaction to cars of that era. What she does notice, and what frightens her considerably, is that she may be feeling fine, and yet will suddenly have an urge to cut herself. At times she has a desire, almost a hunger, to die.

A daily log reveals that these urges frequently occur when driving. At first, therapist and client think this might be because driving allows time for intrusive thoughts and ruminations, but no such thoughts emerge. Knowing what she is looking for—a trigger—allows Roberta to notice finally her reaction to certain cars, ones that are similar to the car in which her father molested her.

In realizing this, Roberta's world begins to change. She no longer feels like a "crazy person" whose self-mutilation and suicidality make no sense. She has a "cognitive life raft" to hold on to, which makes her feel less disoriented and confused. She might or might not have a trauma-based worldview, but she has less of a trauma-based self-view, that is, a sense of herself as unpredictable, as behaving in meaningless ways, and (for many survivors) as malevolent.

Roberta now has choices where she did not before. She cannot avoid such cars: There is no way to predict which cars will drive by. However, using standard behavioral desensitization techniques, she could attempt to habituate to such cars, or she could recognize the affective flashbacks when they occur and self-soothe.

Nor is avoidance, when it is possible, always a dysfunctional option. Whereas unconscious avoidance can result in "posttraumatic decline" (Titchener, 1986), selective, conscious avoidance can be a reasonable choice. For example, a client whose mother was murdered in her own home when the client was a child was forced to continue living in that home when her father refused to move the family. He felt that by staying they would set an example for the community. Each time she or her siblings walked into the kitchen, they had to pass the spot where the mother's raped, shot, and strangled body was found by one of the children. They literally had to walk past the bullet holes in the floor (which the father never repaired). It would have decreased affective flashbacks in children already overwhelmed with trauma if the family had moved.

The specificity of the trigger, its degree of frequency and predictability in the environment, the personal costs of avoiding it—all these will factor into the decision as to whether or not to use avoidance. Unfortunately, unconscious avoidance does not take such factors into account. Some clients, for example, find that their sex lives are significantly improved if they make peace with the fact that certain activities—often oral sex—are too reminiscent of the trauma to enjoy. By avoiding the aversive activities and the affective flashbacks they occasion, they can enjoy sex. The unconscious response would be to avoid sex altogether or to dissociate during it, both of which would impair the client's life more than a more conscious and discriminating use of avoidance.

Conclusions

The survivor's arsenal for reducing pain can be fairly extensive: remaking meaning; developing a cognitive life raft; confronting the internal, perpetrator-based critic; behaviorally desensitizing; and consciously avoiding. Even so, there will still be a need for self-soothing after doing all the pain reduction possible. As in the serenity prayer, the adult survivor must self-soothe that pain that cannot be reduced, reduce that pain that cannot be self-soothed, and develop the wisdom to know the difference.

Then and Now

Sequence

At times, clients enter therapy because they are distressed by the intrusive phase of PTSD: the unbidden memories, the nightmares, the affective flashbacks, the intrusive thoughts. Such clients, well aware of the impact of sexual abuse, set their agenda from the start to shorten its shadow. For these clients, therapy can proceed approximately in the order outlined above. The client begins, on the first day, to tell the tale, and the therapist settles in for the listening.

More commonly, clients enter therapy with "here and now" complaints that may or may not relate to early trauma. For example, a client's marital difficulties could relate to a variety of temperamental or individual differences. Larks and owls, procrastinators and early birds, sexual adventurers and sexual conservatives, fiscal conservatives and fiscal liberals—all may find that the differences that delighted have become the conditions for conflict. When Don Juan marries Emily Dickinson, even sans a history of trauma, the prognosis is guarded. Divorce occurs everywhere but Eden.

So it is with almost any symptom. Trauma may not be implicated. Adult victimization can occur by chance. Alcoholism does run in families. Depression can be occasioned by a dead-end job, by economic stress, by loss or betrayal, or even by chemicals run amok.

Early tasks in therapy, then, are to determine the nature of the problem and the length of its roots. Therapist and client may disagree on both. The problem in the client's view may be simply that her husband is a jerk or even that she is. The problem in the therapist's view may be that the client is afraid of intimacy, avoidant of sexuality, or addicted to abusive men. In many cases, the client may have internalized the offender's point of view and thus will agree more with his formulation than with the therapist's.

Likewise, the client may have never considered the question of whether his current difficulties relate to past trauma. The very nature of posttraumatic defenses—denial, dissociation, avoidance—all work by severing the connection between trauma and the client's conscious awareness. As noted earlier, the defenses may not reduce impact, but they effectively reduce awareness of impact.

Here and Now Versus There and Then. What, then, can one use for guideposts? What buoys or markers can be used to determine which boats are coming from across the bay and which from across the ocean?

The therapist will look first for whether the client is overreacting to current stimuli. A husband comes home late from work without calling. One woman is annoyed. Another is panicky, convinced he has left her or has died. One woman does not like being held down, even playfully; another develops nausea and wants to throw up at the thought. Here-and-now issues generate heat commensurate with the source. Historical issues generate a firestorm from one small match. Thus the therapist is looking first for land mines and the history of their planting.

In addition, certain defenses are typically responses to trauma and are unlikely to be generated for the first time by the ordinary problems of adulthood. Dissociation, amnesia, numbing—all massive defenses, equivalent to military tanks—are not born of adult arguments over finances. They are childhood defenses, produced by conditions of overwhelming trauma. They become automatically used in adulthood in psychologically reminiscent situations.

Finally, certain homegrown solutions to chronic pain are too drastic to be here-and-now responses. The client who loses a job and becomes suicidal probably has a long-standing relationship with rejection. The client whose divorce throws him into a severe depression requiring hospitalization has met abandonment before.

The therapist separates past and present by looking for affect, defenses, or self-medication techniques that are drastically excessive for the current situation. The more extreme the response, the more trivial the insult, the more likely the situation has pushed an internal button.

Affect Bridges. "When have you felt like that before?" the therapist queries. "Tell me about times you've had that feeling." As in the great posttraumatic stress novel *Slaughterhouse Five* (Vonnegut, 1968), which used flashbacks for its main narrative rhythm, the client too must become at least somewhat "unstuck in time" (p. 23). He must move back and forth on affect bridges. The therapist, instead of asking about events, situations, or people, and moving then to the affect they generate, often finds one of the "ancient ones"—the old, powerful, and all-too-familiar affects—and asks the client to go back to other times he felt that way. The mind floats—a radio tuner looking for a station—and then settles. The client is free-associating around an affective pole. The computer is generating a search, using an old emotion. Once the station tunes in, he tells the tale, not from the beginning, but in segments dredged up by current experience. The tale, then, is told in fits and starts as it relates to the present.

Of course, the therapist has begun therapy by asking for a history and has learned early the narrative line of the client's life. But often this surface map does not tell well enough where the sources of heat are. The map the therapist eventually draws will look more like an infrared map than the earlier topographical one. By moving from past to present, the therapist learns the main facts of the client's life, insofar as the client remembers them. By moving from present to past, he learns what is charged, what counts, what still surfaces today after all these years, what fragments of the past cling like stuck debris to bits of the present.

And Back Again. In this way, the client goes back through the old corridors to find what belongs to the past and what belongs to the present. After the affective flashbacks are identified, the tale is told and heard, the meaning remade, and the self-soothing learned, she comes back more fully to the present. Without the excess baggage, real-world problems are more solvable, or at least more manageable. Her relationship may or may not be what she wants—but if she is no longer afraid to be alone, she can leave it if she needs to, stay if she wants to. Because she can leave it, she may not have to. She may feel badly that her job is not going well, but without the cognitive distortion that she is worthless, she may not become clinically depressed. She may still startle when she sees 1950s cars, but knowing that her reaction is an affective flashback may make her anxiety far less severe. She renders to Caesar that which is his and often finds she can accommodate what is left.

Putting It Together

And so goes therapy. The client tells the tale. The therapist listens. The pieces of the quilt are spread out between them.

What ties the past and present together? Why does that memory come up? What does the self-mutilation mean? The wanting to die? Where does the depression come from? The work of meaning-making begins to stitch the divergent patches together.

As each quilt piece is passed back and forth, the therapist handles each one carefully, considers it thoughtfully, and winces when the client rails at it, tears it, tries to discard it. "Oh no," the therapist says, "look at it in this light. It is really quite interesting." And the internalization begins.

"Here," she says, "You'll want to know how to smooth it out yourself." And the work of self-soothing unfolds.

"Well, yes, you can't get all the wrinkles out. How are you going to live with the ones that are left?" And ways to manage chronic pain are considered and brought under conscious control, control that can have the careful specificity of a precision tool. The unconscious, by contrast, favors the indiscriminate stroke of an axe.

And so the quilt takes shape. There are those who would argue for the simplicity of a woven piece—something in the evenness of a fabric that has never been cut and stitched. But quilts came originally not from worn-out clothes, as some think, but from the leftover bits of fabric used to make them. Therapist and client, midwife and survivor, together gather the discarded parts of the self—the leftover, the hidden, the seemingly flawed, the crumpled up and thrown away—and in the teeth of trauma, stitch by stitch, session by session, stubbornly put together not just a pleasing pattern but one that comforts and warms in a way few woven pieces can.

"But is that all?" the disappointed reader says. "You're talking about living with pain. You're talking about pain reduction, not elimination, you're talking about self-soothing. Where is the transformation in that?"

"But there is transformation, there is," I mumble.

She sits in my office, one arm draped casually across the back of the couch. There is always something interesting about her clothes: always understated but with something—a texture, a color, a line—that stands out. "Is this all there is?" she says. "Somehow I thought recovery would be more."

If only she could see, I think, the sureness with which she speaks. If she could see her arm on the back of the couch. I cannot remember, I realize, the last time she averted her gaze.

Her second marriage, a good one, was made long before she started therapy, but she could never enjoy it. Ridden with insecurities, she constantly feared losing her husband. If he was late for dinner—and he was often late—she was alone with chronic pain. Panicky, she railed at him for his insensitivity. He was her transitional object, and she needed him to soothe. Like many independent people, he distanced himself further the more she clung.

The days were a maze of affective flashbacks: the sound of her mother's voice on the phone, a stranger telling her how wonderful her father was, a family picture of the ranch where he raped her in the summers. The depression, at least, she could see. But the constantly critical, hostile perpetrator in her head she could not. She just believed every word she said. "She," because the critic in the family was her mother, an emotionally abusive alcoholic who belittled and humiliated and demeaned. Nurturance came from Daddy, and his eventual betrayal left her decades later with great fears about trusting anybody.

No, she says, her mother does not seem to be much of a problem anymore. Somehow, she's let her go. She laughs. She thinks her mother is a little afraid of her now. It upset her mother, she adds, that she's made such a success of her business. Her mother had always told her she was the stupid one in the family and advised her flatly she could not run a business.

She has made her peace with Joe's lateness. She just doesn't wait. She doesn't like to be late so she takes her car and goes on her own. Sometimes he seems relieved. Sometimes he seems to hurry after her. In any case, she is glad not to always be so angry.

She knows how much he hates the visits to the medical center for her chronic condition, so this time she bought one plane ticket and arranged for a friend to meet her. He was nonplussed. He would as soon go, he said, and called to make his own reservation.

And the depression? She is not sure the last time she was depressed. Yes, it used to be bad, she thinks. Hard to remember, somehow. I remember, though, and yes indeed it was.

I take no extra credit for these changes. There is a reason, I know, that athletes win prizes and not their coaches, although good coaches tend to sleep well at night.

But change it is. And if slowly and carefully and solidly built, it does not feel all that dramatic. It just feels right. And yes, there is still pain and there are still fights and she does have down times.

It's in the tilt of the head, I think. It's in the arm on the back of the couch. She has no idea how much she shines. "For I know," Richard Selzer wrote, "that it is the scarred, and the marred, and the faulty who are subject to grace" (Selzer, 1974, p. 19). And grace she has. And yes—I mumble less now—yes, I say, that is transformation.

Note

1. Excerpt from Valentine, J., *Dream Barker and Other Poems*, New Haven, CT: Yale University Press. Copyright © 1965. Reprinted by permission.

Epilogue
Thoughts on Survivors and Safety
An Essay

T he propane torch swings in front of Deb's face, a metal penis
spitting fire. "Are you afraid, bitch, are you afraid? How'd you
like to get a taste of this, bitch?" He follows her, flicking it at her
hair, her skin. The unsaid words follow her, too. She keeps recognition from her eyes, keeping them flat, slightly harried, a little
distracted. She swings back to the ship's galley, waving the torch
away, casually, dismissingly, and kneads the dough. "Biscuits,"
she says just as silently, "I have biscuits to make, and now look at
this silly interruption." She glances at the clock, brushing her hair
back with a floured hand. "Eleven o'clock already, and I barely
finished breakfast."

Nancy Lieberman rides the subway to Harlem to play pick-up
ball. "Look at that white girl. Where you think she's going?"

"Looking for trouble, that's all I see. Looking for trouble."

"Well, she's gonna find it. You go looking for trouble in this
world, you're gonna find it."

Nancy Lieberman clutches her basketball and stares at the
gum wrapper on the dirty subway floor, barely glancing at the
man nodding off next to her. Over and over she says to herself,

weaving a shawl, a prayer, a litany, "Nobody's gonna mess with me. I've got basketball to play."

Deb moves toward the torch wielder, a bold move. He backs up and she moves around him for more salt. Whose reality will win? Is she cowering victim, deliciously fearful prey? Is he a big, bad, scary rapist, or is he a little boy waiting for the best cook the ship ever had to feed him strawberry shortcake for lunch? A brother teasing a younger sister ("Just kidding, you know. No reason to get upset.")? Or a rapist leaving his calling card? It is being decided now what will happen when the dinner dishes are done, and she walks through the halls, trailing her fingers on the warm metal walls, past the empty storeroom, as women everywhere walk every night. The torch flicks off. The answer is in.

She is 15 years old, a sophomore in high school. She has been set up by a local senior with a date, a college basketball star. She and her friend think God is on their side. He and his friend are southern polite to her parents, "A party at the beach. Yes, ma'am, back early. For sure. Eleven, no later." But there are no other women at the party, just a motel room full of basketball players, one of whom is already down to his underwear.

Now, don't start screaming. You'll get hurt for sure. Figure it out, girl, figure it out. A walk on the beach, definitely a good idea. "No, I can't have sex with you. I'm a virgin. I don't have sex with anybody. No, I don't believe that's what my friend is doing right now."

Keep it casual. Keep that shoulder-rolling-good-buddy-gait. She punches him on the arm, a kid's gesture, a male gesture. He quizzes her crossly. Is she really a virgin? He has qualms, it seems, about gang raping a virgin. Some combination works. It's decided. She and he collude. She's not feeling well, something she ate. They turn back. She and her friend are going home.

Only the very strong and the very weak can ignore camouflage. The grizzly rarely tries to melt into the scenery, and minnows live by luck alone. For the rest of us, it pays not to look like someone's idea of lunch, and sometimes, just sometimes, women get by by pretending it isn't lunchtime at all. Reality is a consensual experience, and every woman knows there are times that a gesture will define it. Was it the floured hand pushing back the errant strand of hair that rescued Deb? Was it Lieberman's rounded back hunched over the basketball? A woman doesn't sit like that, only some crazy basketball nut. Was it the punch in the shoulder or the male walk, that lurching forward, shoulder-rolling gait the teen mimicked that brought her safe to harbor? She didn't have the upper body mass to pull it off, but even a trace of that walk would register, without needing recognition by the conscious mind.

Women cling to that chance to define reality. "You could die," I tell the battered woman in front of me. "You have to understand you could die." "You don't understand, Anna," she tells me. "The moment I leave him he's a shadow outside my door."

The naive and the hopeful will scoff. Call the police. Take out a restraining order. One woman did, against the battering husband who threatened to burn her family and their home if she stayed away. A few days later her parents' barn burned, killing all the animals. "No proof," the police said. "Nothing we can do." She moved back in. For women, safety is always relative, never absolute.

Where does safety lie? Wherever you know enough to survive. I am a safe woman on a basketball court, playing with men half a foot taller and twice my weight. I know how to block out for the rebound, how to brace for the pick I set. I know when to swing in front of a driving player and when to step aside and try to pick his pocket from behind. I know, too, who will go through me and who will go around. My powerful, quick, athletic ex-spouse dislocated his shoulder the first time he joined in.

Philippe Petit, the great French aerialist, is a safe man on a high wire.

> He stretches out on his cable and contemplates the sky. There he gathers his strength, recovers the serenity he may have lost, regains his courage and his faith. . . . The cable is limpid. Your body is silent. Together, they are motionless. Only your leg quivers. You would like to cut it off, to turn your body into a single human wire. But already it no longer belongs to you, is no longer a part of you . . . you close your eyes and see only a magnificent gray wire. (Petit, 1985, pp. 69-70)

Sometimes, switch the frame ever so slightly and you're not safe at all. We were all nervous waiting for Momad, a group of novices waiting for a pro. When he arrived, he threw a practiced eye on all our gear, on the knots and the slings and the ropes and the pitons, checking them all with a glance, and moved off up the mountain like a ferret. No sooner had we reached him than he was off, leaving us scrambling to set up a belay, and hoping, dear God, he didn't fall before we were tied in. At the top, I asked how often he fell, given his speed. "No," he said, "I fell once, and I didn't like it, so I never fell again." I was dumbfounded. This was a world-class climber, a man in the record books for first ascents on this mountain and that.

But he later died while cleaning the inside of a huge vat, working as climbers often do on a high job, thinking he was safe. The sludge became dislodged and fell in an avalanche on a man who could tell an unsafe piton with a look, whether a harness was tied properly at a glance, whether an avalanche was brewing by ways he could not even name—the warmth of the sun on his face that day, the texture of the snow, the single rumbling sound easily discounted—but on a man who did not know the warning signs on the inside of a vat, who did not live with the texture of sludge, the changing temperatures inside a metal can.

And sometimes safety lies in a touch of grace, unowned. In therapy, one can sometimes hear these grace notes resounding across decades. My client's embezzling mother got caught, and the family, too proud to ask for help, never had heat and electricity at the same time again. This child lost 40 pounds that year and would have lost more, but for the teacher who needed her help at recess. "I hate to ask you, because I know you want to play. But I could really use some help erasing the boards, marking these papers." Somehow, the money was always enough for lunch. My client was in her forties before she understood.

Does safety lie in being visible or invisible? Well, it depends. It has been hypothesized that shark attacks on surfers in California are triggered by the configuration that a paddling surfer makes when viewed from below, something alarmingly like a seal. Surfers would be better off looking like surfers, but then again, seals would be better off looking like surfers, too. For my client and her teacher, safety lay in the child being visible and not knowing it, beside a teacher dressed in camouflage. For the sexually abused 4-year-old whose father tells her how much she wants him to fuck her, safety will forever after lie in being visible, in being known, for when she was not, she got hurt. Let people project onto you, and God knows what will happen. Nothing good.

But for the child whose sadistic father closes the curtains when he sees her use the window to dissociate, to leave the abuse behind, safety will forever lie in camouflage, in invisibility. The mother of Henry C. Lucas, the serial killer, asked him as a small child if he loved the family mule. He said he did and so she got the shotgun and killed it. Whatever else that did to Henry Lucas, it also made him appreciate emotional invisibility. Let people know who you really are, what you really care about, and they will kill it. Where does safety lie?

I asked my adult survivors to imagine a safe place. I know they and I will be going into unsafe rooms with unsafe people, into spaces and times they lost memory rather than remember. "A safe place," I say. "And we will use it for solace in the hard times." And sometimes they look blank and I have to say, "Well, can you think of times, of places, of people where you felt a little less afraid?"

Sometimes they can, and in those spaces one can see where safety lies. A woman, raped at age 7 by a 14-year-old brother who kept telling her she was his girlfriend and supposed to like it, finds safety only as a catcher in a softball game—all those pads in front, a net in back, and all those people out there so everybody can see what is going on. So that's it. That's where safety lies, in being seen by one and all, in public places with strangers all around.

But another, forced as an elementary school child to choose which instrument her sadistic father would use to torture her while her mother tied her legs apart and held her hands, finds safety in the image of a tiny speck of a boat on an ocean thousands of miles across. No one could possibly know where she is, and if her father did, the water is so calm for hundreds of miles around that she could see him coming. She keeps high-powered rifles on board just in case. He knew her, you see. He knew what hurt her and he used that knowledge to make it worse. Ah, I see it now. Safety lies in not being seen, in being as close to nonexistent in the world as one can manage. Where does safety lie?

But safety must be more than not being starved or beaten or raped or killed, although for many it would be a start. Can one find safety in therapy? Certainly the therapist can. What could be better? Intimacy without risk, without even exposure, a high-intensity emotional connection wearing a safety harness. I stay firmly planted in my seat while my client skirts chasms, peers in black holes, tap dances on a high wire.

And what of safety for my client? If safety is invisibility, this man has surely found it in my office, for we have sat together six times and I have yet to see a glimpse of him. He watches me intently. A raised eyebrow alone is enough to steer him. Who do I want him to be? He's amenable. He brings in reading lists to show me his intelligence, his dedication, his sincerity. I am impressed. Why, then, won't I tell him what to do, who to be? In desperation he plays, he thinks, a high card. It would be easier, he says shyly, if his therapist weren't so feminine, so attractive. Actually, I say, I don't think it would make any difference at all.

He has not done the "stilling," that great quieting of mind and spirit when one locks the door to one's house and faces the gorilla living there, when one lets go of the outside world, sits down at the kitchen table, and looks around. What do I have? What do I really have? The way the afternoon sun slants through the chair arms, the way the lily leans hard against the vase, this moment, this breath, this ragged hole in my heart, that one, where the edges flap so gently. These are what I have. He has not noticed the silence, how it rushes in when the talking stops. He has not stood his ground and stopped lurching for the phone, for another task, another event, another person—all fodder to stuff in that hole that only seems to grow the more it's filled. He has not stopped his hand in midclutch and just watched it, without judgment, without impatience, until the fingers slowly soften and let go. No, he has done no stilling.

He makes another run instead. "I was very surprised," he says, "that you didn't tell me last time when I asked, that I was abused as a child. And when I questioned you whether my current relationship was love or addiction, you wouldn't say. I'd like to take advantage of your expertise, you know." And behind the aggressive fawning, I hear the anger curling at the edges of his voice. "Goddamn you, goddamn you," he is saying. "Just tell me what you want. I can be it. I know I can."

I must always disappoint. "Does it matter what you label it?" I say. "Whatever you call it, aren't you still left with the feelings?" I have leapt aside again, as I will each time he spins to face me, for I need to be so close beside him he cannot even see me. Is this man safe? Not here or anywhere. He thinks if he could just get hold of me, could grab my shirt and bury his head, he would be. But true safety for him is an eel of a therapist, and I am worn out from trying to be slippery.

But if he cannot find me, I cannot find him either. I am trying to find a radio station that won't tune in. I think if I hear his voice just once I will be able to recognize it, find it again, but in these many weeks, I haven't heard it once. Perhaps I am asking too much, I say. Perhaps I need to listen for a phrase, a word, a syllable that is his own. I listen harder—and stay poised to jump.

So what is safe in this world? Who is safe and who is not? Is a smiling man who is never angry safe? Hardly. Is someone who wants only to please you safe? You'll find him living in your skin. Beyond the lily leaning on the vase, it's a dicey world out there.

In the end, I think I know little of safety, after all—only 57 varieties of risk. But I catch glimpses of her now and then, in a woman's floured hand, a teacher's grace. She brings no fireworks when she comes, sets off no cannons. A mousy guest, she's not one to inspire a toast or draw a rave review: She comes as simply as the breaking of your last remembered fever, as gently as the covers that defined your childhood sleep. One thing's for sure, she's a fickle guest. A nomad, she can leave in the night with the sound of a ringing phone, or move out so slowly it takes years to figure out she's gone.

"Do you know what my plans are?" the client said. "I'm try-ing to string together as many days in a row, like beads on a string, in which nothing bad happens." The days when nothing bad hap-pens. Better yet, the days without fear that something bad will happen. Days our mousy guest resides. I dream of her. I've lost my taste, over the years, for the more theatrical guests.

Stay a while, I coax. String a few more beads. When you are here, "For a moment in the central of our being/The vivid trans-parence that you bring is peace" (Stevens, 1969, p. 380).[1]

Note

1. From *Collected Poems* by Wallace Stevens. Copyright © 1942 by Wallace Stevens. Reprinted by permission of Alfred A. Knopf, Inc.

References

Abel, G. G., Barlow, D. H., Blanchard, E. B., & Guild, D. (1977). The components of rapists' sexual arousal. *Archives of General Psychiatry, 34*(8), 895-903.

Abel, G. G., Becker, J. V., Blanchard, E. B., & Djenderedjian, A. (1978). Differentiating sexual aggressiveness with penile measures. *Criminal Justice and Behavior, 5*(4), 315-332.

Abel, G. G., Becker, J. V., Cunningham-Rathner, J., Mittelman, M., & Rouleau, J. L. (1988). Multiple paraphilic diagnoses among sex offenders. *Bulletin of the American Academy of Psychiatry and the Law, 16*(2), 153-168.

Abel, G. G., Becker, J. V., Cunningham-Rathner, J., Rouleau, J. L., Kaplan, M., & Reich, J. (1984). *The treatment of child molesters.* Unpublished manuscript. (Available from G. G. Abel, Behavior Medicine Institute, 5790 Kingston Cross, Stone Mountain, GA 30087)

Abel, G. G., Becker, J. V., Mittelman, M., Cunningham-Rathner, J., Rouleau, J. L., & Murphy, W. D. (1987). Self-reported sex crimes of nonincarcerated paraphiliacs. *Journal of Interpersonal Violence, 2*(1), 3-25.

Abel, G. G., Becker, J. V., Murphy, W. D., & Flanagan, B. (1981). Identifying dangerous child molesters. In R. Stuart (Ed.), *Violent behavior: Social learning approaches to prediction, management, and treatment* (pp. 116-137). New York: Brunner/Mazel.

Abel, G. G., Mittelman, M. S., & Becker, J. V. (1985). Sexual offenders: Results of assessment and recommendations for treatment. In M. R. Ben-Aron, S. J. Huckle, & C. D. Webster (Eds.), *Clinical criminology: The assessment and treatment of criminal behavior* (pp. 191-205). Toronto: M & M Graphic Ltd.

Abel, G. G., & Rouleau, J. L. (1990). The nature and extent of sexual assault. In W. L. Marshall, D. R. Laws, & H. E. Barbaree (Eds.), *Handbook of sexual assault: Issues, theories, and treatment of the offender* (pp. 9-21). New York: Plenum.

Ageton, S. S. (1983). *Sexual assault among adolescents.* Lexington, MA: Lexington Books.

Alexander, P. C. (1985). A systems theory conceptualization of incest. *Family Process, 24,* 79-87.

Allen, D. M. (1980). Young male prostitutes: A psychosocial study. *Archives of Sexual Behavior, 9*(5), 399-426.

Anderson, G., Yasenik, L., & Ross, C. A. (1993). Dissociative experiences and disorders among women who identify themselves as sexual abuse survivors. *Child Abuse & Neglect, 17*(5), 677-686.

Avery-Clark, C. A., & Laws, D. R. (1984). Differential erection response patterns of sexual child abusers to stimuli describing activities with children. *Behavior Therapy, 15*(1), 71-83.

Awad, G. A., & Saunders, E. B. (1991). Male adolescent sexual assaulters: Clinical observations. *Journal of Interpersonal Violence, 6*(4), 446-460.

Bagley, C., & McDonald, M. (1984). Adult mental health sequels of child sexual abuse, physical abuse and neglect in maternally separated children. *Canadian Journal of Community Mental Health, 3*(1), 15-26.

Bagley, C., & Ramsay, R. (1986). Sexual abuse in childhood: Psychosocial outcomes and implications for social work practice. *Journal of Social Work and Human Sexuality, 4,* 33-47.

Bagley, C., & Young, L. (1987). Juvenile prostitution and child sexual abuse: A controlled study. *Canadian Journal of Community Mental Health, 6*(1), 5-26.

Barbaree, H. E. (1990). Stimulus control of sexual arousal: Its role in sexual assault. In W. L. Marshall, D. R. Laws, & H. E. Barbaree (Eds.), *Handbook of sexual assault: Issues, theories, and treatment of the offender* (pp. 115-142). New York: Plenum.

Barbaree, H. E., Marshall, W. L., & Lanthier, R. D. (1979). Deviant sexual arousal in rapists. *Behaviour Research and Therapy, 17*(3), 215-222.

Barnard, G. W., Fuller, A. K., Robbins, L., & Shaw, T. (1989). *The child molester: An integrated approach to evaluation and treatment.* New York: Brunner/Mazel.

Bass, E., & Davis, L. (1993). *Beginning to heal.* London: Cedar.

Becker, J. V., & Coleman, E. M. (1988). Incest. In V. B. Van Hasselt, R. L. Morrison, A. S. Bellack, & M. Hersen (Eds.), *Handbook of family violence* (pp. 187-205). New York: Plenum.

Becker, J. V., Cunningham-Rathner, J., & Kaplan, M. S. (1986). Adolescent sexual offenders: Demographics, criminal and sexual histories, and recommendations for reducing future offenses. *Journal of Interpersonal Violence, 1*(4), 431-445.

Becker, J. V., & Quinsey, V. L. (1993). Assessing suspected child molesters. *Child Abuse & Neglect, 17*(1), 169-194.

Becker, J. V., Skinner, L. J., Abel, G. G., & Cichon, J. (1986). Level of postassault sexual functioning in rape and incest victims. *Archives of Sexual Behavior, 15*(1), 37-49.

Becker, J. V., Skinner, L. J., Abel, G. G., & Treacy, E. C. (1982). Incidence and types of sexual dysfunctions in rape and incest victims. *Journal of Sex and Marital Therapy, 8*(1), 65-74.

Beitchman, J. H., Zucker, K. J., Hood, J. E., DaCosta, G. A., Akman, D., & Cassavia, E. (1992). A review of the long-term effects of child sexual abuse. *Child Abuse & Neglect, 16*(1), 101-118.

Bender, L., & Blau, A. (1937). The reaction of children to sexual relations with adults. *American Journal of Orthopsychiatry, 7*, 500-518.

Bender, L., & Grugett, A. E. (1952). A follow-up report on children who had atypical sexual experience. *American Journal of Orthopsychiatry, 22*, 825-837.

Bennet, G. (1970). Bristol floods 1968: Controlled survey of effects on health of local community disaster. *British Medical Journal, 3*(70), 454-458.

Benson, C. S., & Heller, K. (1987). Factors in the current adjustment of young adult daughters of alcoholic and problem drinking fathers. *Journal of Abnormal Psychology, 96*(4), 305-312.

Benward, J., & Densen-Gerber, J. (1975). Incest as a causative factor in antisocial behavior: An exploratory study. *Contemporary Drug Problems, 4*(3), 323-340.

Berliner, L., & Williams, L. M. (1994). Memories of child sexual abuse: A response to Lindsay and Read. *Applied Cognitive Psychology, 8,* 379-387.

Bernard, F. (1975). An enquiry among a group of pedophiles. *Journal of Sex Research, 11*(3), 242-255.

Bouhoutsos, J., Holroyd, J., & Lerman, H. E. A. (1983). Sexual intimacy between psychotherapists and patients. *Professional Psychology, 14,* 185-196.

Briere, J. (1984, April). *The effects of childhood sexual abuse on later psychological functioning: Defining a post-sexual abuse syndrome.* Paper presented at the Third National Conference on Sexual Victimization of Children, Washington, DC.

Briere, J. N. (1989). *Therapy for adults molested as children: Beyond survival.* New York: Springer.

Briere, J. N. (1992a). *Child abuse trauma: Theory and treatment of the lasting effects.* Newbury Park, CA: Sage.

Briere, J. N. (1992b). Methodological issues in the study of sexual abuse effects. *Journal of Consulting and Clinical Psychology, 60*(2), 196-203.

Briere, J. N., & Conte, J. R. (1993). Self-reported amnesia for abuse in adults molested as children. *Journal of Traumatic Stress, 6*(1), 21-31.

Briere, J., Evans, D., Runtz, M., & Wall, T. (1988). Symptomatology in men who were molested as children: A comparison study. *American Journal of Orthopsychiatry, 58*(3), 457-461.

Briere, J., & Runtz, M. (1986). Suicidal thoughts and behaviours in former sexual abuse victims. *Canadian Journal of Behavioural Science, 18*(4), 413-423.

Briere, J., & Runtz, M. (1987). Post sexual abuse trauma: Data and implications for clinical practice. *Journal of Interpersonal Violence, 2*(4), 367-379.

Briere, J. N., & Runtz, M. (1988a). Multivariate correlates of childhood psychological and physical maltreatment among university women. *Child Abuse & Neglect, 12*(3), 331-341.

Briere, J. N., & Runtz, M. (1988b). Post sexual abuse trauma. In G. E. Wyatt & G. J. Powell (Eds.), *Lasting effects of child sexual abuse* (pp. 85-99). Newbury Park, CA: Sage.

Briere, J. N., & Runtz, M. (1988c). Symptomatology associated with childhood sexual victimization in a nonclinical adult sample. *Child Abuse & Neglect, 12*(1), 51-59.

Briere, J., & Runtz, M. (1990). Augmenting Hopkins SCL scales to measure dissociative symptoms: Data from two nonclinical samples. *Journal of Personality Assessment, 55*(1-2), 376-379.

Briere, J. N., & Runtz, M. (1993). Childhood sexual abuse: Long-term sequelae and implications for psychological assessment. *Journal of Interpersonal Violence, 8*(3), 312-330.

Briere, J., & Zaidi, L. Y. (1989). Sexual abuse histories and sequelae in female psychiatric emergency room patients. *American Journal of Psychiatry, 146*(12), 1602-1606.

Browne, A., & Finkelhor, D. (1986a). Impact of child sexual abuse: A review of the research. *Psychological Bulletin, 99*(1), 66-77.

Browne, A., & Finkelhor, D. (1986b). Initial and long-term effects: A review of the research. In D. Finkelhor (Ed.), *A sourcebook on child sexual abuse* (pp. 143-179). Newbury Park, CA: Sage.

Brunold, H. (1964). Observations after sexual traumata suffered in childhood. *Excerpta Criminologica, 11*, 5-8.

Bryer, J. B., Nelson, B. A., Miller, J. B., & Krol, P. A. (1987). Childhood sexual and physical abuse as factors in adult psychiatric illness. *American Journal of Psychiatry, 144*(11), 1426-1430.

Burgess, A. W., & Holmstrom, L. L. (1979). Adaptive strategies and recovery from rape. *American Journal of Psychiatry, 136*(10), 1278-1282.

Carnes, P. (1983). *Out of the shadows: Understanding sexual addiction.* Minneapolis, MN: Compcare.

Cavaiola, A. A., & Schiff, M. (1988). Behavioral sequelae of physical and/or sexual abuse in adolescents. *Child Abuse & Neglect, 12*(2), 181-188.

Cavaiola, A. A., & Schiff, M. (1989). Self-esteem in abused chemically dependent adolescents. *Child Abuse & Neglect, 13*(3), 327-334.

Ceci, S. J., & Bruck, M. (1993). Child witnesses: Translating research into policy. *Social Policy Report: Society for Research in Child Development, 7*(3), 1-30.

Ceci, S. J., Toglia, M. P., & Ross, D. E. (1987). *Children's eyewitness memory.* New York: Springer-Verlag.

Christiansen, J. R., & Blake, R. H. (1990). The grooming process in father-daughter incest. In A. L. Horton, B. L. Johnson, L. M.

Roundy, & D. Williams (Eds.), *The incest perpetrator: A family member no one wants to treat* (pp. 88-98). Newbury Park, CA: Sage.

Christie, M. M., Marshall, W. L., & Lanthier, R. D. (1979). *A descriptive study of incarcerated rapists and pedophiles.* Report to the Solicitor General, Government of Canada, Ottawa.

Chu, J. A., & Dill, D. L. (1990). Dissociative symptoms in relation to childhood physical and sexual abuse. *American Journal of Psychiatry, 147*(7), 887-892.

Cole, C. B. (1986, May). *Differential long-term effects of child sexual and physical abuse.* Paper presented at the Fourth National Conference on Sexual Victimization of Children, New Orleans, LA.

Conte, J. R., & Schuerman, J. R. (1987). The effects of sexual abuse on children: A multidimensional view. *Journal of Interpersonal Violence, 2*(4), 381-390.

Cummings, C., Gordon, J. R., & Marlatt, G. A. (1980). Relapse: Strategies of prevention and prediction. In W. R. Miller (Ed.), *The addictive behaviors* (pp. 291-321). Oxford, UK: Pergamon.

Daly, R. J. (1983). Samuel Pepys and post-traumatic stress disorder. *British Journal of Psychiatry, 143,* 64-68.

Day, D. M., Miner, M. H., Nafpaktitis, M. K., & Murphy, J. F. (1987). *Development of a situational competency test for sex offenders.* Unpublished manuscript. (Available from David M. Day, California Department of Mental Health, 1600 Ninth Street, Sacramento, CA 95814)

De Francis, V. (1969). *Protecting the child victim of sex crimes committed by adults.* Denver, CO: American Humane Association.

DeMott, B. (1980). The pro-incest lobby. *Psychology Today, 13*(10), 11-12, 15-16.

Derosis, H., Hamilton, J. A., Morrison, E., & Strauss, M. (1987). More on psychiatrist-patient sexual contact. *American Journal of Psychiatry, 144*(5), 688-689.

de Young, M. (1982). *The sexual victimization of children.* Jefferson, NC: McFarland.

de Young, M. (1983). Case reports: The sexual exploitation of victims by helping professionals. *Victimology, 6,* 92-98.

Didion, J. (1979). *The white album.* New York: Simon & Schuster.

Dillard, A. (1974). *Pilgrim at Tinker Creek.* New York: Bantam Books.

DiTomasso, M. J., & Routh, D. K. (1993). Recall of abuse in childhood and three measures of dissociation. *Child Abuse & Neglect, 17*(4), 477-485.

Donaldson, M. A. (1983, November). *Incest victims years after: Methods and techniques for treatment.* Paper presented at the annual meeting of the National Association of Social Workers, Washington, DC.

Donaldson, M. A., & Gardner, R. (1985). Diagnosis and treatment of traumatic stress among women after childhood incest. In C. R. Figley (Ed.), *Trauma and its wake* (Vol. 1, pp. 356-377). New York: Brunner/Mazel.

Dubowitz, H., Black, M., Harrington, D., & Verschoore, A. (1993). A follow-up study of behavior problems associated with child sexual abuse. *Child Abuse & Neglect, 17*(6), 743-754.

Eldridge, H. (in press). Identifying and breaking patterns of adult male sexual offending—Implications for assessment, intervention and maintenance. In M. Cardoza, D. Fisher, & B. Print (Eds.), *Sex offenders: Towards improved practice.* London: Whiting and Birch.

Elliott, D. M., & Briere, J. (1991a, August). *Multivariate impacts of parental incest, physical maltreatment, and substance abuse.* Paper presented at the annual meeting of the American Psychological Association, San Francisco.

Elliott, D. M., & Briere, J. (1991b). Studying the long term effects of sexual abuse: The Trauma Symptom Checklist (TSC) scales. In A. W. Burgess (Ed.), *Rape and sexual assault: A research handbook* (Vol. 3, pp. 57-74). New York: Garland.

Elliott, D. M., and Briere, J. (1992). Sexual abuse trauma among professional women: Validating the Trauma Symptom Checklist-40 (TSC-40). *Child Abuse & Neglect, 16*(3), 391-398.

Erichsen, J. E. (1882). *On concussion of the spine: Nervous shock and other obscure injuries of the nervous system in their clinical and medico-legal aspects.* London: Longmans, Green.

Eth, S., & Pynoos, R. S. (Eds.). (1985). *Post-traumatic stress disorder in children.* Washington, DC: American Psychiatric Press.

Faller, K. C. (1990). Sexual abuse by paternal caretakers: A comparison of abusers who are biological fathers in intact families, stepfathers, and noncustodial fathers. In A. L. Horton, B. L.

Johnson, L. M. Roundy, & D. Williams (Eds.), *The incest perpetrator: A family member no one wants to treat* (pp. 65-73). Newbury Park, CA: Sage.

Famularo, R., Kinscherff, R., & Fenton, T. (1990). Symptom differences in acute and chronic presentation of childhood post-traumatic stress disorder. *Child Abuse & Neglect, 14*(3), 439-444.

Father knows best. (1992, July). *Reader's Digest*, p. 27.

Feldman-Summers, S., & Pope, K. S. (1994). The experience of "forgetting" childhood abuse: A national survey of psychologists. *Journal of Consulting and Clinical Psychology, 62*(3), 636-639.

Feltman, R. I. (1985). *A controlled, correlational study of the psychological functioning of female paternal incest victims.* Unpublished doctoral dissertation, University of Missouri, St. Louis.

Ferenczi, S. (1933/1949). Confusion of tongues between adults and the child. *International Journal of Psychoanalysis, 30,* 225-230.

Fields, P. J. (1980). *Parent-child relationshps, childhood sexual abuse, and adult interpersonal behavior in female prostitutes.* Unpublished doctoral dissertation, California School of Professional Psychology, Los Angeles.

Fine, C. G. (1990). The cognitive sequelae of incest. In R. P. Kluft (Ed.), *Incest related syndromes of adult psychopathology* (pp. 161-182). Washington, DC: American Psychiatric Press.

Finkelhor, D. (1979). *Sexually victimized children.* New York: Free Press.

Finkelhor, D. (1984). *Child sexual abuse: New theory and research.* New York: Free Press.

Finkelhor, D. (1986). *A sourcebook on child sexual abuse.* Newbury Park, CA: Sage.

Finkelhor, D. (1988). The trauma of child sexual abuse: Two models. In G. E. Wyatt & G. J. Powell (Eds.), *Lasting effects of child sexual abuse* (pp. 61-82). Newbury Park, CA: Sage.

Finkelhor, D., & Baron, L. (1986). High-risk children. In D. Finkelhor (Ed.), *A sourcebook on child sexual abuse* (pp. 60-88). Newbury Park, CA: Sage.

Finkelhor, D., Hotaling, G. T., Lewis, I. A., & Smith, C. (1989). Sexual abuse and its relationship to later sexual satisfaction, marital status, religion, and attitudes. *Journal of Interpersonal Violence, 4*(4), 379-399.

Foa, E. B., Rothbaum, B. O., & Steketee, G. S. (1993). Treatment of rape victims. *Journal of Interpersonal Violence, 8*(2), 256-276.

Forster, J. (1969). *The life of Charles Dickens.* London: J. M. Dent and Sons.

Frederick, C. J. (1985). Children traumatized by catastrophic situations. In S. Eth & R. S. Pynoos (Eds.), *Post-traumatic stress disorder in children* (pp. 73-99). Washington, DC: American Psychiatric Press.

Freeman-Longo, R. E. (1985). *Incidence of self-reported sex crimes among incarcerated rapists and child molesters.* Unpublished manuscript.

Fremont, J. (1975). Rapists speak for themselves. In D. E. H. Russell (Ed.), *The politics of rape: The victim's perspective* (pp. 243-256). New York: Stein and Day.

Freund, K. (1967). Erotic preference in pedophilia. *Behaviour Research and Therapy, 5,* 339-348.

Freund, K. (1990). Courtship disorder. In W. L. Marshall, D. R. Laws, & H. E. Barbaree (Eds.), *Handbook of sexual assault: Issues, theories, and treatment of the offender* (pp. 195-207). New York: Plenum.

Freund, K., & Kuban, M. (1993). Toward a testable developmental model of pedophilia: The development of erotic age preference. *Child Abuse & Neglect, 17*(2), 315-324.

Friedrich, W. N. (1988). Behavior problems in sexually abused children: An adaptational perspective. In G. E. Wyatt & G. J. Powell (Eds.), *Lasting effects of child sexual abuse* (pp. 171-191). Newbury Park, CA: Sage.

Frisbie, L. V., Vanasek, F. J., & Dingman, H. F. (1967). The self and the ideal self: Methodological study of pedophiles. *Psychological Reports, 20,* 699-706.

Fromuth, M. E. (1983). *The long term psychological impact of childhood sexual abuse.* Unpublished doctoral dissertation, Auburn University, Auburn, GA.

Fromuth, M. E. (1986). The relationship of childhood sexual abuse with later psychological and sexual adjustment in a sample of college women. *Child Abuse & Neglect, 10*(1), 5-15.

Fromuth, M. E., & Burkhart, B. R. (1989). Long-term psychological correlates of childhood sexual abuse in two samples of college men. *Child Abuse & Neglect, 13*(4), 533-542.

Furby, L., Weinrott, M. R., & Blackshaw, L. (1989). Sex offender recidivism: A review. *Psychological Bulletin, 105*(1), 3-30.

Gagnon, J. H. (1965). Female child victims of sex offenses. *Social Problems, 13*(2), 176-192.

Gartrell, N., Herman, J., Olarte, S., Feldstein, M., & Localio, R. (1986). Psychiatrist-patient sexual contact: Results of a national survey, I: Prevalence. *American Journal of Psychiatry, 143*(9), 1126-1131.

Gayford, J. J. (1975). Wife battering: A preliminary survey of 100 cases. *British Medical Journal, 1*(5951), 194-197.

Gebhard, P. H., Gagnon, J. H., Pomeroy, W. B., & Christenson, C. V. (1965). *Sex offenders: An analysis of types.* New York: Harper & Row.

Gelinas, D. J. (1981). Identification and treatment of incest victims. In E. Howell & M. Bayes (Eds.), *Women and mental health* (pp. 481-496). New York: Basic Books.

Gelinas, D. (1992, June). *On being the chosen one in a malevolent family environment.* Paper presented at a conference titled Psychological Trauma: Maturational Processes and Therapeutic Interventions, Boston.

Giarretto, H. (1982). *Integrated treatment of child sexual abuse.* Palo Alto, CA: Science and Behavior Books.

Gil, E. (1988). *Treatment of adult survivors of childhood abuse.* Walnut Creek, CA: Launch Press.

Gil, E. (1991). *The healing power of play: Working with abused children.* New York: Guilford.

Gold, E. R. (1986). Long-term effects of sexual victimization in childhood: An attributional approach. *Journal of Consulting and Clinical Psychology, 54*(4), 471-475.

Gold, S. R., Milan, L. D., Mayall, A., & Johnson, A. E. (1994). A cross-validation study of the Trauma Symptom Checklist: The role of mediating variables. *Journal of Interpersonal Violence, 9*(1), 12-26.

Goodwin, J. (1985a). Credibility problems in multiple personality disorder patients and abused children. In R. P. Kluft (Ed.), *Childhood antecedents of multiple personality* (pp. 1-19). Washington, DC: American Psychiatric Press.

Goodwin, J. (1985b). Post-traumatic symptoms in incest victims. In S. Eth & R. S. Pynoos (Eds.), *Post-traumatic stress disorder in children* (pp. 157-168). Washington, DC: American Psychiatric Press.

Goodwin, J. M. (1990). Applying to adult incest victims what we have learned from victimized children. In R. P. Kluft (Ed.), *Incest related syndromes of adult psychopathology* (pp. 55-74). Washington, DC: American Psychiatric Press.

Goodwin, J. M. (1993). Human vectors of trauma: Illustrations from the Marquis de Sade. In J. M. Goodwin (Ed.), *Rediscovering childhood trauma: Historical casebook and clinical applications* (pp. 95-111). Washington, DC: American Psychiatric Press.

Goodwin, J. M. (1994). Credibility problems in sadistic abuse. *Journal of Psychohistory, 21*(4), 479-496.

Gore, A. (1992). *Earth in the balance: Ecology and the human spirit.* Boston: Houghton Mifflin.

Grassberger, R. (1964). Der exhibitionismus. *Kriminalstik in Österrich, 18,* 557-562.

Greenwald, A. G. (1980). The totalitarian ego: Fabrication and revision of personal history. *American Psychologist, 35*(7), 603-618.

Greenwald, E., & Leitenberg, H. (1990). Posttraumatic stress disorder in a nonclinical and nonstudent sample of adult women sexually abused as children. *Journal of Interpersonal Violence, 5*(2), 217-228.

Greenwald, E., Leitenberg, H., Cado, S., & Tarran, M. J. (1990). Childhood sexual abuse: Long-term effects on psychological and sexual functioning in a nonclinical and nonstudent sample of adult women. *Child Abuse & Neglect, 14*(4), 503-514.

Groth, A. N. (1979). *Men who rape: The psychology of the offender.* New York: Plenum.

Groth, A. N., & Burgess, A. W. (1977). Rape: A sexual deviation. *American Journal of Orthopsychiatry, 47*(3), 400-406.

Groth, A. N., Hobson, W. F., & Gary, T. S. (1982). The child molester: Clinical observations. In J. R. Conte & D. A. Shore (Eds.), *Social work and child sexual abuse* (pp. 129-144). Binghamton, NY: Haworth.

Groth, A. N., Longo, R. E., & McFadin, J. B. (1982). Undetected recidivism among rapists and child molesters. *Crime & Delinquency, 28*(3), 450-458.

Gruber, K. J., & Jones, R. J. (1983). Identifying determinants of risk of sexual victimization of youth. *Child Abuse & Neglect, 7,* 17-24.

Gutheil, T. G., & Avery, N. C. (1977). Multiple overt incest as family defense against loss. *Family Process, 16*(1), 105-116.

Guttmacher, M. S., & Weihofen, H. (1952). *Psychiatry and the law.* New York: Norton.

Haley, J. (Ed.). (1985). *Conversations with Milton Erickson: Changing individuals.* New York: Triangle Press.

Hannah, S. (1982, January 17). A judge's remarks: A look at the case. *Milwaukee Journal,* p. 1.

Hare, R. D. (1980). A research scale for the assessment of psychopathy in criminal populations. *Personality and Individual Differences, 1,* 111-119.

Harlan, S., Rogers, L., & Slattery, B. (1981). *Male and female adolescent prostitutes.* Washington, DC: Huckleberry House Sexual Minority Youth Services Project, Youth Development Bureau, U.S. Department of Human Services.

Harris, T. (1969). *I'm OK, you're OK.* New York: Harper & Row.

Hawthorne, N. (1850/1986). *The scarlet letter.* New York: Bantam.

Heilbroner, D. (1993, August). Serial murder and sexual repression. *Playboy, 78,* 147-150.

Henderson, J. (1983). Is incest harmful? *Canadian Journal of Psychiatry, 28*(1), 34-40.

Henn, F. A. (1978). The aggressive sexual offender. In I. L. Kutash, S. B. Kutash, & L. B. Schlesinger (Eds.), *Violence: Perspective on murder and aggression.* San Francisco: Jossey-Bass.

Henschel, D., Briere, J., Magallanes, M., & Smiljamich, K. (1990, April). *Sexual abuse related attributions: Probing the role of "traumagenic factors."* Paper presented at the annual meeting of the Western Psychological Association, Los Angeles.

Herman, J. L. (1981). *Father-daughter incest.* Cambridge, MA: Harvard University Press.

Herman, J. L. (1990). Sex offenders: A feminist perspective. In W. L. Marshall, D. R. Laws, & H. E. Barbaree (Eds.), *Handbook of sexual assault: Issues, theories, and treatment of the offender* (pp. 177-193). New York: Plenum.

Herman, J. L. (1992). *Trauma and recovery.* New York: Basic Books.

Herman, J. L., & Schatzow, E. (1987). Recovery and verification of memories of childhood sexual trauma. *Psychoanalytic Quarterly, 4*(1), 1-14.

Hibbard, S. (1989). Personality and object relational pathology in young adult children of alcoholics. *Psychotherapy, 26*(4), 504-509.

Hilberman, E., & Munson, M. (1978). Sixty battered women. *Victimology*, *2*, 460-471.

Hindman, J. (1989). *Just before dawn*. Boise, ID: AlexAndria Associates.

Holmes, R. M., & De Burger, J. (1988). *Serial murder*. Newbury Park, CA: Sage.

Holroyd, J. C., & Brodsky, A. M. (1977). Psychologists' attitudes and practices regarding erotic and non-erotic physical contact with patients. *American Psychologists*, *32*(10), 843-849.

Horowitz, M. (1976). *Stress response syndromes*. New York: Aronson.

James, B., & Nasjleti, M. (1983). *Treating sexually abused children and their families*. Palo Alto, CA: Consulting Psychologists Press.

James, J., & Meyerding, J. (1977). Early sexual experience and prostitution. *American Journal of Psychiatry*, *134*(12), 1381-1385.

Janoff-Bulman, R. (1979). Characterological versus behavioral self-blame: Inquiries into depression and rape. *Journal of Personality and Social Psychology*, *37*(10), 1798-1809.

Janoff-Bulman, R. (1992). *Shattered assumptions: Towards a new psychology of trauma*. New York: Free Press.

Janoff-Bulman, R., & Frieze, I. H. (1983). A theoretical perspective for understanding reactions to victimization. *Journal of Social Issues*, *39*(2), 1-17.

Janoff-Bulman, R. M., Madden, M., & Timki, C. (1983). Victims' reactions to aid: The role of perceived vulnerability. In A. Nadler, J. D. Fisher, & B. DePaulo (Eds.), *New directions in helping: Applied perspectives in help-seeking and -receiving* (Vol. 3, pp. 21-42). New York: Academic Press.

Janus, M. D., Scanlon, B., & Price, V. (1984). Youth prostitution. In A. W. Burgess (Ed.), *Child pornography and sex rings* (pp. 127-146). Lexington, MA: Lexington Books.

Jehu, D., & Gazan, M. (1983). Psychosocial adjustment of women who were sexually victimized in childhood or adolescence. *Canadian Journal of Community Mental Health*, *2*(2), 71-82.

Jenkins-Hall, K. D. (1989). Cognitive restructuring. In D. R. Laws (Ed.), *Relapse prevention with sex offenders* (pp. 207-215). New York: Guilford.

Jenkins-Hall, K. D., & Marlatt, G. A. (1989). Apparently irrelevant decisions in the relapse process. In D. R. Laws (Ed.), *Relapse prevention with sex offenders* (pp. 47-55). New York: Guilford.

Johnson, B. K., & Kenkel, M. B. (1991). Stress, coping, and adjustment in female adolescent incest victims. *Child Abuse & Neglect, 15*(3), 293-305.

Kanin, E. J. (1985). Date rapists: Differential sexual socialization and relative deprivation. *Archives of Sexual Behavior, 14*(3), 218-232.

Kaplan, M. S. (1985). *The impact of parolees' perceptions of confidentiality on the reporting of their urges to interact sexually with children.* Unpublished doctoral dissertation, New York University.

Kardener, S. H., Fuller, M., & Mensh, I. N. (1973). A survey of physicians' attitudes and practices regarding erotic and non-erotic contact with patients. *American Journal of Psychiatry, 130*(10), 1077-1081.

Kaufman, I., Peck, A., & Tagiuri, C. K. (1954). The family constellation and overt incestuous relations between father and daughter. *American Journal of Orthopsychiatry, 24*, 266-279.

Kernberg, O., Selzer, M. A., Koenigsberg, H., & Carr, A. C. (1989). *Psychodynamic psychotherapy of borderline patients.* New York: Basic Books.

Kidder, L. H., Boell, J. L., & Moyer, M. M. (1983). Rights consciousness and victimization prevention: Personal defense training and assertiveness training. *Journal of Social Issues, 39*(2), 153-168.

Kierkegaard, S. (1959). *Either/or.* Garden City, NY: Anchor.

Kilpatrick, D. G., Amick-McMullan, A., Best, C. L., Burke, M. M., & Saunders, B. E. (1986, May). *Impact of child sexual abuse: Recent research findings.* Paper presented to the Fourth National Conference on the Sexual Victimization of Children, New Orleans, LA.

Kilpatrick, D. G., Saunders, B. E., Amick-McMullan, A., Best, C. L., Veronen, L. J., & Resnick, H. (1989). Victim and crime factors associated with the development of crime-related post-traumatic stress disorder. *Behavior Therapy, 20*(2), 199-214.

Kilpatrick, D. G., Saunders, B. E., Best, C. L., Von, J. M., & Veronen, L. J. (1987). Criminal victimization: Lifetime prevalence, reporting to police, and psychological impact. *Crime & Delinquency, 33*(4), 479-489.

Kluft, R. P. (1990a). Incest and subsequent revictimization: The case of therapist-patient sexual exploitation, with a description of the sitting duck syndrome. In R. P. Kluft (Ed.), *Incest related syndromes of adult psychopathology* (pp. 263-287). Washington, DC: American Psychiatric Press.

Kluft, R. P. (1990b). On the apparent invisibility of incest: A personal reflection on things known and forgotten. In R. P. Kluft (Ed.), *Incest related syndromes of adult psychopathology* (pp. 11-34). Washington, DC: American Psychiatric Press.

Knight, R. A., & Prentky, R. A. (1990). Classifying sexual offenders: The development and corroboration of taxonomic models. In W. L. Marshall, D. R. Laws, & H. E. Barbaree (Eds.), *Handbook of sexual assault: Issues, theories, and treatment of the offender* (pp. 23-52). New York: Plenum.

Knight, R., Rosenberg, R., & Schneider, B. (1985). Classification of sex offenders: Perspectives, methods, and validation. In A. W. Burgess (Ed.), *Rape and sexual assault: A research handbook* (pp. 223-293). New York: Garland.

Knopp, F. H. (1984). *Retraining adult sex offenders: Methods and models.* Orwell, VT: Safer Society Press.

Koss, M. P., Gidycz, C. A., & Wisniewski, N. (1987). The scope of rape: Incidence and prevalence of sexual aggression and victimization in a national sample of higher education students. *Journal of Consulting and Clinical Psychology, 55*(2), 162-170.

Koverola, C., Pound, J., Heger, A., & Lytle, C. (1993). Relationship of child sexual abuse to depression. *Child Abuse & Neglect, 17*(3), 393-400.

Landis, J. T. (1956). Experiences of 500 children with adult sexual deviation. *Psychiatric Quarterly Supplement, 30*(Part 1), 91-109.

Langer, E. J. (1975). The illusion of control. *Journal of Personality and Social Psychology, 32*(2), 311-328.

Langevin, R. (1990). Sexual anomalies and the brain. In W. L. Marshall, D. R. Laws, & H. E. Barbaree (Eds.), *Handbook of sexual assault: Issues, theories, and treatment of the offender* (pp. 103-113). New York: Plenum.

Lanktree, C., Briere, J., & Zaidi, L. (1991). Incidence and impact of sexual abuse in a child outpatient sample: The role of direct inquiry. *Child Abuse & Neglect, 15*(4), 447-453.

Lanning, K. V. (1987). Child molesters: A behavioral analysis for law enforcement. In R. R. Hazelwood & A. W. Burgess (Eds.), *Practical aspects of rape investigation: A multidisciplinary approach* (pp. 201-256). New York: Elsevier.

Laws, D. R. (Ed.). (1989). *Relapse prevention with sex offenders.* New York: Guilford.

Lawson, L., & Chaffin, M. (1992). False negatives in sexual abuse disclosure interviews: Incidence and influence of caretaker's belief in abuse in cases of accidental abuse discovery by diagnosis of STD. *Journal of Interpersonal Violence, 7*(4), 532-542.

Lerner, M. J. (1980). *The belief in a just world: A fundamental delusion.* New York: Plenum.

Lerner, M. J., & Miller, D. T. (1978). Just world research and the attribution process: Looking back and ahead. *Psychological Bulletin, 85*(5), 1030-1051.

Lewis, D. O., Shanock, S. S., & Pincus, J. H. (1979). Juvenile male sexual assaulters. *American Journal of Psychiatry, 136*, 1194-1196.

Leyton, E. (1986). *Hunting humans: Inside the minds of mass murderers.* New York: Pocket Books.

Lifton, R. J. (1967). *Death in life: Survivors of Hiroshima.* New York: Simon & Schuster.

Lifton, R. J. (1963). Psychological effects of the atomic bomb in Hiroshima: The theme of death. *Daedalus, 92*, 462-497.

Lindberg, F. H., & Distad, L. J. (1985). Post-traumatic stress disorders in women who experienced childhood incest. *Child Abuse & Neglect, 9*(3), 329-334.

Loftus, E. F. (1993). The reality of repressed memories. *American Psychologist, 48*(5), 518-537.

Loftus, E. F., & Davies, G. M. (1984). Distortions in the memory of children. *Journal of Social Issues, 40*(2), 51-67.

Longo, R. E., & Groth, A. N. (1983). Juvenile sexual offenses in the history of adult rapists and child molesters. *International Journal of Offender Therapy and Comparative Criminology, 27*(2), 150-155.

Longo, R. E., & McFadin, J. B. (1981). Inappropriate behavior development in the sexual offender. *Law and Order Magazine, 19*, 21-23.

Lutz, S. E., & Medway, J. P. (1984). Contextual family therapy with the victims of incest. *Journal of Adolescence, 7*, 319-327.

Malamuth, N. M. (1989). The attraction to sexual aggression scale: Part 2. *Journal of Sex Research, 26*, 324-354.

Maletzky, B. M. (1991). *Treating the sexual offender.* Newbury Park, CA: Sage.

Maltz, W. (1988). Identifying and treating the sexual repercussions of incest: A couples therapy approach. *Journal of Sex and Marital Therapy, 14*(2), 142-170.

Maltz, W., & Holman, B. (1987). *Incest and sexuality: A guide to understanding and healing.* Lexington, MA: Lexington Books.

Mannarino, A. P., Cohen, J. A., & Berman, S. R. (1994). The relationship between preabuse factors and psychological symptomatology in sexually abused girls. *Child Abuse & Neglect, 18*(1), 63-71.

Marlatt, G. A. (1989a). Feeding the PIG: The problem of immediate gratification. In D. R. Laws (Ed.), *Relapse prevention with sex offenders* (pp. 56-62). New York: Guilford.

Marlatt, G. A. (1989b). How to handle the PIG. In D. R. Laws (Ed.), *Relapse prevention with sex offenders* (pp. 227-235). New York: Guilford.

Marlatt, G. A., & Gordon, J. R. (1980). Determinants of relapse: Implications for the maintenance of behavior change. In P. O. Davidson & S. M. Davidson (Eds.), *Behavioral medicine: Changing health lifestyles* (pp. 410-450). New York: Brunner/Mazel.

Marques, J. K., Day, D. M., Nelson, C., & Miner, M. H. (1989). The sex offender treatment and evaluation project: California's relapse prevention program. In D. R. Laws (Ed.), *Relapse prevention with sex offenders* (pp. 247-267). New York: Guilford.

Marques, J. K., & Nelson, C. (1989a). Elements of high-risk situations for sex offenders. In D. R. Laws (Ed.), *Relapse prevention with sex offenders* (pp. 35-46). New York: Guilford.

Marques, J. K., & Nelson, C. (1989b). Understanding and preventing relapse in sex offenders. In M. Gossop (Ed.), *Relapse and addictive behavior* (pp. 96-106). Beckenham, Kent, UK: Routledge.

Marshall, W. L., Barbaree, H. E., & Eccles, A. (1991). Early onset and deviant sexuality in child molesters. *Journal of Interpersonal Violence, 6*(3), 323-335.

Marshall, W. L., Laws, D. R., & Barbaree, H. E. (Eds.). (1990). *Handbook of sexual assault: Issues, theories, and treatment of the offender.* New York: Plenum.

Matlin, M. W., & Stang, D. (1978). *The Pollyanna principle: Selectivity in language, memory, and thought.* Cambridge, MA: Schenkman.

McCann, I. L., & Pearlman, L. A. (1990). *Psychological trauma and the adult survivor: Theory, therapy, and transformation.* New York: Brunner/Mazel.

McLeer, S. V., Deblinger, E., Atkins, M. S., Foa, E. B., & Ralphe, D. L. (1988). Post-traumatic stress disorder in sexually abused children. *Journal of the American Academy of Child and Adolescent Psychiatry, 27*(5), 650-654.

Meiselman, K. C. (1978). *Incest: A psychological study of causes and effects with treatment recommendations.* San Francisco: Jossey-Bass.

Miller, A. (1990). *The untouched key: Tracing childhood trauma in creativity and destructiveness.* New York: Doubleday.

Miller, P. (1976). *Blaming the victim of child molestation: An empirical analysis.* Unpublished doctoral dissertation, Northwestern University, Evanston, IL.

Miller, W. R. (1980). The addictive behaviors. In W. R. Miller (Ed.), *The addictive behaviors: Treatment of alcoholism, drug abuse, smoking and obesity.* New York: Pergamon.

Morrison, T. (1987). *Beloved.* New York: Plume.

Morrow, K. B. (1991). Attributions of female adolescent incest victims regarding their molestation. *Child Abuse & Neglect, 15*(4), 477-483.

Mott, F. W. (1919). *War neuroses and shell shock.* London: Oxford Medical Publications.

Mrazek, P. B., & Bentovim, A. (1981). Incest and the dysfunctional family system. In P. B. Mrazek & C. H. Kempe (Eds.), *Sexually abused children and their families* (pp. 167-177). New York: Pergamon.

Mrazek, P. B., & Mrazek, D. A. (1981). The effects of child sexual abuse: Methodological considerations. In P. B. Mrazek & C. H. Kempe (Eds.), *Sexually abused children and their families* (pp. 235-245). New York: Pergamon.

Mullen, P. E. (1993). Child sexual abuse and adult mental health. *Journal of Interpersonal Violence, 8*(3), 429-431.

Murphy, S. M., Kilpatrick, D. G., Amick-McMullan, A., Veronen, L. J., Paduhovich, J., Best, C. L., Villeponteaux, L. A., & Saunders, B. E. (1988). Current psychological functioning of child sexual assault survivors. *Journal of Interpersonal Violence, 3*(1), 55-79.

Murphy, W. D. (1990). Assessment and modification of cognitive distortions in sex offenders. In W. L. Marshall, D. R. Laws, &

H. E. Barbaree (Eds.), *Handbook of sexual assault: Issues, theories, and treatment of the offender* (pp. 331-342). New York: Plenum.

Myers, C. S. (1940). *Shell shock in France, 1914-1918.* Cambridge, UK: Cambridge University Press.

Myers, J. E. B., Bays, J., Becker, J., Berliner, L., Corwin, D. L., & Saywitz, K. J. (1989). Expert testimony in child sexual abuse litigation. *Nebraska Law Review, 68*(1 & 2), 1-145.

Newman, C. J. (1976). Children of disaster: Clinical observations at Buffalo Creek. *American Journal of Psychiatry, 133*(3), 306-312.

Nichols, H. R., & Molinder, I. (1984). *Multiphasic Sex Inventory manual.* Tacoma, WA: Author.

Nir, Y. (1985). Post-traumatic stress disorder in children with cancer. In S. Eth & R. S. Pynoos (Eds.), *Post-traumatic stress disorder in children* (pp. 123-132). Washington, DC: American Psychiatric Press.

Norris, F. H. (1992). Epidemiology of trauma: Frequency and impact of different potentially traumatic events on different demographic groups. *Journal of Consulting and Clinical Psychology, 60*(3), 409-418.

Norris, J. (1988). *Serial killers.* New York: Doubleday.

Page, H. W. (1883). *Injuries of the spine and spinal cord without apparent mechanical lesion, and nervous shock, in their surgical and medicolegal aspects.* London: J. & A. Churchill.

Parker, D. A., & Harford, T. C. (1988). Alcohol-related problems, marital disruptions and depressive symptoms among adult children of alcohol abusers in the United States. *Journal of Studies on Alcohol, 49*(4), 306-313.

Perloff, L. S. (1983). Perceptions of vulnerability to victimization. *Journal of Social Issues, 39*(2), 41-62.

Peters, S. D. (1984). *The relationship between childhood sexual victimization and adult depression among Afro-American and white women.* Unpublished doctoral dissertation, University of California, Los Angeles.

Peters, S. D. (1988). Child sexual abuse and later psychological problems. In G. E. Wyatt & G. J. Powell (Eds.), *Lasting effects of child sexual abuse* (pp. 101-117). Newbury Park, CA: Sage.

Peterson, C., Schwartz, S. M., & Seligman, M. E. (1981). Self-blame and depressive symptoms. *Journal of Personality and Social Psychology, 41*(2), 253-259.

Petit, P. (1985). *On the high wire.* New York: Random House.

Pithers, W. D. (1990). Relapse prevention with sexual aggressors: A method for maintaining therapeutic gain and enhancing external supervision. In W. L. Marshall, D. R. Laws, & H. E. Barbaree (Eds.), *Handbook of sexual assault: Issues, theories, and treatment of the offender* (pp. 343-361). New York: Plenum.

Pithers, W. D., Beal, L. S., Armstrong, J., & Petty, J. (1989). Identification of risk factors through clinical interviews and analysis of records. In D. R. Laws (Ed.), *Relapse prevention with sex offenders* (pp. 77-87). New York: Guilford.

Pithers, W. D., Buell, M. M., Kashima, K. M., Cumming, G. F., & Beal, L. S. (1987). Precursors to sexual offenses. In *Proceedings of the First Annual Meeting of the Association for the Behavioral Treatment of Sexual Aggressors,* Newport, OR.

Pithers, W. D., Kashima, K. M., Cumming, G. F., & Beal, L. S. (1988). Relapse prevention: A method of enhancing maintenance of change in sex offenders. In A. C. Salter (Ed.), *Treating child sex offenders and victims: A practical guide* (pp. 131-170). Newbury Park, CA: Sage.

Pithers, W. D., Marques, J. K., Gibat, C. C., & Marlatt, G. A. (1983). Relapse prevention with sexual aggressives: A self-control model of treatment and maintenance of change. In J. G. Greer & I. R. Stuart (Eds.), *The sexual aggressor: Current perspectives on treatment* (pp. 214-239). New York: Van Nostrand Reinhold.

Pope, K. S., & Bouhoutsos, J. C. (1986). *Sexual intimacy between therapists and patients.* New York: Praeger.

Pope, K. S., Levenson, H., & Schover, L. R. (1979). Sexual intimacy in psychology training: Results and implications of a national survey. *American Psychologists, 34*(8), 682-689.

Prentky, R. A., Burgess, A. W., & Carter, D. L. (1986). Victim responses by rapist type: An empirical and clinical analysis. *Journal of Interpersonal Violence, 1*(1), 73-98.

Prentky, R. A., & Knight, R. A. (1991). Identifying critical dimensions for discriminating among rapists. *Journal of Consulting and Clinical Psychology, 59*(5), 643-661.

Putnam, F. W. (1989). *Diagnosis and treatment of multiple personality disorder.* New York: Guilford.

Putnam, F. W. (1990). Disturbances of "self" in victims of childhood sexual abuse. In R. P. Kluft (Ed.), *Incest related syndromes of adult psychopathology* (pp. 113-131). Washington, DC: American Psychiatric Press.

Pynoos, R. S., & Eth, S. (1985). Children traumatized by witnessing acts of personal violence: Homicide, rape, or suicide behavior. In S. Eth & R. S. Pynoos (Eds.), *Post-traumatic stress disorder in children* (pp. 19-43). Washington, DC: American Psychiatric Press.

Quarantelli, E. L. (1985). An assessment of conflicting views on mental health: The consequences of traumatic events. In C. R. Figley (Ed.), *Trauma and its wake: The study and treatment of post-traumatic stress disorder* (pp. 173-215). New York: Brunner/Mazel.

Queen's Bench Foundation. (1976). *Rape: Prevention and resistance.* San Francisco: Author.

Quinsey, V. L. (1977). The assessment and treatment of child molesters: A review. *Canadian Psychological Review, 18*(3), 204-220.

Quinsey, V. L., & Chaplin, T. C. (1984). Stimulus control of rapists and non-sex offenders' sexual arousal. *Behavioral Assessment, 6*(2), 169-176.

Quinsey, V. L., & Chaplin, T. C. (1988). Penile responses of child molesters and normals to descriptions of encounters with children involving sex and violence. *Journal of Interpersonal Violence, 3*(3), 259-274.

Quinsey, V. L., Chaplin, T. C., & Upfold, D. (1984). Sexual arousal to nonsexual violence and sadomasochistic themes among rapists and non-sex-offenders. *Journal of Consulting and Clinical Psychology, 52*(4), 651-657.

Quinsey, V. L., Harris, G. T., Rice, M. E., & Lalumière, M. L. (1993). Assessing treatment efficacy in outcome studies of sex offenders. *Journal of Interpersonal Violence, 8*(4), 512-523.

Quinsey, V. L., & Marshall, W. L. (1983). Procedures for reducing inappropriate sexual arousal: An evaluation review. In J. G. Greer & I. R. Stuart (Eds.), *The sexual aggressor* (pp. 267-289). New York: Van Nostrand Reinhold.

Rada, R. T. (Ed.). (1978). *Clinical aspects of the rapist.* New York: Grune & Stratton.

Rapaport, K. (1984). *Sexually aggressive males: Characterological features and sexual responsiveness to rape depictions.* Unpublished doctoral dissertation, Auburn University, Auburn, GA.

Rascovsky, M., & Rascovsky, A. (1950). On consummated incest. *Journal of Psychoanalysis, 31*, 42-47.

Rasmussen, A. (1934). The importance of sexual attacks on children less than fourteen years of age for the development of mental disease and character anomalies. *Acta Psychiatrica et Neurologica, 9,* 351-434.

Redfield, J. (1993). *The celestine prophecy: An adventure.* New York: Warner.

Remembering "repressed" abuse. (1992). *APS Observer, 5*(4), 6-7.

Resick, P. A. (1993). The psychological impact of rape. *Journal of Interpersonal Violence, 8*(2), 223-255.

Resnick, H. S., Kilpatrick, D. G., Dansky, B. S., Saunders, B. E., & Best, C. L. (1993). Prevalence of civilian trauma and posttraumatic stress disorder in a representative national sample of women. *Journal of Consulting and Clinical Psychology, 61*(6), 984-991.

Ressler, R. K., Burgess, A. W., & Douglas, J. E. (1988). *Sexual homicide: Patterns and motives.* Lexington, MA: Lexington Books.

Ressler, R. K., Burgess, A. W., Douglas, J. E., Hartman, C. R., & D'Agostino, R. B. (1986). Sexual killers and their victims: Identifying patterns through crime scene analysis. *Journal of Interpersonal Violence, 1*(3), 288-308.

Rice, M. E., Harris, G. T., & Quinsey, V. L. (1990). A follow-up of rapists assessed in a maximum-security psychiatric facility. *Journal of Interpersonal Violence, 5*(4), 435-448.

Rooth, G. (1973). Exhibitionism, sexual violence and pedophilia. *British Journal of Psychiatry, 122,* 705-710.

Rosenberg, R., Knight, R. A., Prentky, R. A., & Lee, A. (1988). Validating the components of a taxonomic system for rapists: A path analytic approach. *Bulletin of American Academy of Psychiatry and the Law, 16*(2), 169-185.

Rosenfeld, A. A. (1979). Incidence of a history of incest among 18 female psychiatric patients. *American Journal of Psychiatry, 136*(6), 791-795.

Ross, C. A. (1989). *Multiple personality disorder: Diagnosis, clinical features, and treatment.* New York: John Wiley.

Ross, M. (1988). *Pillars of flame.* New York: Harper & Row.

Rossi, E. L. (Ed.). (1980). *The nature of hypnosis and suggestion: The collected papers of Milton H. Erickson on hypnosis.* New York: Irvington.

Roth, S., & Newman, E. (1993). The process of coping with incest for adult survivors: Measurement and implications for treatment and research. *Journal of Interpersonal Violence, 8*(3), 363-377.

Rowan, A. B., Foy, D. W., Rodriguez, N., & Ryan, S. (1994). Posttraumatic stress disorder in a clinical sample of adults sexually abused as children. *Child Abuse & Neglect, 18*(1), 51-61.

Rule, A. (1980). *The stranger beside me.* New York: Norton.

Runtz, M. (1987a). *The psychosocial adjustment of women who were sexually and physically abused during childhood and early adulthood: A focus on revictimization.* Unpublished master's thesis, University of Manitoba, Canada.

Runtz, M. G. (1987b, June). *The sexual victimization of women: The link between child abuse and revictimization.* Paper presented at the annual meeting of the Canadian Psychological Association, Vancouver, BC.

Rush, F. (1980). *The best kept secret: Sexual abuse of children.* New York: McGraw-Hill.

Russell, D. E. H. (1984). *Sexual exploitation: Rape, child sexual abuse, and workplace harassment.* Beverly Hills, CA: Sage.

Russell, D. E. H. (1986). *The secret trauma: Incest in the lives of girls and women.* New York: Basic Books.

Salter, A. C. (1988). *Treating child sex offenders and victims: A practical guide.* Newbury Park, CA: Sage.

Salter, A. C. (1992). *Epidemiology of child sexual abuse.* New York: Lawrence Erlbaum.

Salter, A. C., Kairys, S., & Richardson, C. (1990). *Correlates of sexual offenders: Psychopathology, empathy and life stress.* Unpublished manuscript.

Saunders, B. E., Hanson, R. F., Kilpatrick, D. G., Resnick, H., Best, C. L. (1991, March). *Prevalence, case characteristics, and long-term psychological correlates of child rape among women: A national survey.* Paper presented at the annual meeting of the American Orthopsychiatry Association, Toronto, Canada.

Saunders, B. E., Villeponteaux, L. A., Lipovsky, J. A., Kilpatrick, D. G., & Veronen, L. J. (1992). Child sexual assault as a risk factor for mental disorders among women: A community study. *Journal of Interpersonal Violence, 7*(2), 189-204.

Sauzier, M. (1989). Disclosure of child sexual abuse. For better or for worse. *Psychiatric Clinics of North America, 12*(2), 455-469.

Scheppele, K. L., & Bart, P. B. (1983). Through women's eyes: Defining danger in the wake of sexual assault. *Journal of Social Issues, 39*(2), 63-80.

Schetky, D. H. (1990). A review of the literature on the long-term effects of childhood sexual abuse. In R. P. Kluft (Ed.), *Incest related syndromes of adult psychopathology.* Washington, DC: American Psychiatric Press.

Sedney, M. A., & Brooks, B. (1984). Factors associated with a history of childhood sexual experience in a nonclinical female population. *Journal of the American Academy of Child Psychiatry, 23*(2), 215-218.

Selzer, R. (1974). *Mortal lessons: Notes on the art of surgery.* New York: Simon & Schuster.

Sexton, A. (1966). *Live or die.* Boston: Houghton Mifflin.

Sgroi, S. M., & Sargent, N. H. (1993). Impact and treatment issues for victims of childhood sexual abuse by female perpetrators. In M. Elliott (Ed.), *Female sexual abuse of children: The ultimate taboo* (pp. 15-38). London: Longman.

Shostak, M. (1981). *Nisa: The life and words of a !Kung woman.* New York: Vintage Books.

Silbert, M. H., & Pines, A. M. (1981). Sexual child abuse as an antecedent to prostitution. *Child Abuse & Neglect, 5,* 407-411.

Silver, R. L., Boon, C., & Stones, M. H. (1983). Searching for meaning in misfortune: Making sense of incest. *Journal of Social Issues, 39*(2), 81-101.

Singer, M. I., Petchers, M. K., & Hussey, D. (1989). The relationship between sexual abuse and substance abuse among psychiatrically hospitalized adolescents. *Child Abuse & Neglect, 13*(3), 319-325.

Sloane, P., & Karpinski, E. (1942). Effects of incest on the participants. *American Journal of Orthopsychiatry, 12,* 666-673.

Smukler, A. J., & Schiebel, D. (1975). Personality characteristics of exhibitionists. *Diseases of the Nervous System, 36,* 600-603.

Sorensen, T., & Snow, B. (1991). How children tell: The process of disclosure in child sexual abuse. *Child Welfare League of America, 70*(1), 3-15.

Spiegel, D. (1990). Trauma, dissociation, and hypnosis. In R. P. Kluft (Ed.), *Incest related syndromes of adult psychopathology* (pp. 247-261). Washington, DC: American Psychiatric Press.

Stein, J. A., Golding, J. M., Siegel, J. M., Burnam, M. A., & Sorenson, S. B. (1988). Long-term psychological sequelae of child sexual abuse: The Los Angeles Epidemiologic Catchment Area Study. In G. E. Wyatt & G. J. Powell (Eds.), *Lasting effects of child sexual abuse* (pp. 135-154). Newbury Park, CA: Sage.

Stevens, W. (1969). *The collected poems of Wallace Stevens.* New York: Alfred A. Knopf.

Sullivan, H. S. (1953). *The interpersonal theory of psychiatry.* New York: Norton.

Sullivan, J. (1986). Background information regarding child sexual offenders (Training brochure). Washington, DC: Child Pornography and Protection Unit (CPPU), U.S. Customs Service Headquarters.

Summit, R. C. (1983). The child sexual abuse accommodation syndrome. *International Journal of Child Abuse and Neglect, 7,* 177-193.

Summit, R. (1988). Hidden victims, hidden pain: Societal avoidance of child sexual abuse. In G. E. Wyatt & G. J. Powell (Eds.), *Lasting effects of child sexual abuse* (pp. 39-60). Newbury Park, CA: Sage.

Svalastoga, K. (1962). Rape and social structure. *Pacific Sociological Review, 5*(1), 48-53.

Swett, C., & Halpert, M. (1993). Reported history of physical and sexual abuse in relation to dissociation and other symptomatology in women psychiatric inpatients. *Journal of Interpersonal Violence, 8*(4), 545-555.

Taylor, R. L. (1984). Marital therapy in the treatment of incest. *Social Casework, 65*(4), 195-202.

Taylor, S. E. (1989). *Positive illusions: Creative self-deceptions and the healthy mind.* New York: Basic Books.

Taylor, S. E., & Brown, J. D. (1988). Illusion and well-being: A social-psychological perspective on mental health. *Psychological Bulletin, 103*(2), 193-210.

Terr, L. C. (1985a). Children traumatized in small groups. In S. Eth & R. S. Pynoos (Eds.), *Post-traumatic stress disorder in children* (pp. 47-70). Washington, DC: American Psychiatric Press.

Terr, L. C. (1985b). Psychic trauma in children and adolescents. *Psychiatric Clinics of North America, 8*(4), 815-835.

Terr, L. C. (1987). Childhood trauma and the creative product: A look at the early lives and later works of Poe, Wharton, Magritte, Hitchcock, and Bergman. *Psychoanalytic Study of the Child, 42,* 545-572.

Terr, L. (1990). *Too scared to cry.* New York: Harper & Row.

Terr, L. (1994). *Unchained memories: True stories of traumatic memories, lost and found.* New York: Basic Books.

Tiger, L. (1979). *Optimism: The biology of hope.* New York: Simon & Schuster.

Titchener, J. L. (1986). Post-traumatic decline: A consequence of unresolved destructive drives. In C. R. Figley (Ed.), *Trauma and its wake: Traumatic stress, theory, research, and intervention* (Vol. 11, pp. 5-19). New York: Brunner/Mazel.

Trepper, T. S., & Barrett, M. J. (1989). *Systemic treatment of incest.* New York: Brunner/Mazel.

Trimble, M. R. (1985). Post-traumatic stress disorder: History of a concept. In C. R. Figley (Ed.), *Trauma and its wake: The study and treatment of post-traumatic stress disorder* (Vol. 1, pp. 5-14). New York: Brunner/Mazel.

Tsai, M., Feldman-Summers, S., & Edgar, M. (1979). Childhood molestation: Variables related to differential impacts on psychosexual functioning in adult women. *Journal of Abnormal Psychology, 88*(4), 407-417.

Vaillant, G. E. (1993). *The wisdom of the ego.* Cambridge, MA: Harvard University Press.

Valentine, J. (1965). *Dream barker and other poems.* New York: AMS Press.

van der Kolk, B. A. (1987). *Psychological trauma.* Washington, DC: American Psychiatric Press.

van der Kolk, B. A., Perry, J. C., & Herman, J. L. (1991). Childhood origins of self-destructive behavior. *American Journal of Psychiatry, 148*(12), 1665-1671.

Vissing, Y. M., Straus, M. A., Gelles, R. J., & Harrop, J. W. (1991). Verbal aggression by parents and psychosocial problems of children. *Child Abuse & Neglect, 15*(3), 223-238.

Vonnegut, K. (1968). *Slaughterhouse five.* New York: Dell.

Walsh, B. W., & Rosen, P. M. (1988). Self-mutilation: Theory, research and treatment. New York: Guilford.

Warner-Kearney, D. (1987, February). *The nature of grooming behavior used by sexual offenders in father-daughter incest.* Paper presented at the Western Criminology Association, Las Vegas, NV.

Weinrott, M. R., & Saylor, M. (1991). Self-report of crimes committed by sex offenders. *Journal of Interpersonal Violence, 6*(3), 286-300.

Weiss, J., Rogers, E., Darwin, M. R., & Dutton, C. E. (1955). A study of girl sex victims. *Psychiatric Quarterly, 29,* 1-27.

Wheeler, J. R., & Berliner, L. (1988). Treating the effects of sexual abuse on children. In G. E. Wyatt & G. J. Powell (Eds.), *Lasting effects of child sexual abuse* (pp. 227-247). Newbury Park, CA: Sage.

Williams, L. M. (1992). Adult memories of childhood abuse: Preliminary findings from a longitudinal study. *APSAC Advisor, 5*(3), 19-22.

Williams, L. M. (1993, October). *Recovered memories of abuse in women with documented child sexual victimization histories.* Paper presented at the annual meeting of the American Society of Criminology, Phoenix, AZ.

Williams, L. M. (in press-a). Recall of childhood trauma: A prospective study of women's memories of child sexual abuse. *Journal of Consulting and Clinical Psychology.*

Williams, L. M. (in press-b). What does it mean to forget child sexual abuse? A reply to Loftus, Garry and Feldman. *Journal of Consulting and Clinical Psychology.*

Wilson, C., & Seaman, D. (1992). *The serial killers.* London: Virgin.

Winnicott, D. W. (1965). *The maturational processes and the facilitating environment.* New York: International Universities Press.

Wolfe, D. A., Sas, L., & Wekerle, C. (1994). Factors associated with the development of posttraumatic stress disorder among child victims of sexual abuse. *Child Abuse & Neglect, 18*(1), 37-50.

Wormith, J. S. (1983). A survey of incarcerated sexual offenders. *Canadian Journal of Criminology, 25*(4), 379-390.

Wortman, C. B. (1975). Some determinants of perceived control. *Journal of Personality and Social Psychology, 31,* 282-294.

Wortman, C. B. (1976). Casual attributions and personal control. In W. J. H. Harvey, W. J. Ickes, & R. F. Kidd (Eds.), *New directions in attribution research* (pp. 23-52). Hillsdale, NJ: Lawrence Erlbaum.

Wozencraft, T., Wagner, W., & Pellegrin, A. (1991). Depression and suicidal ideation in sexually abused children. *Child Abuse & Neglect, 15*(4), 505-511.

Wright, R. (1980). *Rape and physical violence.* Cambridge, UK: Institute of Criminology.

Wyatt, G. E. (1985). The sexual abuse of Afro-American and White-American women in childhood. *Child Abuse & Neglect, 9*(4), 507-519.

Wyatt, G. E., Guthrie, D., & Notgrass, C. M. (1992). Differential effects of women's child sexual abuse and subsequent sexual revictimization. *Journal of Consulting and Clinical Psychology, 60*(2), 167-173.

Yalom, I. D. (1960). Aggression and forbiddenness in voyeurism. *Archives of General Psychiatry, 3*, 305-319.

Yochelson, S., & Samenow, S. E. (1976). *The criminal personality: A profile for change.* New York: Jason Aronson.

Yorukoglu, A., & Kemph, J. P. (1966). Children not severely damaged by incest with a parent. *Journal of the American Academy of Child Psychiatry, 5*(1), 111-124.

Index

About the Author

Anna C. Salter is in private practice in Lebanon, New Hampshire, and on the adjunct faculty of Dartmouth Medical School in the Departments of Pediatrics and Psychiatry. Prior to entering private practice in 1988, she was on the full-time faculty of Dart-

mouth Medical School in Psychiatry and Maternal and Child Health. She was Director of Parents in Distress Program, Assistant Director of the Children at Risk Program, Co-Director of the Parenting Clinic, Director of Psychosocial Education for the Pediatric Residency Program, and Director of Child Psychiatry Inpatient Consultation. She has also developed a training curriculum for the National Institute of Corrections that has been used nationwide to develop sex offender treatment specialists. She lectures and consults throughout the country and abroad on sex offenders as well as on adult and child victims of sexual abuse. She is the author of *Treating Child Sex Offenders and Victims: A Practical Guide* (Sage, 1988).

About the Contributors

Hilary Eldridge, Dip. SW, CQSW, is Clinical Director of the Faithfull Foundation, a child protection agency that provides a range of therapeutic facilities for child and adult survivors of sexual abuse and their families, engages in assessment and intervention with sex offenders, and has a major role in the training of professional groups in work with sexual abuse. After completing postgraduate training at Leicester University School of Social Work, Ms. Eldridge worked as a probation officer for 13 years, specializing in work with sexual abuse. Ms. Eldridge is a member of the National Executive Committee of NOTA (National Association for the Development of Work With Sex Offenders) and has published material relating to sexual abuse, including a relapse prevention manual titled *Maintaining Change.*

Jenny Still, Dip. App. Soc. Studs, CQSW, qualified as a social worker in 1974. She has specialized in working with child abuse since 1977 as a practitioner, consultant, teacher, and then as Head of a Special Unit (Child Protection) for the National Society for Prevention of Cruelty to Children. As a Senior Lecturer at the University of London (Institute of Child Health), she was responsible for setting up and running the government-sponsored national training program on child sexual abuse. She was a cofounder of the Gracewell Clinic, set up in 1988 to provide an intensive residential assessment and therapy program for sex offenders, and has worked extensively with offenders, children who have been sexually abused, and their nonoffending parents and families. She is now Deputy Clinical Director with Gracewell's successor organization, the Faithfull Foundation.

Date Due

BRODART, INC.   Cat. No. 23 233   Printed in U S A